A FAN FOR

Following the 75 year history of Toronto's

ALL SEASONS

Maple Leafs through the Eyes of a Fan

Tom Gaston with Kevin Shea

Foreword by Ron Ellis

Fenn Publishing Company Ltd.
Bolton, Canada

A FAN FOR ALL SEASONS

A Fenn Publishing Book / October 2001

Fenn Publishing Company Ltd.
Bolton, Ontario, Canada

Distributed in Canada by H. B. Fenn and Company Ltd.
Bolton, Ontario, Canada, L7E 1W2

visit us on the World Wide Web at www.hbfenn.com

National Library of Canada Cataloguing in Publication Data

Gaston, Tom
    A fan for all seasons : following the history of Toronto's Maple Leafs
through the eyes of their most recognized fan

ISBN 1-55168-262-1

1. Toronto Maple Leafs (Hockey team) 2. Gaston, Tom
I. Shea, Kevin, 1956- . II. Title.

GV848.T6G38 2001   796.962'64'09713541   C2001-901727-8

Printed and bound in Canada

This book is dedicated with love
to the memory of my dear wife Ruth–my best friend,
wife and hockey partner for 55 years.

CONTENTS

FOREWORD

After my time on the organizing committee for the 1991 Canada Cup, I joined the staff of the Hockey Hall of Fame, which in those days was located on the Canadian National Exhibition grounds in Toronto.

I was looking forward with great anticipation to my new career, especially the opportunity to work with some wonderful people. The Hall staff, led at that time by Scotty Morrison, was young, full of enthusiasm, and they all had a passion for the game of hockey.

One day I met an extraordinary elderly couple by the name of Tom and Ruth Gaston, who volunteered their time in the Hockey Hall of Fame's Resource Centre. I thought to myself, "Isn't that good of the Hall to give this couple an opportunity as volunteers." I quickly changed my tune, however, as I came to realize the contribution they made to the library and Resource Centre. They both possessed knowledge of the Toronto Maple Leafs, and the game in general, that amazed me. Tommy was particularly adept at identifying players in recently donated photos from the old days that left the rest of the staff stumped.

As a former player with the Leafs, a fact that impresses me is that Tommy has watched his beloved team perform in all three arenas – Mutual Street, Maple Leaf Gardens and the Air Canada Centre. He was able to give me a much clearer picture of those great Leafs of the past whom I admired, including Clancy, Conacher, Primeau, Horner, Barilko – and most of all, Ace Bailey, who gave me the honour of letting me wear his retired number 6. Tommy and I have spent many hours at the coffee machine discussing these players, and I always enjoy his unique insights.

During our talks and from the rest of the staff, I soon found that, apart from being loyal Leaf fans, this couple was special in many ways. I detected a devotion to one another that was refreshing in this day and age. After hearing about Tom's eye accident, I realized that Ruth had stood by her man during a very difficult time in his life. With Ruth's support, Tommy has made his life count, as he has touched many lives as he pursued his various interests.

In closing, I know my life is richer for having had the privilege of spending time with this wonderful couple. I look forward to many more chats with Tommy.

Ron Ellis
Director, Public Affairs
Hockey Hall of Fame

ACKNOWLEDGEMENTS

Tommy Gaston and Kevin Shea wish to thank all those who helped in the preparation of A Fan for All Seasons. Specific thanks, first, to Jordan Fenn and Heidi Winter at Fenn Publishing for their enthusiasm toward this project, and the confidence they showed in allowing us to do it. Thanks also to Kari Atwell for her ideas and energies. We thank the entire team at H.B. Fenn and Company for their efforts on behalf of our dream.

A special thank you to Lloyd Davis for his outstanding editing skills. We couldn't have been more pleased to discover your talents and love of hockey, and thank you for the contributions you made to the manuscript.

Many people contributed anecdotes and tributes to A Fan for All Seasons, and we want them to know how much their time and memories were appreciated.

To Ron Ellis, the warmest of thanks for your longtime friendship, through good times and challenging times. Your writing the foreword meant the world to us both.

To Philip Pritchard and Craig Campbell of the Hockey Hall of Fame, we want you to know how much we both enjoy working with you, and to thank you for taking the time to offer your unique perspectives to the book.

We would like to express special appreciation to Lefty Reid, Scotty Morrison and Jeff Denomme – three gentlemen who have kept the Hockey Hall of Fame vital and exciting through the years. Your friendship and support in writing this book is most appreciated.

Brian Conacher, a former Leaf as both player and executive, gave us a wonderful tribute as well as valuable background information on his amazing family. Thank you very, very much Brian.

Like his father, King, Terry Clancy, played for the Toronto Maple Leafs, and we thank him for offering a wonderful perspective on his legendary Dad.

We've known both Christine Simpson and Nick Kypreos for a number of years. Christine worked at the Hockey Hall of Fame, while Nick wore the blue and white sweater of the Leafs. Both now work in television at Sportsnet, and both supplied us with wonderful anecdotes and tributes for the book. Thank you ever so much. We'll be watching!

Frank Selke Jr. gave us added background on a young Tommy Gaston and the neighbourhood in which the Gaston and Selke families grew up. Thank you for your contribution.

Anne Klisanich, whose brother Bill Barilko played a significant role in Toronto Maple Leafs history, is a volunteer at the Hockey Hall of Fame. Her excitement and addition to the book was most appreciated.

Andrew Podnieks is a co-worker, a fellow fan and an author of many hockey books in his own write, and we thank him warmly for contributing to our project.

Bruce Barker's status as one of Toronto's leading figures in the sports media is huge, but his friendship is even greater. Thank you.

Jimmy Holmstrom took time out of his busy teaching schedule to share his story about the Maple Leafs' "Memories and Dreams" parade, and we appreciate it! Jimmy is in charge of the music at the Air Canada Centre. Do you take requests?

We thank the Reverend Dr. G. Malcolm Sinclair for taking time from his duties at Metropolitan United Church in Toronto to reminisce so eloquently about Ruth and Tom.

Susan Pearce, a Leaside neighbour, added a flavour to A Fan for All Seasons that we wouldn't ordinarily have had. Warm thanks.

Extra-special love to Tom's daughters, Jayne Asselstine and Gayle Osborne. Both showed us why the Gaston family is special. They were delightful and helpful in compiling the book.

Several others contributed to the completion of A Fan for All Seasons, and we want to acknowledge their help as well: Tyler Wolosewich, Marilyn Robbins and all of our great friends at the Hockey Hall of Fame; Ken Dryden, Ann Clark, Nancy Gilks and all the wonderful folks at Maple Leaf Sports and Entertainment; the Toronto Sun's brilliant columnist Peter Worthington for giving us permission to use his exclusive, firsthand account of visiting the fuselage of the Barilko/Hudson airplane in 1962; Shelley Stertz, Jake Gold, and the members of The Tragically Hip for allowing us to use lyrics from "Fifty Mission Cap" in the Barilko chapter; Thelma Morrison, town archivist of Wasaga Beach, Ontario; hockey historian Brian McFarlane for his encouragement; and Bob Haggert, the former trainer for the Toronto Maple Leafs.

Tom Gaston is indebted to the only other surviving member of the Gaston family, his brother Bill. Thank you for your friendship.

Kevin Shea wishes to thank the team that supports him unconditionally: his mom and stepfather, Margaret and Gerry England, his brother Dale, and his many wonderful friends.

And finally, both Tom Gaston and Kevin Shea thank the Toronto Maple Leafs hockey team for decades of enjoyment. Having given us great excitement for so many years, we wish them every success as they go into a new season.

TOMMY GASTON'S ODE TO THE LEAFS

I went down to the Arena Gardens, found there on Mutual
    Street
To sit and cheer our hockey team-a game was quite a treat.
We'd park our car and find our seat, all dressed in shirt and
    tie
And watch the skills of all the players-we really liked Babe
    Dye.

And then one day, young Connie Smythe-he of suit and spats
He came along on Valentine's and bought the home St. Pat's
The weary Toronto sports fans were given great relief
When on that day in '27 the Pats became the Leafs.

On forward they had Bailey, on defense there was Hap Day.
We yelled and cheered for each great play, with dreams of
    Cups one day.
As years went on, we added stars who'd wear the white and
    blue
Like Conacher and Busher Jackson-Joseph Primeau too.

Then Smythe had an idea. It really was quite clever.
'Let's build a rink-a palace with ice!' The skeptics they sighed
    'Never!'
But Smythe showed determination. He'd refuse to ever be
    beat
He convinced the Eaton folks to sell him space on Carlton
    Street.

Now the Depression made it challenging, but Frank Selke
   showed he cares
He convinced the mighty union men to work, in part, for
   shares.
They dug and sawed and hammered too, and let the con-
   crete harden
We watched in awe as from the ground rose the incredible
   Maple Leaf Gardens.

And six months after shovels hit, the palatial Gardens shone.
The toast of all Toronto and a tribute to our Conn.
On November 12 in '31, the Leafs pulled on their socks.
And skated out to meet the force of the Windy City's Hawks.

The politicians on they droned, they had to have their say
But the crowd felt it should get a voice-they yelled, "Let's go-
   let's play!"
The puck was dropped and 2:30 in, the very first goal was
   scored.
But it was the Hawks Mush March, not the blue and white,
   who entered history's lore.

The first game ended quietly, the score was two to one
And though the Hawks won the game that night, it was ever
   so much fun.
The season ended wonderfully-the city, it grew up.
As on the ice, the mighty Leafs were handed Stanley's Cup.

The Kid Line was so famous, they almost scored at will
And Horner kept them honest too-he'd leave them standing
   still.
Chabot, the goalie blocked the net-to his mates he was a
   hero.
It wasn't odd to see opposing teams lose several goals to zero.

But the Cup was so elusive, and it avoided the white and
   blue
Toronto didn't sip champagne again until the spring of '42
But that one, it was wonderful. In fact, I'd say it was great.
After being down three games to none, the Leafs, they won
   four straight.

And then the war broke out in Europe, Smythe asked them
    to enlist.
Guys like Broda, Apps and Goldham-I assure you, they were
    missed.
Hap Day, he ran the team alone with Conny 'across the
    pond.'
He used some schoolboys, full of zip, and waved a magic
    wand.

As the Second World War was raging, the allies flew and dived
The Stanley Cup returned to Toronto in nineteen forty five.
The city was so excited, how really do you explain
That the Silver Bowl was brought back home by Ulcers,
    Windy and McLean?

After missing out on playoff action in nineteen forty six
The Leafs returned, with soldiers back, and a bag chock full
    of tricks.
And Syl and Turk, they led their team-no longer boys, but men
And then, in nineteen forty seven, the Leafs, they won again!

But this was just the first of magic tricks with hats and rabbits
For the next three years, we won the Cup-it became a regu-
    lar habit.
The Maple Leafs had won the Cup-a dynasty was founded
The city cheered, the directors danced and jubilation
    abounded.

And then in nineteen fifty, folks, you know the tale by now.
Prone and bleeding by the boards was the Red Wings' Gordie
    Howe.
Was it from a butt end, or a trip? We do not really know.
But the Red Wings rallied 'round their star, and the Leafs lost
    to their foe.

Then, miracles on ice came true in ninety fifty one
When Bill Barilko scored his goal! The Leafs were back-we'd
    won!
The handsome boy who scored that goal in overtime by then
Flew off that summer to fish for trout...and was never seen
    again.

The fifties were dark as the puck itself-we couldn't seem to win
The fans were forced to reminisce about victories that had been.
We often missed the playoffs-the feeling not close to heaven
It seemed the tide turned right around with the forming of the Silver Seven

Pal Hal and Staff, they ran the team-they bought it from Staff's Dad.
John Bassett was the third partner-it made Conn raging mad.
The trio had a major plan, they mapped it out so slow.
The first of several things to do? Hap Day-he had to go.

The Maple Leafs needed resurrecting-it really was no hunch
So Stafford and his partner Hal, they hired a coach named Punch.
Another change? 'We need a netminder who can mind the goal."
So quickly Johnny Bower was secured to satisfy that role.

The Marlies and St.Mike's played a part in building the team too.
They sent the Leafs Brewer, Baun and Keon-just to name a few.
And the fortunes of our hockey team began to turn around.
In sixty two, the Stanley Cup, to its rightful spot was found.

In sixty three and sixty four, the victories would repeat
The gleaming Stanley Cup would make the trip up old Bay Street.
Then with a cast of characters who looked grizzled and old in the mirror
The Stanley Cup came home again to Toronto in Centennial Year.

Expansion helped to split apart the team we knew so well.
In sixty eight the team played bad-in fact they played like hell.
To the Flyers and the L.A.Kings, we'd not expect to lose.
We couldn't beat the Seals or Stars, the Penguins or the Blues

And then in nineteen seventy one, Staff Smythe lost a valiant
 fight.
Harold Ballard bought the team right then, the new owner of
 the blue and white
And so began a chapter full of anguish and of woe
A cast of characters came and went, the morale it was quite
 low.

He heard about Yolanda, and the dog named T.C.Puck
But with them coming into The Gardens, well—out went all
 our luck.
We loved the guys like Turnbull, Tiger, Lanny and Palmateer
And Sittler, with his ten point night, was grinning ear to ear.

But slowly and methodically, they tried to make him quit
Trading Lanny and the Tiger caused the city to throw a fit.
But Darryl was a trooper with maple syrup in his veins
He stayed and did his best to lead the team that then re-
 mains.

The Leafs had been dismantled, and the press was growing
 tired
The charade continued until Sittler caved-he agreed to be a
 Flyer.
The city picketed MLG. 'You can't do that to us!'
But Ballard did, and on they went, in spite of all the fuss.

With the eighties arriving on the scene, the team remained
 quite thrifty
But along came Vaive for the Maple Leafs, he was the first to
 reach goal fifty
Ken Wregget and little Bester teamed to plug the spot in goal
Then Wendel Clark was drafted—fought and scored-that was
 his role.

Gord Stellick, the GM in '88, certainly left his mark
For Courtnall we got Kordic, hoping to add a needed spark
Well, he added that, but a whole lot more-a troubled man at
 best
It wasn't long before we was gone-in peace, we hope he'll
 rest.

With run and gun the featured play, it suited Gary Leeman
In 1990, he scored fifty, and left the city beamin'
Harold Ballard died in ninety, and it changed the Blue and
   White
They brought in Fletcher, gave him reigns and told him
   'Make it right.'

It wasn't long before Cliff called and said he'd found a cure.
For Damphousse, Ing to Edmonton, we got Anderson and
   Fuhr.
And then there was a bigger deal, ten players changed their
   sweater
With Gilmour coming to the Leafs, we instantly got better.

Dougie had this way about him, he played with such desire
In 93, we came a cut away from going to the wire.
Wendel, Doug and Felix led the way in '94
Again, we went to the third round-but the city wanted more.

In '95, Fletcher took a chance that the chemistry he'd wreck
He sent crowd favourite Wendel Clark to the Nordiques of
   Quebec.
With Sundin down the middle and Doug Gilmour's fire on
   ice
The Maple Leafs made the playoffs again-not just once but
   twice.

Then the puck was dropped to start the year in the fall of 96
There was something wrong, the team wasn't right, and they
   tried for a quick fix.
Gilmour was sent to Jersey, though his play had been quite
   stellar
But the Mighty Leafs had a terrible year and they ended in
   the cellar.

The next year, in came Dryden, hired to save the hurting
   team.
He got us moved to the Eastern Conference, a move which
   made fans beam.
Then in the fall of '98, the directive was to win
So Dryden called the BC home of former Leaf, Pat Quinn.

The results were instantaneous-the Leafs turned right around
From missing out on playoff action to reaching the second
　　round.
But the story isn't over, the ending not abrupt
We won't be satisfied until the team brings home the Cup.

But there'll be one thing that is missing if you want to know
　　the truth.
A Stanley Cup won't feel as good to me without my Ruth.
She always sat beside me, cheering the boys on the frozen
　　pond
I have no doubt she's up with King cheering from the Great
　　Beyond.

And so dear fans, you wonder why I've hung in oh so long
Cause missing out on a Stanley Cup would make it seem so
　　wrong.
I've seen all of eleven, and don't worry about my health
Cause they'll never take me from this earth until I see a
　　twelfth.

Tom Gaston with Kevin Shea

CHAPTER ONE

Beginnings

Friday, February 19, 1999, was an auspicious date in the history of the Toronto Maple Leafs, as the franchise prepared to leave venerable Maple Leaf Gardens behind and make the official move into their brand new home, the Air Canada Centre. Six days earlier, on February 13, the team had played its final game at the Gardens – a deflating 6-2 loss to the Chicago Blackhawks. In a moving postgame ceremony, many of those who had proudly donned a Maple Leafs sweater over the years set foot on the ice one last time. Having paid homage to the past, the organization was now about to celebrate its future. Players from the past and present would take part in a parade between the Gardens and the "ACC."

The event symbolized a passing of the torch. The fans who looked on were no doubt dreaming that, at some point in the not-too-distant future they might once again line the streets of Toronto, but this time to help the current Maple Leafs celebrate a Stanley Cup victory. After all, the Toronto Maple Leafs won the Stanley Cup in their first year at the Gardens. Why not in their first year at the new building?

A convoy of blue and white Ford Mustang convertibles made its way west from 60 Carlton Street to Yonge. In one car sat Gaye Stewart, Gus Mortson and Fleming MacKell, members of the great Leaf teams of the 1940s; in another, Eddie Shack, Jim Pappin and Frank Mahovlich of the '60s dynasty; and Tie Domi shared a ride with popular alumni Tiger Williams and Brad Smith. The Stanley Cup rode in a car with Hockey Hall of Fame manager Craig Campbell. Turning south, the cars inched slowly toward Lake Ontario – and the Hockey Hall of Fame, in front of which a magnificent ice sculpture had been placed. The parade slipped west along Front to York Street before heading south toward the magnificent new building.

In the midst of the procession was a massive flatbed trailer, beautifully done up in blue and white. Half of it was reserved for the Maple Leafs' organist and audio expert, Jimmy Holmstrom. There, with his keyboard in tow, Holmstrom worked the fanatical crowd, enticing the thousands of fans gathered along the route to cheer, "Go Leafs Go!" The other half of this ornately decorated trailer was dedicated to the fans, and there, representing all Toronto Maple Leaf supporters, was the one person singled out for his lifelong dedication to the blue and white: Tom Gaston.

Holmstrom remembers the event vividly. "I've known Tom forever, it seems. He's a living legend – the rest of us diehard, lifelong, bleed-blue, never-off-the-bandwagon fans are just shadows up against Tommy. The first time we met face to face was at the Leaf parade to the Air Canada Centre, where we both told each other what an honour it was to be associated with the other – go figure!

"During that trip, Tom got to see what he has always only heard. There I was, playing my favourite Maple Leaf tunes, and there was Tom, dancing and clapping to the game soundtrack instead of sitting and cheering from his regular Maple Leaf Gardens seat. After the trip, we were congratulated for braving the cold – minus-4 degrees! – and both of us responded, 'Cold? What cold?' It was an honour, privilege and lifelong ambition for both of us kindred spirits to ever be connected, in any way, with our Toronto Maple Leafs."

Tom considers it one of the great events of his life. "It was an incredible thrill for me – I still can't believe it to this day! I guess the Leafs could have chosen just about anybody, but they picked me to represent all the fans. I was called and asked how I would like to be in a parade with the Leafs. I told them I'd be pleased. That was about a month before the closing of the Gardens. Closer to the date, I was told to show up at the Gardens on February 19 at 9 a.m. I asked, 'How do you want me to dress?' The lady said, 'Oh, Tom, you always know how to dress.'

"When I got there, I was taken to a long row of tables in the Hot Stove Lounge. A lot of the Leaf players were already there. We were to pick out one of each item on the tables. There was a Leaf watch first, then a jacket, T-shirts, gloves, toques and boots. They dressed me the same way that the players were dressed that day: in a blue and white toque, a beautiful blue leather bomber jacket with the Leafs logo on the left breast, blue track pants with white stripes down the side, and boots with the Leafs emblem embossed in the side. I went to the visitor's dressing room and changed into my new 'uniform' beside Brian Conacher, who had played with the Leafs when they won the Stanley Cup in 1967. On the walls of the dressing room were the signatures of a lot of the Chicago Blackhawks, who had used the room last. It was strange to see Dougie Gilmour's autograph there on the visitor's wall after his great years in Toronto.

"The Leaf folks took me out to the parade vehicles. They showed me the float I was going to ride on. There was a huge sign with 'Tommy Gaston – Superfan' on it. I felt like a million bucks sitting up there on the float, waving to all my fellow fans. There were thousands of them, and I couldn't believe how many called out my name and waved to me. People even ran out onto the street and wanted my autograph!"

But why was Tom Gaston chosen to represent all fans of the Toronto Maple Leafs? Because he is without question the club's most ardent supporter. You may not see a Leaf logo shaved into his thatch of white hair, but he is as passionate about his team as any fan could dream of being. Tom Gaston has seen the Maple Leafs play in three arenas: the Arena Gardens (often called the Mutual Street Arena), Maple Leaf Gardens and the Air Canada Centre. He has attended games every year since 1930, and has held his own season tickets since 1940. Tom has cheered for eleven Stanley Cup winning teams, and has seen all the greats of the game skate in front of him, including Clancy, Conacher, Kennedy, Keon, Clark and CuJo. He has rubbed shoulders with Leafs players and management, and has been present when many were laid to rest. As a volunteer at the Hockey Hall of Fame, Tom has been to more than twenty induction ceremonies, honouring the greatest players ever to lace up a pair of skates.

The 2001-02 season marks the seventy-fifth anniversary of the Toronto Maple Leaf franchise. It also marks the seventieth anniversary of the first Stanley Cup victory Toronto won as the Maple Leafs. In this historic season, it is only appropriate that we honour the Leaf most closely tied to the history of the team.

In essence, Tom Gaston represents every fan. Scoffed at by sports reporters, Tommy is part of that breed of fan that is fiercely loyal to the death. That doesn't mean he likes everything he has seen on the ice through the years, but he would never think of cheering for any other team. When callers to open-line radio shows try to rally the fans into boycotting games to protest rising ticket prices, Tom Gaston just shrugs, pulls his sweater over his narrow shoulders and ambles down to the bus stop on his journey to yet another Leaf game. Tom Gaston is truly a fan for all seasons.

Given his fierce loyalty to his favourite hockey team, a visit to the quiet Leaside bungalow where Tom Gaston lives doesn't reveal any surprises. There are reminders of his love for the Leafs everywhere you turn – a plaque here, a photo there, sweaters hanging in the closets. Photos of his grandchildren show that they too are dressed in the same blue and white favoured by Grandpa. One grandchild is even named Wendell, although that is more a coincidence than a tribute to the Leafs' popular number 17. There's an autograph from Danny Markov on Tom's refrigerator, and game sticks used by Rick Vaive, Borje Salming, Dave Burrows and Tie Domi in his recreation room. Throughout the tidy home there are photos of Tom and his beautiful, late wife Ruth, and each of them is tagged with a hockey story. "That's Ruth and me at the Hockey Hall of Fame on our fiftieth wedding anniversary. That's Ruth and me up in Picton – look at our Leaf shirts. That's Ruth, me, and our two girls. I had bought them both a Leaf sweater and had the number 1/2 put on the back." Tommy is no name-dropper, but his speech is inevitably peppered with the names of Maple Leafs past and present. "I was in the elevator at the Hockey Hall of Fame the other day and I got a good poke in the ribs. I turned around – it was George Armstrong."

Tom Gaston was born a Leaf fan. With a birthdate of May 16, 1917, he is older than the National Hockey League itself – the NHL was officially formed on November 26, 1917, six months after the Gaston family welcomed their third child, Thomas Roberts Gaston, into the world. "My dad, Thomas Gaston, worked for a company called Milnes Fuel," begins Tommy. "Part of his job was to deliver coal to homes around the area. One day, Dad was delivering coal to a lady's house just like any other day. But the lady's daughter, Emily Roberts, was home with the chicken pox. Dad laid eyes on Emily and fell in love. They started to date, and it wasn't too long before the couple became Thomas and Emily Gaston – my parents. Hard to believe it started over a lump of coal."

Thomas was born in the family home at 25 Merton Street. His eldest brother, Joseph, was born in 1913, followed by William, in 1915. A sister, Emily, came along in 1919. There weren't many hospitals in the area at that time, so all four Gaston children were born at home. Milnes Fuel, the senior Tom Gaston's employer, owned the house, and the family rented it from them. The house is long gone; today, the property houses Mount Pleasant Glass & Mirror.

"I was named Thomas after my father, and my middle name – Roberts – was my mother's maiden name. I was always a little guy, and pretty timid, too. My brothers all kept an eye on me, as did the neighbourhood boys. In fact, I can remember the Stark family, who owned the gas station at Merton and Mount Pleasant, being especially watchful over me in the school playground." Joe Stark, who came from a family of nine boys and two girls, would play a significant role in Tommy Gaston's life. "He was a pretty good athlete in our neighbourhood. Later on he was a practice goalkeeper for the Toronto Maple Leafs and Chicago Blackhawks. As a matter of fact, Joe got his name inscribed on the Stanley Cup with the Blackhawks when they won in 1933-34. He backed up Charlie Gardiner in net. Anyway, we all went to Davisville [Public School], and if I got picked on by the bigger boys, Joe Stark was always there to stand up for me. Years later, he was the passenger in a car that hit the shoulder of Highway 2 near Whitby and rolled several times. Both he and the driver were killed instantly. It was too bad-he was a great friend."

Tommy smiles proudly as he reminisces about his father. "My dad was really good at football and baseball. He was born in the Forest Hill district of Toronto, but took a job with Bethlehem Steel in Bethlehem, Pennsylvania, around 1905. While he was there, he played organized football in a local league. He played competitive baseball, too, and was just a step or two away from the major leagues.

"Me, I never did too much, just played playground sports. Both my brothers wore the skates I had before I got them. Dad took an old pair of my boots, and screwed skate blades onto them. They served the purpose very nicely. I remember I really wanted a pair of hockey pants like the Leafs wore, so my mom cut the legs off an old pair of blue trousers and sewed a strip of material from a shirt to look like a white stripe down the sides. God bless her. In my mind, they were just as good as any hockey pants ever.

"My brother William played some senior hockey around Toronto, and I played a little intermediate," remembers Gaston. "I loved the game, but I was never going to go very far. I had a teammate, Jack Crawford, who went on to play with the Boston Bruins. Anyway, he advised me to give up competitive hockey. I just wasn't cut out for it. I was too small and too timid. He told me that as long as I chose to play, he'd watch over me, but that I should really pack it in." Crawford was an oddity in the National Hockey League when he broke in with the Bruins in 1937: he was one of the only players who wore a helmet. As a youngster, he had developed an infection from the paint on a football helmet, and it caused his hair to fall out. Crawford wore a helmet his entire hockey career – for protection as much as to disguise his bald head.

"I was a better lacrosse player than I was a hockey player – which still isn't saying much," Tom laughs as he continues. "I was a goalkeeper in lacrosse. I wore an old baseball catcher's chest protector, hockey shin guards, hockey gloves and a peaked cap. Here was this little bit of a guy standing in front of the net with all these huge guys bearing down and propelling that Indian rubber ball at incredible speeds.

"One year in the city finals, a player on the other team threw the ball at me, after the whistle had blown the play dead, and broke my tooth. I complained to the ref like crazy, but he didn't do anything, so I took the officiating into my own hands. Next time that player came near my net, I stepped out of the crease and swatted him in the chest with my lacrosse racquet for all I was worth. He went down like a ton of bricks, and laid there gasping for breath. I know he broke some ribs. One of my defencemen came back, stood over top of him and said, 'Don't even try to stand up or I'll knock you right back down. You deserved everything you got and more!' I may have been somewhat timid, but nobody was going to get away with that nonsense. When it comes to sports, it's often frontier justice – maybe even the Golden Rule: Do unto others as they would do unto you."

Tom attended Davisville, Hodgson and Eglinton public schools, all of which were located in what was once the separate town of North Toronto. For a brief time, he also went to Northern Vocational, but like many boys his age during the Great Depression of the 1930s, formal education ended with public school, after which it was time to get a job and bring in some money to cover the family's needs. At the age of thirteen, Tommy was cutting lawns and doing chores for neighbours to earn a little money. Then he and a friend started an egg business, "Tom & Wilbert Eggs." They would buy hams and bacon from Canada Packers on St. Clair Avenue West, and eggs from local farmers, and sell their goods door-to-door. A city inspector stopped the boys one day, asking to see their licence.

"Oh, boy, were we nervous," remembers Tom. "We didn't have any peddler's licence. We just bought the meat and eggs and resold them to our customers. The inspector told us he wouldn't fine us if we went down to City Hall to pay for a licence. We went downtown to get one, but it would have cost us $25, and we didn't have that kind of money, so we folded our little egg business."

Tom took a job delivering paint for Sherwin-Williams at Yonge Street and St. Clair Avenue. The paint cans would be loaded into the carrier of his bicycle and he would head off to deliver them. "One day, a customer came into the store while I was loading up the paint. He needed an assistant to help him look after some buildings. I took the job, and for three years I was assistant caretaker doing odd jobs around the building.

"One of the tenants thought I did a nice job around the building, and recommended that her husband hire me," Tom modestly recalls. "He worked at the Canadian Fairbanks Morse plant, and on his wife's recommendation, he offered me the job as a stock keeper. I accepted the position, and after giving my notice with the building superintendent, I showed up for the first day of my new job. Canadian Fairbanks Morse was on Front Street, just west of where the Hockey Hall of Fame is now located. It's funny, but for the better part of my working life, I was in the Yonge and Front area – and now, as a volunteer at the Hockey Hall of Fame, I'm still in that neighbourhood. In fact, back when I was working, I banked at the Bank of Montreal branch which now houses the Hockey Hall of Fame's Great Hall."

CHAPTER TWO

From Mutual Street to MLG

Long before Maple Leaf Gardens was ever conceived, Toronto had been home to a host of hockey arenas. One of the earliest was the Toronto Curling and Skating Rink, built in 1877 and gone ten years later. The Granite Club Ice Rink, located at 519 Church Street, opened its doors in 1880. Five years later, the Caledonia Rink was constructed on the Mutual Street site that Arena Gardens would one day occupy. And in 1887, the Victoria Rink on Huron Street opened up. It would be enjoyed by generations of Torontonians until 1962.

By the early teens, skating and hockey had grown exponentially in popularity. Whereas these activities had previously been carried out on curling rinks, arenas designed specifically for blades and sticks were now beginning to spring up across the city. The Elmdale Rink was built at 239 Bathurst Street. In the Dovercourt area, kids could take their skates to the Old Orchard Rink. At Prospect and Ontario streets stood the Prospect Park Rink. North Riverdale Arena, close to the corner of Danforth and Broadview avenues, was prominent in the 1910s. Further south, at 275 Broadview, the Broadview Rink was built. The Maple Leaf Rink, at 325 Pape Avenue, was built in the early teens as well, and the Beaches boasted the Kenilworth Rink, constructed at 1945 Queen Street East.

Several arenas emerged as important breeding grounds for To-ronto's early hockey development. The Aura Lee Athletic Club and Skating Rink, located at 205 Avenue Road near Davenport, became home to an outstanding junior hockey program that spawned such players as Lionel Conacher. St. Mary's Arena hosted a junior team, run by Frank Selke, that later became the Toronto Marlboros. That rink was at 558 Adelaide Street West, near Bathurst. At the turn of the twentieth century, Varsity Arena was built at Bloor Street and Devonshire Place. There was a skating rink with an adjoining hockey facility, and it was there that the University of Toronto's successful hockey program was developed. In 1926, the current Varsity Arena was built right next to the stadium; in addition to hosting U of T's hockey teams, it housed the Toronto Toros of the World Hockey Association during the 1973-74 season.

Tommy Gaston remembers the last hockey game in which he played, one that took place at that same Varsity Arena. "We used to play our company hockey games at Varsity. The gang from Fairbanks would meet down at the stadium, and the married guys played the single guys. If you weren't playing, you usually would go and watch the game, so we would have a good little crowd. Afterward, everyone would go back to someone's home for coffee and sandwiches, and we'd dance and talk down in the basement. Anyway, I usually played defence, but on this evening the referee came over to me and said I was to take the face-off at centre ice. I shrugged and skated up to the face-off circle. The ref dropped the puck right onto my stick, and grabbed the other guy's stick so he couldn't get at the puck. My wingers skated ahead and took out the other team's defencemen, and I kept on skating with the puck. As I broke in on goal, the referee knocked the goalie down and I fired the puck into an empty net.

"Everybody cheered, and the ref picked up the puck and brought it over to me. He handed me the puck and said, 'Tommy, you're now officially retired. We're afraid you could lose your other eye [Tommy lost the vision in his right eye in a workplace accident in 1940], so now you're the team's manager.' That was the last game of hockey I ever played. Nice to leave on a high note though, isn't it?"

The Ravina Ice Arena was built in 1911 at 50 Rowland Street, near Keele and Annette streets, right by Humberside Collegiate Institute. It was torn down and Ravina Gardens went up in its place. Destroyed in 1961 – the site is now occupied by a football field – the rink played a significant role in Toronto's hockey heritage. When Frank Selke wasn't working as an electrician at the University of Toronto, he could be found at Ravina Gardens, scouting young prospects for his Marlboros. Several future Maple Leafs, including Joe Primeau and Carl Voss, played with the Toronto Ravinas in 1927-28. During the 1940s Ravina Gardens hosted the Toronto Mercantile league, and Toronto's NHL teams made steady use of it as a practice rink over the years. When Conn Smythe was putting together the New York Rangers in 1926, he held the new club's training camp at Ravina Gardens.

"I tried out for intermediate hockey at Ravina Gardens," Tommy Gaston says, pulling another memory from his impressive collection. "The dressing room was so cold they had a pot-bellied stove in the middle of the dressing room, and we'd pull chairs up close to the heat as we got dressed."

When Arena Gardens opened, it was the first artificial ice rink in Canada built east of Vancouver. It occupied the site of the old Caledonia Rink at 60 Mutual Street, and it officially opened on October 7, 1912. Silent movie star Marie Dressler, who had appeared with Charlie Chaplin in a number of short films, was in attendance on opening night. Dressler was a native of Cobourg, Ontario, but was living in Hollywood at the time.

Financed by a group of businessmen that included Sir Henry Pellatt, owner of Toronto's splendid Casa Loma, Arena Gardens cost $500,000 and seated just under 8,000 fans. When the National Hockey League was formed in 1917, the Toronto Arenas were a charter member, along with the Montreal Canadiens, Montreal Wanderers and Ottawa Senators. Playing out of Arena Gardens, the Toronto Arenas won their opening night game against Ottawa, 11-4, and proceeded to win the Stanley Cup in the NHL's first season. Incidentally, player salaries for that first year totalled $6,500.

The consortium that owned the Arenas, desperate to rid themselves of a money-losing proposition, sold the team in 1919 for $5,000. The new owners, headed by Charlie Querrie and J.P. Bickell, changed the club's nickname to the St. Patricks, although the team was always referred to as the St. Pats. In keeping with their Irish name, the team wore green sweaters, and they brought another Stanley Cup championship to Toronto in 1922.

In the midst of the 1926 training camp he was running at Ravina Gardens, Toronto native Conn Smythe was fired as coach of the New York Rangers. The team had decided to go with a better-known coach, hiring Lester Patrick in Smythe's place. Smythe was furious, and when he was presented with the chance to buy the St. Pats, Smythe was more than eager. But the asking price – $200,000 – was $190,000 more than Smythe had received from the Rangers as his severance pay. Conn turned to Ed Bickle and Peter Campbell and convinced them to contribute to the purchase, but the $160,000 the sportsmen managed to raise was still shy of the goal. Undaunted,

Smythe talked the St. Pats' owners into selling him and his colleagues the team for $75,000 cash and a promise to pay $85,000 within thirty days. On February 17, 1927, the team skated onto the ice at Arena Gardens with new owners, new sweaters (white with a green leaf on the chest, across which the word TORONTO was embroidered in white) and a new name: the Toronto Maple Leafs. The first game played as the Leafs was a 4-1 victory over the New York Americans.

Under new ownership and management, the team did not immediately rise to the top of the standings and provide Smythe with a measure of revenge against his former bosses; in fact, the Leafs hovered around the middle of the pack for the next few seasons. (Meanwhile, the Ranger club that Smythe had had a hand in building was an overnight success, placing first in its maiden season and winning the Stanley Cup in its second.) But Conn was busy assembling a roster that fit his vision of a championship team. Hap Day and Ace Bailey, both talented holdovers from the St. Pats, anchored the lineup, and in short order Smythe added Lorne Chabot, Andy Blair and Harold "Baldy" Cotton. At the same time, the Leaf-affiliated Toronto Marlboros organization was developing a bumper crop of junior players who would star with the major-league club, including Red Horner, Charlie Conacher and Harvey Jackson.

In the late 1920s, teams around the NHL were spending vast sums of money to acquire star players. The New York Americans spent $20,000 to get goaltender Roy Worters from Pittsburgh. The Rangers offered the Montreal Canadiens $50,000 for scoring sensation Howie Morenz – the Habs declined. And salaries were skyrocketing: defensive star Eddie Shore demanded $25,000 a year from the Boston Bruins – and got it! The money being thrown around was astronomical! ("Yeah," Tommy harumphs, "Conn Smythe would roll over in his grave if he got wind of the paycheques today. Hell, players won't even do an autograph signing for $25,000!")

The Leafs realized that, in order to be truly competitive, they too would have to spend some cash, but the onset of the Great Depression after the stock market crash of 1929 meant that money was scarce. Smythe was sure that he needed only one more player – albeit a headliner who could lead the club – in order to make a real run for the Cup. He set his sights on the cash-strapped Ottawa Senators, whose lineup boasted just the player he was looking for: a defenceman named Francis "King" Clancy.

"King was my favourite player," Gaston announces proudly. "I called him the 'human dynamo.' He had a funny skating style, but boy, could he move up the ice! He was a great defender, but he could also really add offence to the attack. You know, they called him King after his father. His father was a big man – over six feet and 200 pounds. The King, as we know, was pretty small – five foot six or seven and around 150 pounds.

"The senior Clancy really made a name for himself in football. He was a great player with the Ottawa Rough Riders in the late 1800s. Back then, you didn't snap the ball to the quarterback – you 'heeled' the ball. Clancy senior was great at it. You faced the other team, dropped the ball and heeled it back to the quarterback. Clancy – his name was Tom, too – was so good at it that he got to be known as the 'King of the Heelers.' And that got shortened to 'King.' When Francis came along, they called him King, too – it had nothing to do with the fact he was a great hockey player. That came later.

"I always liked him when he played for the Senators, but I loved it when he came to Toronto."

Ottawa wasn't interested in trading Clancy for a player of equal talent – the Senators had a surplus of players. What they desperately needed was money. The price they quoted was high; Smythe placed a five-day option on Clancy and proceeded to sell his board of directors on the benefits of securing the outstanding defenceman. The board approved, but made only $20,000 available to Smythe. "The big rumour has always been that Mr. Smythe made about $14,000 at Woodbine Racetrack betting on a longshot named Rare Jewel," Tommy says. "He had bought the horse for $250 – it had never won a race. But that day, the horse won, and it paid $214.40 for a $2 bet. He won about $11,000 on his bet – and he got the purse, which was close to $4,000. He used that money from Rare Jewel, added it to the $20,000 the board of directors was willing to spend, and purchased King Clancy."

On October 11, 1930, just a month before the season was to begin, the Leafs sent Eric Pettinger, Art Smith and $35,000 to the Ottawa Senators for Clancy. Other teams denounced the deal, saying the Leafs paid too high a price for King and thus inflated the going rate for star players, but Smythe and the Leaf fans knew it was worth the hefty investment.

The Leafs began the 1930-31 season with Lorne Chabot in goal; Clancy, Hap Day, Red Horner and Art Duncan on defence; and forwards Joe Primeau, Andy Blair, Ace Bailey, Baldy Cotton, Charlie Conacher and Harvey "Busher" Jackson. Late in the season, Alex Levinsky and Bob Gracie were added to the lineup. Seven of those players would go on to become members of the Hockey Hall of Fame: King Clancy was inducted in 1958, Day and Conacher in 1961, Primeau in 1963, Horner in 1965, Jackson in 1971 and Bailey in 1975. A formidable lineup.

"At Christmas, my mom bought me a miniature hockey stick at Simpson's," Tommy smiles. "She heard a couple of the Leafs were going to be in the store signing autographs, so she lined up and got them to sign the stick. The players were Charlie Conacher and Hap Day. Those were the first autographs I ever got. I shellacked the stick so that the autographs would be safe, and I used it to play road hockey."

Tom recalls his very first visit to Arena Gardens. "The arena was an old brick building on Mutual Street, near Shuter, right downtown. I remember thinking they kept the place up pretty nice. I guess it held about 8,000 people, and the Leafs were a big deal, so even though money was scarce and the Leafs weren't a great team, the place was usually full and it was tough to get seats. A friend of my brother's had tickets, and when he didn't want to go, he'd let my brother Joe have them. Anyway, I got the tickets for Christmas in 1930, and I was so excited.

"I went to the game with my brother Joe. I couldn't believe I was going to see a real hockey game. I was only thirteen, but none of my friends had ever been to a game, so it was a big deal. The arena was oval-shaped at the ends. All the seats were wooden benches, kind of like church pews. At one end were the cheap seats, and there was standing room in tiers. Chicken wire kept the people in standing room from trying to move down into the seats.

"The game was against the Montreal Maroons. I'm pretty sure it was January 8 – it was early January, anyway. The Leafs won 1-0 on a goal by Andy Blair, and Chabot got the shutout. Both Conachers played – Charlie for the Leafs and Lionel for the Maroons. I was as thrilled as any kid could be to see a real NHL game.

"That particular game has taken on a greater meaning over the years – after all, not many people are still around who can say they saw the Leafs play at Mutual Street. And to see the Conacher brothers, Ace Bailey, Lorne Chabot, King Clancy, Happy Day – there's not many of us left anymore."

Arena Gardens was a fully functional, multipurpose facility that was used for all manner of events other than hockey. History was made there on June 10, 1925, when Methodists, Congegationalists and most of Canada's Presbyterians joined forces to form the United Church of Canada. Many top musical acts performed there, and everything from boxing matches to curling bonspiels to six-day marathon bicycle races took place within its walls. But Clancy and the Leafs were the main attraction, and they had outgrown the building. Conn Smythe knew he would need a much larger arena to generate the revenue needed to compete in the NHL of the 1930s. After all, teams in Montreal, New York, Boston, Chicago and Detroit were all playing in larger, more modern rinks.

Smythe was aware of the formidable challenge that building a new arena would present. "He had his engineering degree from the University of Toronto, so he knew enough about buildings that he could figure the cost pretty close to the actual dollars spent," Gaston points out. Selling his business partners on the idea of a new arena was one thing, but in 1930, money was hard to come by. Smythe and his team persuaded, cajoled and twisted the arms of anybody who had money, and they were able to come up with nearly all of the necessary funds. Frank Selke, who by this time was on the Smythe payroll, made a suggestion that has become the stuff of legend: to keep down the cost of labour, perhaps the construction workers might be willing to forgo part of their wages in favour of stock in the new arena. At the eleventh hour, Selke – who was a member of the electricians' union – made an impassioned plea to his union brethren, and they agreed to the compromise. "After all," Tommy reminds us, "many of the boys wouldn't have been working at all, and some money was better than no money."

With financing secured and the unions on board, the Leafs' braintrust began to look for a site for the new arena, which Smythe had already begun to call "Maple Leaf Gardens." The first location was on the Toronto waterfront near the foot of Yonge Street, but the real estate was too expensive, so that idea was vetoed. A site on Spadina Avenue, just north of College Street – where Knox College is located – was considered, but residents of the neighbourhood were bitterly opposed to the idea, and Smythe looked elsewhere. The T. Eaton Company offered to sell Smythe some property near Wood and Church streets, but Conn had his eye on a plot at the corner of Church and Carlton instead. That property, also owned by Eaton's, was perfect for Smythe's needs – located on the Carlton and the Church streetcar lines, and only a block away from the Yonge streetcars. J.J. Vaughn, the president of Eaton's, approved the sale, and in exchange for $350,000 and shares in the new venture, Maple Leaf Gardens had found its home.

The architectural firm of Ross and MacDonald, which had designed such Toronto landmarks as the Royal York Hotel and Union Station, drafted the blueprints. After the buildings on the site were razed, ground was broken on May 16, 1931. Incredibly, just six months later, the brilliant new edifice was open for business, and the first puck was dropped at Maple Leaf Gardens on November 12, 1931.

While construction was underway, Conn Smythe sent word to the staff at Arena Gardens that he had jobs for everyone. He let them know in no uncertain terms that he saw no future for them at the old rink, and they would have but one chance to join him at the new rink. The entire staff quit Arena Gardens that day to take jobs at Maple Leaf Gardens. In so doing, they left the ice-making equipment at Mutual Street unattended, and when the furnace went out, the pipes froze and burst. That equipment was never repaired, and there would never be another hockey game played at Arena Gardens.

Tom Gaston had been having some problems with his ear, and he spent a few days in the hospital in August 1931. His father picked him up one day and asked if he'd like to watch the men build Maple Leaf Gardens. "I guess my Dad must have taken a chance, but we pulled up near the construction site and asked if we could see Conn Smythe. Mr. Smythe came out to the front, and my Dad asked if we could see the building. Mr. Smythe said, 'Show the boy what he'd like to see, but stay out of the way of the workers.' Then he went back to his office. My Dad and I walked in – I couldn't believe how big it was, it seemed so huge! Where the ice surface would be, there was nothing but mud. They were just pouring the cement for the tiers where the seats would be. The whole thing was so impressive. We went back two or three times while the Gardens was being built.

"I had a friend who was the water boy on the construction site. His job was to carry a pail of water and a tin cup and walk around to the workers so they could get a drink as they worked. He received some shares in Maple Leaf Gardens for his work, and he never sold them. He still has them today," Tom enthuses. Those shares no longer have any financial value, as Steve Stavro took the company private in 1996, but it's a sure thing that there are countless collectors and Leaf fans who would dearly love to have such a keepsake.

Nobody could have imagined the new arena would be finished in time for the start of the 1931-32 hockey season, but on the evening of November 12, 1931, the NHL's newest shrine opened its doors for the first time. "There was still some minor construction work being done, but on opening night, the building was about as beautiful as anything I'd seen."

The Maple Leafs' move left Arena Gardens without its principal tenant, but it continued to host a wide range of events. As the Depression wore on, however, its owners ran into financial difficulties, and the City of Toronto acquired control. In 1938, William Dickson leased the historic building from the city and renamed it the Mutual Street Arena. Seven years later, he bought the building. The Mutual Street Arena came to be known as one of the city's better concert venues, hosting Glenn Miller and his Orchestra in 1942 and Frank Sinatra in 1948. Duke Ellington also played there later. In 1962, the Mutual Street Arena was remodelled extensively and converted into a roller skating rink called The Terrace. In 1989, the historic building was demolished, and a housing co-op now stands where Foster Hewitt first announced a hockey game, where King Clancy starred, where Hap Day and Ace Bailey played for the St. Pats, and where Red Horner, Joe Primeau, Busher Jackson and Charlie Conacher began their professional careers.

CHAPTER THREE

The Kid Line

"Primeau, Conacher and Jackson – that Kid Line was as good as any line that ever played." There is a wistful tone in Tom Gaston's voice as he recalls the trio of homegrown forwards who put the Toronto Maple Leafs firmly on the hockey map.

"Gentleman Joe" Primeau was the first player ever signed by the newly reorganized Maple Leaf franchise. Born Alfred Joseph Primeau on January 29, 1906 in Lindsay, Ontario, he moved with his family to Toronto at a young age. Early in his athletic career, Joe developed a reputation as quite a baseball player, pitching for St. Francis of Assisi School in Toronto's west end. The ball club was very competitive, and the managers wanted to keep the boys together and in shape during the winter months, so they organized a hockey team.

Primeau progressed rapidly in his new sport, and when he attended St. Michael's College School in downtown Toronto, he made their Junior A team. Frank Selke noticed the 18-year-old and invited him to join the St. Mary's team he was managing. Joe played with that club for the next three years – prior to the 1926-27 season they were renamed the Toronto Marlboros. During that last season with the Marlies, Joe was also playing in the Toronto Mercantile League, a rough-and-tumble circuit based out of Ravina Gardens.

Over the years, Conn Smythe had made a name for himself in Toronto hockey circles. In 1914-15 he captained the University of Toronto Varsity Blues junior team to the Ontario Hockey Association championship. After returning from World War I, he helped U of T win the Allan Cup, emblematic of excellence in senior hockey, in 1920-21. By 1926, the Blues were playing out of the new Varsity Arena and Smythe was their coach. Under his tutelage, they were intercollegiate champions and Allan Cup finalists. Members of the team included Dave Trottier, who went on to a decade-long career with the Montreal Maroons, Hugh Plaxton and the captain, Lou Hudson. Conn Smythe once said of Hudson, "I've had some great captains in my day, men like Syl Apps and Ted Kennedy, and [Hudson] sits right alongside them." Hudson is significant to Toronto Maple Leaf history in another way: his brother Henry died in the 1951 airplane crash that also claimed the life of Leaf defenceman Bill Barilko.

Word of Smythe's hockey acumen reached Colonel John Hammond, president of Madison Square Garden, and Tex Rickard, owner of the New York Rangers – a franchise that was set to join the NHL, along with teams in Detroit and Chicago, for the 1926-27 season. They recruited him to build a hockey team from scratch. Smythe went to work and assembled a stellar cast. In goal, he had Lorne Chabot, whom he had discovered in Port Arthur (now Thunder Bay). Chabot backstopped the team that had beaten Smythe's Varsity squad for the 1926 Allan Cup title. Next came defencemen Ching Johnson and Taffy Abel, who were plying their trade in Minnesota, and high-scoring brothers Bill and Bun Cook were purchased from Saskatoon. Classy centre Frank Boucher was signed from Vancouver of the Western Hockey League. Perhaps to add a touch of youth to this veteran lineup, Smythe signed Joe Primeau, who had scored 15 goals in seven games with the St. Mary's juniors, to a personal services contract.

The Rangers held their first training camp at Ravina Gardens in Toronto's west end, but before the season had even begun, Smythe was fired. Colonel Hammond felt there wasn't enough marquee value in the players who had been signed, so Conn was cut loose in favour of Lester Patrick. With his brother Frank, Lester Patrick had organized a league, the Pacific Coast Hockey Association, that rivalled the NHL through the late teens and early '20s. (Patrick was available because major-league hockey in western Canada was no longer viable.) Although Patrick led the Rangers to a first-place finish in the American Division that season, followed by a Stanley Cup championship in 1927-28, it was the players Conn Smythe had recruited who did the job. Boucher, the Cook brothers and Ching Johnson were all eventually inducted into the Hockey Hall of Fame.

New York settled with Conn Smythe by giving him cash and the rights to Joe Primeau. On February 14, 1927, still fuming from his dismissal from the Rangers, Smythe purchased the Toronto St. Patricks, renamed them the Maple Leafs, and changed the team colours to, in Smythe's words, "the blue of the waters and the white of the clouds that surround this great country we live in."

Although Joe Primeau was the first player the Toronto Maple Leafs signed, it would be some time before he played regularly with the club. He got into his first two NHL games early in the 1927-28 season, but was sent to the Toronto Ravinas of the Can-Pro league for further seasoning. There, after scoring 26 goals in 41 games, he seemed a sure bet to break in with the Leafs in 1928, but he was again farmed out to the Can-Pro league, this time with the London Panthers. Primeau's coach in London was Bert "Pig Iron" Corbeau, a character who always wore a black derby hat whenever he wasn't on the ice.

In addition to coaching, Bert Corbeau managed and occasionally played for the Panthers. During games he would be dressed in full hockey equipment, just in case he was needed. In Ed Fitkin's book The "Gashouse Gang" of Hockey, the story is told that when something went wrong on the ice, Corbeau would kick the wooden boards so hard that his skate would get stuck in them. As the play continued on the ice, Corbeau would spend the next several minutes extricating his skate from the bottom of the boards.

Fitkin also recounts the story of how Bert Corbeau retired from playing. With just minutes left in a 0-0 deadlock between the London Panthers and the Detroit Olympics on Christmas night 1928, Joe Primeau broke his skate blade, a frequent occurrence in the first half of the century. So Pig Iron moved defenceman Carl Voss – who, after becoming the first player ever selected as the NHL's rookie of the year, would go on to become an Honoured Member of the Hockey Hall of Fame – to centre. Corbeau himself took Voss's place on the blueline. In the two minutes it took Primeau to replace his skate blade, Detroit had gone ahead 3-0. The Olympics skated around Corbeau like a pylon, and the crowd grew so disgusted that they were screaming at him to get off the ice, throwing programs and other objects at him. At the end of the game, a London loss, Bert Corbeau stormed into the dressing room and slammed his skates against the wall, vowing he'd never put them on again.

In 1929-30, Joe Primeau finally became a regular with the Toronto Maple Leafs. The smooth-skating centre wasn't very big, but he made up for his lack of weight with his remarkable playmaking abilities.

The right winger on the Kid Line, Charlie Conacher, was born December 20, 1909, in a rented house – long since demolished – at 48 Davenport Road in Toronto. The location of the Conacher home, across the street from Jesse Ketchum Public School, is now occupied by a health club. It seems fitting that this site, which nurtured some of the finest athletes the city of Toronto has ever known, should continue to be associated with athletics.

Like the rest of his nine siblings, Charlie attended Ketchum. The neighbourhood around Avenue Road and Davenport is now considered upscale, but in the early part of the twentieth century it was a depressed area. The principal, William Kirk, saw sports as a way to keep his charges out of trouble, so he insisted that every one of his pupils get involved in athletics. Following the example set by his older brother Lionel, Charlie excelled in baseball, rugby, soccer, swimming and golf. Charlie also took after Lionel in that he struggled with hockey, particularly the skating, early on. Like many poor skaters, Charlie was relegated to playing goal at first, but with his brother's encouragement he worked hard and improved significantly.

Lionel Conacher was nine years older than Charlie, and his sporting exploits had already made him a legend throughout the city. Charlie idolized him, and followed him around like a puppy. By the time Lionel made his NHL debut with the Pittsburgh Pirates in 1925, Charlie had quit school and was playing pickup hockey at Jesse Ketchum Park with other men and boys who were out of work. He worked diligently on his skating, and he had an exceptionally hard shot – a gift he would employ to great effect throughout his NHL career.

Conacher was chosen to play with the North Toronto Juniors in 1926, before joining the Toronto Marlboros for 1927-28. Charlie scored 11 goals in nine games that season, adding 15 more goals in 11 playoff games. The Marlies entertained hopes of a Memorial Cup title, but the Ottawa Gunners surprised everyone, defeating the Marlboros before losing to the Regina Monarchs in the finals.

In 1928-29, playing on a line with future Leaf great Harvey Jackson on left wing and Eddie Convey at centre, Conacher tore up the OHA junior ranks. In eight games, he led the league with 18 goals and 21 points. He became the Marlies' captain when the Leafs promoted Red Horner. The Marlboros, coached by Frank Selke, reached the Memorial Cup finals this year, hosting the Elmwood Millionaires from Winnipeg in a best-of-three series at Arena Gardens and winning the first two games and the title. Conacher again dominated, leading the playoffs in both goals (28) and points (36) over the course of 15 games. By any measure, Charlie Conacher was the most prominent player in Canadian junior hockey.

The Leafs had put Conacher on their reserve list, but it wasn't easy to sign him. Brother Lionel, who was by now the playing coach of the New York Americans, lobbied for seven months to get the NHL to grant Charlie's rights to his team, but the league declined, and so Charlie's fate rested with Conn Smythe's Maple Leafs. Lionel reasoned that, if he couldn't land his younger brother for the Americans, it was best that he play close to home, and so he took it upon himself to negotiate Charlie's contract with the Leafs: a two-year deal at an annual salary of $10,000, plus a $5,000 signing bonus. At the time, it was huge money. In a display of flash that would typify the rest of his life, Charlie bought a yellow Buick coupe with a rumble seat, picked up his mom, dad, twin brothers Roy and Bert, sister Mary and the twin girls, Nora and Kay, and took them all for a picnic in a ravine near Yonge Street.

On November 14, 1929, Charlie Conacher played his first game with the Maple Leafs. He was placed at right wing on a line with Eric Pettinger and Baldy Cotton. In the March 16, 1957, issue of Maclean's, Charlie Conacher described his first goal. "I got a pass from Pettinger near the boards. I faked to my left as though I was going to try to split the defence, and when [Taffy] Abel moved to his right to block me, I cut to my right, skated wide around him and broke clear in on [Charlie] Gardiner and scored my first NHL goal." That goal came in Conacher's first NHL game, a 2-2 tie against the Blackhawks.

Conacher's first victim, Charlie Gardiner, was a superb goaltender. During a phenomenal seven-year career, all with the Blackhawks, he won the Vezina Trophy twice, was chosen to the NHL's First All-Star Team three times and was named to the Second Team once. He was also one of the few goalies ever to be named captain of an NHL team. After Gardiner and the Blackhawks won the Stanley Cup on April 10, 1934, the netminder went home to Winnipeg where, on June 13, he died of a brain hemorrhage. After an encounter with Conacher, some reporters asked Gardiner how hard the Leaf winger could shoot the puck. Without a word, Gardiner removed his sweater, chest protector and undershirt to reveal a massive purple bruise that covered his lower chest and abdomen. Once satisfied that the reporters had had time to survey the carnage, Gardiner looked up slowly and said: "And he wasn't even bearing down!"

Harvey Jackson was born in Toronto on January 19, 1911. He honed his hockey skills on frozen Grenadier Pond in High Park. As a teenager, Jackson hung around Ravina Gardens, offering to shovel the ice surface after games in return for a few hours of ice time early in the morning before school. Frank Selke, who spent long hours at Ravina Gardens monitoring talent, watched the young Jackson dart around the ice. When Selke first asked if the boy would like to play for the Toronto Marlboros, Jackson declined – he was playing for his high school, Humberside Collegiate. But once Selke convinced Jackson that he would get lots of practice and, perhaps more important, lots of ice time, he relented and joined the Junior A Marlboros in 1927. Teamed with Charlie Conacher and Eddie Convey, Harvey Jackson scored four goals in four games during the regular season, then went on a tear in the playoffs, notching a league-best 7 goals and 9 points in three games. The next season, 1928-29, Jackson scored 10 goals and 14 points in nine games. In those nine games, the Conacher-Convey-Jackson line combined for 44 points. In the Marlies' successful Memorial Cup run, Jackson scored 15 goals and 25 points in 13 games, while Conacher added the aforementioned 28 goals and 36 points. Convey added 8 goals and 20 points to give the dominant line an aggregate 51 goals and 81 points.

When the Maple Leafs called Conacher up, the younger Jackson was angry, feeling that he, too, deserved a shot at the NHL. He refused to re-sign with the Marlboros, making plans instead to play for a senior team in Toronto. A rumour circulated that he had challenged Conn Smythe to sign him to the Leafs, pledging that he could help turn the team around. In any event, on December 6, 1929, Jackson signed with the Maple Leafs, and he saw his first NHL action the very next night, against the Montreal Canadiens. Late in this game, there was a hint of great things to come. With the Habs leading, coach Conn Smythe tried to even the score by putting out a makeshift line of Joe Primeau, Charlie Conacher and Harvey Jackson. Although the threesome didn't score, they produced a number of spectacular chances, only to be thwarted by the Canadiens' goalie, the great George Hainsworth.

It would be several more weeks before the Kid Line was officially formed. Jackson suffered a charley horse in that first game, then Conacher was laid up with tonsillitis. While Jackson was out of the lineup, he was tagged with the nickname he would carry for the rest of his life. Before the team's next game, against the New York Americans, Leaf trainer Tim Daly asked the injured Jackson to help him look after the sticks. Jackson glared at the trainer and responded that he was an NHL player now, and so he was not about to look after anybody's sticks because it wasn't his job. Daly did a double take that almost gave him whiplash, then barked, "Well, if you ain't the cockiest busher I ever met!" The term "busher," coined by the legendary sportswriter Ring Lardner, described a player whose attitude was brash and cocky. From that moment, Harvey Jackson was known as Busher, a handle he quite enjoyed.

The Kid Line was officially born on Sunday, December 29, 1929. The three youngsters, all healthy now, were sent out to start a game in Chicago against the Blackhawks. According to Fitkin in The "Gashouse Gang" of Hockey, Leaf goalie Lorne Chabot gave Jackson a tap and said, "Good luck, kid!" Jackson, whose cockiness hadn't diminished one iota, responded with, "Don't you worry about me, Chabot. You just keep 'em out. I'll put 'em in." The game ended with a 4-3 Leaf victory – Jackson and Conacher each scored a goal, and Primeau assisted on both of them. In the next three games, Primeau scored a goal and two assists, Conacher added two goals and two assists, and Jackson netted three goals. The Kid Line had arrived. Tom Gaston remembers the Kid Line well: "Primeau made the bullets and Jackson and Conacher fired them!"

"Gentleman Joe," recalls Gaston. "Now there was a classy player! Won the Lady Byng Trophy in 1932. Boy, was he a smooth skater. And unselfish, too. He was happy to let Jackson and Conacher score the goals. He'd skate from his own blueline to the other team's blueline with the puck, then when the opposing team came at him he would dish off to one of his linemates and they'd go in to score.

"I met him at King Clancy's funeral in November 1986. By then he was a very successful businessman. Had his own concrete business. He was sitting up in the choir loft by himself. Said he wasn't feeling well.

"Now, Jackson was a beautiful skater – just like a hula dancer on skates. He had this great manoeuvrability; he could just go through that defence like nobody's business. He wasn't really a tough guy, but he could take care of himself if he had to. And boy, did the girls love him. He looked just like a Hollywood movie star.

"Jackson was drinking," recalls Tom. "Smythe kept it out of the papers back then, but I think he and Conacher were living pretty high. Good-looking boys, huge hockey stars. I remember in that

Stanley Cup season of 1932, the Kid Line almost finished one-two-three in scoring. Jackson came in first [with 53 points], Primeau was second [with 50] and Howie Morenz nudged Conacher out of third. Morenz had 49 points and Charlie had 48.

"They should have put the Kid Line in the Hockey Hall of Fame together. Connie Smythe kept Busher out because of his lifestyle. A player's outside life shouldn't impact on his selection as an athlete, but back then six guys controlled everything and those owners were incredibly powerful. Charlie Conacher was inducted into the Hockey Hall of Fame in 1961. Joe Primeau was inducted in '63. But Jackson didn't get selected until 1971, and that was only after Conn Smythe had relinquished his ownership. Busher Jackson died in 1966, so he never got to see his dream of entering the Hall come true."

CHAPTER FOUR

Hockey's First Family

Over the years there have been some incredible stories about the fathers, sons, brothers, uncles and nephews who have made substantial contributions to the game of hockey – so many, in fact, that the Hockey Hall of Fame in Toronto features a section dedicated to hockey families.

Brothers Frank and Lester Patrick helped build the present-day National Hockey League by forming the Pacific Coast Hockey Association in 1911-12. Both Frank and Lester owned, managed, coached and played for their respective PCHA clubs. Frank enjoyed success with his Vancouver Millionaires, who won the Stanley Cup in 1914-15. Lester's team was the Victoria Aristocrats, who later changed their name to the Cougars. By 1924, the PCHA was reduced to two teams, so the Patrick brothers took their teams into the Western Canada Hockey League. When that league folded after the 1925-26 season, the Patricks sold their players to NHL clubs. The brothers also brought their expertise east, Frank going on to coach the Boston Bruins while Lester joined the New York Rangers as coach and general manager – and even playing one celebrated game in goal during the 1928 Stanley Cup finals, a series the Rangers won. Lester's sons, Lynn and Muzz, both played for the Rangers during the 1930s and '40s and, like their father, they moved into hockey management. Lynn, Lester and Frank are all Honoured Members of the Hockey Hall of Fame. Lynn's sons, Craig and Glenn, both played in the NHL in the 1970s before following their father, grandfather and great uncle into hockey management. In 2001, it was Craig's turn to be inducted into the Hall of Fame.

The Boucher family of Ottawa had four boys who played in the NHL. Billy had a seven-year career in the 1920s, which included a Stanley Cup victory with the Montreal Canadiens in 1923-24. Bobby, often called "Shorty," played his only NHL season alongside Billy on the Cup-winning '24 Montreal Canadiens. Frank Boucher played thirteen seasons with the New York Rangers between 1926-27 and 1943-44, winning the Stanley Cup twice during his tenure. He went on to coach and manage the Rangers, and is an Honoured Member of the Hockey Hall of Fame. The fourth brother, Georges, was always called "Buck"; he too is an Honoured Member of the Hall. Best remembered as a twelve-year veteran of the Ottawa Senators, Buck contributed to four Stanley Cup titles for his hometown team.

Bryan Hextall came out of Saskatchewan to star with the New York Rangers in the 1930s. During his eleven-year stint, the elder Hextall was a four-time All-Star, and is an Honoured Member of the Hall of Fame. His boys, Bryan Jr. and Dennis, both had long careers in the NHL and, like their dad, both played for the New York Rangers at one time. Ron Hextall, the Vezina Trophy-winning All-Star goalie, is the son of Bryan Jr. and the grandson of Bryan Sr.

The Sutter family was a phenomenon unto itself. The pride of Viking, Alberta, the Sutters overcame incomprehensible odds in sending six brothers to the National Hockey League. Brian, the eldest, joined the St. Louis Blues in 1976; next came Darryl, who broke in with Chicago in 1979, and Duane, who became a New York Islander the same year; Brent joined Duane on Long Island in 1980; and finally, twins Ron and Rich made the grade, Ron with the Philadelphia Flyers in 1981 and Rich with the Pittsburgh Penguins a year later. All played a gritty, honest, no-holds-barred brand of hockey, and Brian, Darryl and Duane have parlayed that reputation into coaching careers.

Hall of Famer Gordie Howe was joined briefly in the NHL by his brother Vic, who played 33 games with the New York Rangers in the early 1950s. In 1973, Gordie's sons Mark and Marty got the unique opportunity to play with their dad, first with the Houston Aeros of the World Hockey Association and later with the New England Whalers of the same league. When the NHL absorbed four WHA teams in 1979-80, the three Howes played one season together with the renamed Hartford Whalers.

Maurice and Henri Richard spent their entire careers with the Montreal Canadiens; both were captains of the team and both have been inducted into the Hockey Hall of Fame. The "Rocket" won the Stanley Cup eight times during his eighteen-year NHL career. Henri, dubbed the "Pocket Rocket," won eleven Stanley Cup titles in a twenty-year career. A third brother, Claude, who journalists tagged

"The Vest Pocket Rocket,"attended a Canadiens training camp as a right winger, but he never played an NHL game.

Between 1964 and 1972, Bobby Hull played for the Chicago Blackhawks with his brother Dennis. A third Hull brother, Garry, tried out for the Ottawa Nationals of the WHA in 1972, but he was cut from the team before the season began. Bobby's son Brett has enjoyed an incredible career, surpassing the "Golden Jet's" career goal-scoring total early in the 2000-01 season.

In 1999, Wayne Gretzky retired after scoring 894 goals in 1,487 NHL games. Younger brother Brent added one more goal to the Gretzky family legend during a 13-game NHL career with the Tampa Bay Lightning. Between the brothers, they have won four Stanley Cups (although the scale is decidedly tilted in the direction of the elder brother).

But there is one family that has eclipsed all of these in terms of sheer numbers. The Conacher family has placed an astonishing seven members in the National Hockey League – three brothers, a brother-in-law and three nephews. And though the question of which family has been most significant to the league's history, it would be difficult to overlook the Conachers. Three are Honoured Members of the Hockey Hall of Fame, and the seven have played on seven Stanley Cup-winning teams. Collectively, they have won three scoring titles and earned five nominations to the NHL's First All-Star Team and four selections to the Second Team. Tom Gaston states emphatically that "the Conachers are truly the first family of hockey."

Brian Conacher, the youngest of five children born to Hall of Famer Lionel Conacher and his wife Dorothy, played his first game with the Leafs during the 1961-62 season, but he retained his amateur status and played for the Canadian national team until he rejoined the Leafs in 1965-66. Brian was a Stanley Cup winner with the Toronto Maple Leafs in 1966-67, his first full season in the NHL. After splitting the 1971-72 season between the Detroit Red Wings and Fort Worth of the Central league, he joined the Ottawa Nationals of the WHA the next season. Brian Conacher played in 155 NHL games, scoring 28 goals and 28 assists for 56 points. He has been an author and was vice president of building operations with the Toronto Maple Leafs.

Pete Conacher was born Charles Conacher Jr. He went by his middle name, Pete, to avoid the inevitable comparisons to his fabled father. Pete was a member of the Chicago Blackhawks organization during his junior years, and he finally cracked the big club's lineup in 1951-52, when he played two games. After bouncing between the National and American leagues, Pete stuck, remaining with Chicago until they traded him to the New York Rangers in 1954. From 1956 until he retired in 1966, Pete played almost exclusively for Buffalo and Hershey of the American Hockey League, except for a five-game stint with the Toronto Maple Leafs during the 1957-58 season. Pete Conacher played in 229 NHL games, scoring 47 goals and assisting on 39 others for 86 total points.

Murray Henderson was an eight-year veteran of the Boston Bruins. The big, strong defenceman joined the Bruins in 1944, and his NHL career ended with the final buzzer of the 1951-52 season. During that period, "Moe" scored 24 goals and assisted on 62 for a total of 86 points in 405 games. Murray Henderson is the son of Dolly (Conacher) Henderson, the eldest sister of Lionel, Charlie and Roy. Murray Henderson and his Uncle Roy were teammates on the Boston Bruins during the 1945-46 season.

No discussion of the Conacher family would be truly complete without mention of Lionel's brother-in-law, Harold "Baldy" Cotton, who married Marion Kennedy, the sister of Lionel's wife, Dorothy. Cotton entered the NHL along with Lionel when the Pittsburgh Pirates were added to the league in 1925. He later played with the Maple Leafs and, with Charlie Conacher, was part of the Toronto team that christened Maple Leaf Gardens with a Stanley Cup victory in 1931-32. Baldy retired in 1937 after finishing his career with the New York Americans. In 503 NHL games, Cotton scored 101 goals and assisted on 103 others for 204 points. He was a longtime member of the Hot Stove League, a group of hockey enthusiasts who discussed events related to the sport during the intermissions of Maple Leaf radio broadcasts. The present-day "Satellite Hot Stove" on CBC Television's Hockey Night in Canada is fashioned after that earlier radio version. Baldy Cotton scouted for the Boston Bruins for many years after his playing days were done.

"The Conachers really were the royal family of Toronto sports," Tommy says. "During the Depression, sports got a lot of families through some terrible times. When all of our families were worried about putting food on the table and a roof over our heads in the '30s, it was the great sports stories of families like the Conachers that took our minds off these concerns, it made our problems bearable. The story of the Conacher family and its rise from poverty gave us all just a little more hope."

THE BIG TRAIN

Tom Gaston's father was an acquaintance of Benjamin Conacher, the patriarch of the Conacher family. "My father used to deliver coal for Milnes Fuel, and the Conachers were living on Macpherson Street, next door to a coal yard," explains Tom. "Benjamin Conacher was a teamster, and he drove his horse and wagon around the city doing various jobs. For years, we had heard about the Conacher family and their sporting exploits around the Cottingham Square area of Toronto. Lionel was especially well known and loved in the city for his incredible athletic abilities."

Tom had another connection to the Conacher family. "My cousin lived on Marlborough Street, not far from the Conachers' home. I'd meet him at his house sometimes, and the odd time, we'd see the Conachers around. My cousin was a lacrosse player – he played for the old Toronto Tecumsehs, and he played with and against Lionel when the 'Big Train' was playing for the Maitlands. Lionel was a great athlete. He could play anything and be great at it.

"The first NHL game I ever saw was at the old Arena Gardens between the Leafs and the Montreal Maroons," recalls Tommy. "It was the 1930-31 season, and Lionel Conacher was playing for the Maroons and Charlie was with the Leafs. I got the tickets for Christmas. I went with my Dad and my brother Joe, and we sat way up high in the cheap seats. Toronto was always excited when Lionel Conacher came to town. I can't recall much about the game, but I do remember that Charlie and Lionel got into a scuffle. They were both sent to the penalty box. Back then, penalized players from both teams sat in the same penalty box. The two of them continued fighting in the penalty box, and the cops came over and stepped in between them. I clearly remember that Charlie kept fighting, and he wound up trying to slug Lionel, but he cold-cocked a policeman by mistake!"

Lionel Conacher was so revered for his incredible athleticism that he was chosen Canada's athlete of the half-century for the first half of the twentieth century. He was also inducted into the Canadian Sports Hall of Fame in 1955, the Canadian Football Hall of Fame in 1963 and the Canadian Lacrosse Hall of Fame in 1966. One of the proudest moments in Tom Gaston's hockey life was the day Lionel was inducted into the Hockey Hall of Fame in 1994.

"I always respected Lionel for being such a great athlete. One day, I was thinking that it was a crime that Lionel Conacher wasn't in the Hockey Hall of Fame. I think a lot of people must have assumed he was, but he wasn't. I don't know whether he was just overlooked in error, or forgotten because he had played in the 1930s, or whether somebody had kept him out because he used to drink a fair bit at one time, but he wasn't an Honoured Member. So a friend who volunteered with us at the Hall, Jim Hughes, and I put forward a nomination. First we talked to Brian Conacher, Lionel's son, and got his blessing.

"Lionel Conacher was a brainy hockey player. He was a big, rug-ged defenceman – and he had a great nickname, the 'Big Train.' Lionel was a popular brand of model trains, and as a hockey player, Lionel was just like a locomotive. He won back-to-back Stanley Cups – in 1934 with Chicago and in 1935 with the Maroons. He was on the NHL's First All-Star Team in 1934 and on the Second All-Star Team twice, in 1933 and again in '37. So Jim and I felt he was qualified to be in the Hockey Hall of Fame.

"We presented our case for Lionel in 1993, but he wasn't selected that first year. We tried again in 1994, and the committee voted him in. We were so happy, and the Conacher family was so appreciative. Even today, every time I see Brian Conacher, he always thanks me for getting his Dad into the Hall of Fame. At the induction cer-emony, the family invited me to sit with them in the Great Hall. That was a huge thrill, because only very special people ever get to witness an induction from the Great Hall."

Lionel Conacher excelled in baseball, football, lacrosse, boxing, soccer, wrestling and hockey. In fact, it has often been observed that hockey may very well have been Lionel's weakest sport. Red Burnett of the Toronto Star wrote, "If you listed Conacher's feats and sent the story to Hollywood, they'd turn them down as too fantastic!" Milt Dunnell, also of the Star, wrote, "He was the international sym-bol of greatness in athletics."

Lionel Pretoria Conacher was born May 24, 1900, the third of ten children born to Benjamin and Elizabeth Conacher. Benjamin had come to Canada from Scotland, while his wife, Elizabeth Black, was an Irish immigrant who had found work as a maid. The couple married in 1894. His first name honoured a distant ancestor, while

Pretoria was chosen because it was the name of the South African city in which the British had won a decisive battle in the Boer War.

Lionel was born in the family home at 48 Davenport Road. In a Toronto Star article, Lionel's daughter Deanne recalled that her father's family was "poor as church mice." According to Charlie Conacher, the neighbourhood in those days was "one of Toronto's higher-class slums." Directly across the street was Jesse Ketchum Public School, where all the Conacher children were encouraged to participate in sporting activities. Lionel left school at the age of twelve to work with his father as a labourer, and he was able to contribute an extra dollar a week to the family coffers by delivering sod from the Don Valley.

According to the Toronto Star, "Though Lionel played no games other than road hockey until he was 13 – he couldn't afford skates and other equipment – in five years he became known as the best all-around athlete in Toronto." Lionel Conacher didn't just participate in a vast number of sports, he dominated them all. His favourite, as he often repeated, was football. In 1921, the Toronto Argonauts recruited Lionel, and in his first game he scored 23 of the Argos' 27 points. He led his league, the "Big Four," in scoring that season with 85 points, including 14 touchdowns, in a six-game season! The Argos won all six games, scoring 167 points and allowing only 35, and went on to win the Grey Cup with a 23-0 victory over Edmonton. In the Grey Cup game, Lionel scored two touchdowns, two singles, and a drop-kick field goal – good for 15 points, which set a record for points scored in one game that stood for seventeen years. What made Conacher's feat even more remarkable is that he didn't play the whole game. With the game well in hand, Lionel left during the third quarter so that he could join the Aura Lee junior hockey team in a game against the Toronto Granites. In the third period of that game, he scored the winning goal.

In 1922, Conacher was named captain of the Argonauts, and he rushed for 950 yards in six games. After racking up a 5-0-1 record in league play, the Boatmen lost the eastern final, 12-11, to Queen's University of Kingston, Ontario. Early in the season, during a game against Montreal, a player named Allan Arless was killed while attempting to tackle Conacher, although Lionel denied that he was the ball carrier on that play. Several weeks later, the teams played a charity game that raised $12,000 for Arless's widow.

Lionel also played soccer – he joined the Toronto Scottish soccer team in 1919 as a fullback – until he was warned that he might lose his amateur status if he continued to play with the professionals on the Scots team.

And he was undefeated as a light-heavyweight boxer. In 1922, Conacher fought a four-round exhibition bout against heavyweight champion Jack Dempsey to raise funds for Toronto's Christie Street Hospital. At the age of 16, Lionel was Ontario's amateur lightweight wrestling champion, and he turned to professional wrestling in 1932.

During the summers, Lionel juggled baseball and lacrosse schedules. In 1921, he played outfield for the Toronto Hillcrests, helping them win the city senior baseball championship with his powerful bat. Each member of the team earned a gold medallion. On June 4, 1921, Conacher batted in the winning run with a double in the bottom of the ninth inning to give the Toronto Hillcrests a 6-3 victory over St. Francis in a Western City Baseball League game at Willowvale Park at the corner of Bloor and Christie streets. With that game over, Lionel rushed to Scarborough Beach Stadium at the other end of town, where he joined the Maitlands, his Ontario Amateur Lacrosse Association team, in a game that was already in progress. When Lionel arrived at halftime, the Brampton Excelsiors were leading 2-1, but Conacher scored two unassisted goals and assisted on another to lead his team to a 5-3 victory. The Toronto Telegram commented on Conacher's lacrosse prowess:

"He is, without a doubt, the greatest player in the game. Connie has faults as a lacrosse player. His style of play, as it is at present, does not make for good teamwork. If he knew just when to break and when to pass, there is no reason why he would not average at least five goals and five assists per match. However, as he stands on this season's work, he is the most brilliant individual performer in the sport."

The Toronto Hillcrests won a second consecutive baseball championship in 1922 with Lionel Conacher leading the team in batting. In 1926, he played three games in the outfield for the Toronto Maple Leafs of the Triple-A International League. The Maple Leafs won the pennant and the Little World Series championship that year.

When it came to hockey, Lionel Conacher was a late bloomer. He learned to skate for the first time in 1916, at the age of sixteen. Most of his peers had been playing hockey for almost ten years by that point, but Conacher's outstanding all-around athleticism helped him make up for lost time. In his first season, he played midget hockey with the Toronto Century Rovers. He worked diligently and moved up to the Toronto Aura Lee Junior A club. (The Aura Lee Athletic Club was on Avenue Road, just north of Davenport – a short walk from the Conacher home.) In 1918, that team went to the OHA finals, and the Toronto St. Patricks of the NHL offered Lionel a $3,000 contract – at least double the average salary in those days. Turning pro would have rendered him ineligible to play football, which was still an amateur sport, even at the elite level.

In 1920, Lionel helped the Toronto Canoe Club Paddlers win the Memorial Cup as Canadian junior hockey champions. Roy Worters and Billy Burch, with whom Lionel would eventually play on the New York Americans, were also on that squad. After that victory, Lionel moved up to the senior ranks. On February 18, 1922, as a member of the North Toronto Seniors, he took part in a historic game against Midland. It was the first game every broadcast over the radio. Conacher scored four goals to lead his team to a 16-4 victory.

Conacher received another invitation to join the NHL, this time from the Montreal Canadiens, who offered him $5,000 and his own business. He again declined the offer in order to remain eligible for football.

Since July of 1923, the word had spread that Lionel would be moving to Pittsburgh to play hockey and attend Bellefonte Academy, a noted prep school in central Pennsylvania, and by September the rumours were confirmed. Ultimately, he would attend Duquesne University, where he originally planned to earn an arts degree in hopes of one day studying medicine, but he later changed his major to economics. A freshman rule prohibited first-year students from playing football for the university team, which kept Conacher off the gridiron, although he was given permission to work out with the team. He also played for the school's hockey team, which held exhibition games against Yale, Harvard and Princeton. And he was named playing coach of the Pittsburgh Yellow Jackets of the United States Amateur Hockey Association, to which he lured a number of friends from Ontario who hadn't yet turned pro. All the players on the Yellow Jackets were Canadian, and the roster included co-coach Dick Carroll, who had been with the Toronto St. Pats, as well as goaltender Roy Worters and forwards Harold Cotton, Herb Drury, Hib Milks, Duke McCurry and Harold Darragh. All of those players went on to the National Hockey League.

Prior to Conacher's move to Pittsburgh, his friends in the Toronto sporting world arranged appropriate farewells. In his final baseball game with the Hillcrests on September 15, Conacher went

2-for-4, leading the way to a 10-2 win over the Westmorelands. The game was played before 3,000 fans at Hampden Park at Shaw and College streets. It was the Toronto Amateur Baseball Association's championship game. Mayor Alf Maguire presented Conacher with a leather travel bag on behalf of the city. The president of the Hillcrest Baseball Club, Harry "Clare" Settell, presented Conacher with a floral horseshoe, which he and the team placed over Conacher's shoulders.

The president of the Maitlands Lacrosse Club, Harris Ardiel, held a going-away party for Conacher at his home at 67 Lynwood Avenue. Unknown to all but a handful of people, it was here that Lionel Conacher and Dorothy Kennedy were married on that very evening. The front page of the Tuesday, September 18 edition of the Toronto Telegram bore a headline announcing the wedding:

CONACHER VICTIM CUPID'S DART – WEDS BEFORE LEAVING CITY

Many have seen his sparkling fifty and sixty yard runs through a broken field of tacklers on the gridiron or in carrying the ball on the lacrosse field, and he has often belted the ball out of the ballground. But the last bit of history Conacher made before he left Toronto stands as the greatest in his life. For Connie was married just twenty minutes before the train left Toronto. And the happiest young lady in Toronto today is Mrs. Lionel Pretoria Conacher, formerly Miss Dorothy Kennedy.

The marriage caused a scandal in Toronto, for although Lionel was loved by his fans, Dorothy was only seventeen at the time of their wedding. The bride's father was furious, but he eventually became very close with his son-in-law. Harry Deacon's Orchestra entertained, later playing Mendelssohn's Wedding March while Conacher rushed to pack for Pittsburgh. The train was scheduled to leave Union Station at 7:15 p.m., but it had to be held a few minutes for Conacher's party. As the Telegram reported: "Smiling and happy, Connie rushed through a group of friends, straight to his little wife who, with his younger brother, Charlie Conacher, were waiting for a last word with husband and brother. Connie soon took his wife in his arms, and with little Charlie hanging on to the couple, crying and heartbroken at the thought of his big brother leaving, they walked to the coach, where he had just enough time to wave goodbye, and Toronto had seen the last of her greatest athlete until around Christmas time."

The Yellow Jackets, who were paying Conacher's tuition, board and expenses, won the USAHA championship in 1924 and 1925. The autumn of 1925 would see the Yellow Jackets join the NHL, with its roster intact, as the Pittsburgh Pirates. On November 11, Lionel Conacher signed an NHL contract and finally became a professional athlete. When the Pirates visited Toronto on December 9, Conacher was greeted with a chorus of boos as he skated out for his first shift – the fans cared more about their St. Pats than the return of their prodigal sporting hero. Lionel and his Pirates exacted a measure of revenge, winning the game 6-3.

In their first season, the Pirates finished third in the NHL with a record of 19-16-1. Just nine games into his second pro season, the Pirates traded Conacher to the New York Americans for Charlie Langlois and $2,000. Conacher was paired on defence with "Bullet Joe" Simpson, from whom he learned much more about the intricacies of professional hockey. Unfortunately, New York also offered him the chance to learn about life in the fast lane, and he earned a reputation as a heavy drinker. The Americans missed the playoffs in 1926-27 and 1927-28, and Lionel was struggling off the ice as well. One night, while playing cards with his teammates, Conacher was hit in the eye by an apple core thrown by Red Green. Conacher overturned the card table and chased Green through the hallways of the hotel. Green ducked behind a closed door, but that didn't stop Conacher, who took his shoulder to the door and knocked down a portion of the wall in the process. Tempers cooled eventually, but the team was charged a substantial sum to repair the damage. Conacher was named playing coach of the Americans in 1929-30 but, locked in a battle with his personal demons, the big defenceman contributed just 10 points during the regular season, and New York failed to make the playoffs for the fourth time in their five-year history.

In part to save Lionel from himself, the Americans sold Conacher to the Montreal Maroons on November 5, 1930. Charlie Conacher was only half kidding when he stated that his brother took the advertising slogan "Drink Canada Dry" literally. Lionel again struggled, with just 7 points in 1930-31. The Maroons, sensing the Big Train's hockey days might be over, were prepared to waive him through the league, but Lionel begged for a reprieve and was kept on. During that season, Lionel became a father with the birth of a girl, Constance, on November 25. The new family responsibilities, combined with the realization that his career had been in jeopardy, triggered a new commitment to both his wife and his game.

"It was in 1930 that I experienced my hardest battle as an athlete. I was an unwanted veteran with the Maroons, who were trying, unsuccessfully, to waive me out of the league. I promptly decided to quit drinking, and it was the training of many gruelling years in sport – making the old will power say 'uncle' – that stood me in good stead. It was a tough fight getting out of the broken-down, has-been rut, and none realize the job it was better than myself." (Macleans, September 1, 1932)

With a renewed work ethic, and now living with his young family in a mansion at 55 Teddington Park Avenue in Toronto, Lionel was voted Most Valuable Maroon by his teammates in 1931-32. The next season, with a second daughter, Diane, in the fold, Lionel Conacher had his most productive NHL season, scoring 7 goals and 21 assists for 28 points, and was named to the NHL's Second All-Star Team.

In the summer of 1933, Conacher returned to Toronto and helped organize Canada's first professional football league. Having turned pro in hockey, wrestling, lacrosse and baseball, he was ineligible to play for teams like the Argonauts, which were still strictly amateur. It had been ten years since Conacher had played football in Canada, and a league was organized that included teams in Toronto, Buffalo and Rochester. Lionel captained Toronto's Crosse and Blackwell Chefs (the team sponsor was a food supply company), for which brother Charlie also played.

The Maroons traded Conacher to the Chicago Blackhawks in time for the start of the 1933-34 season. The deal shocked Lionel, but there was a bright side: he would be rejoining coach Tommy Gorman, who had been his mentor with the 1928-29 New York Americans. Upon his arrival, Lionel was named captain of the Blackhawks, an honour he repaid by working exceptionally hard, recording 23 points during the regular season and helping the Hawks to their first-ever Stanley Cup title. It was also Lionel's first championship. He was named to the First All-Star Team, and was second to the Canadiens' Aurel Joliat in the most valuable player voting. That summer, Lionel returned to Toronto and his football team, which had changed sponsors and was now known as the Wrigley Aromints. It would be Lionel's last season of football.

On October 3, 1934, Lionel Conacher was traded again – this time, twice in the same day. The Hawks sent him to the Montreal Canadiens with Leroy Goldsworthy and Roger Jenkins in return for Howie Morenz, Marty Burke and Lorne Chabot. Later that day, the Canadiens swung a deal with the Maroons, sending Conacher and Herb Cain to the Maroons for Nels Crutchfield. Oddly enough, this trade would yet again reunite Lionel with Tommy Gorman, who had left Chicago for the job behind the Maroons' bench. Conacher enjoyed a solid season, even acting as playing coach for several games when Gorman's health failed. The Maroons finished in second place in the Canadian Division, then charged through the playoffs to win the Stanley Cup, the second title in a row for both Conacher and Gorman.

In 1935-36, the Maroons finished first in the Canadian Division, but they were eliminated in the semifinals by the Detroit Red Wings, who won the Stanley Cup. The next season, Lionel's last in the NHL, was a productive one: his 25 points were the second-highest total of his career. For the second time, he was runner-up for the Hart Trophy (the award given to the NHL's most valuable player), this time to Babe Siebert of the Canadiens. Lionel was also selected to the Second All-Star Team at the end of the season. On April 3, 1937, Lionel Conacher played his final game in the National Hockey League. In his twelve NHL seasons, Lionel Conacher played in 498 regular-season games, scored 80 goals and assisted on 105 others for a total of 185 points. He was also charged with 882 penalty minutes. In 35 playoff games he contributed two goals and two assists for four points, along with 40 minutes in penalties.

Throughout his celebrated career, Conacher broke his nose eight times, broke bones in his arm, leg and both hands, suffered cracked ribs, and collected more than 600 stitches – sixteen of which closed a gash across his jugular vein from a skate blade. For his contributions to his team and to hockey, Lionel Conacher was inducted, posthumously, into the Hockey Hall of Fame in 1994.

When Lionel Conacher left the hockey arena, he entered the political arena. In October 1937, Conacher was elected to the Ontario Legislature as the Liberal MPP – Member of Provincial Parliament – for the Toronto riding of Bracondale. He defeated the Conservative incumbent by a slim 37-vote margin. His constituency office was located in the Conacher Brothers Service Station and Garage, a block away from where he had been born. In 1938, Lionel –

a natural for the position – was selected as chairman of the Ontario Athletic Commission, and during the Second World War he was director of recreation for the Royal Canadian Air Force.

When a provincial election was called for the summer of 1943, Lionel had hoped to stand for re-election, but in a shocking turn, he failed to win the party's nomination in his riding. He tried to enter federal politics in the election of 1945, but again was unsuccessful. Finally, in the federal election of June 1949, Lionel Conacher was elected to the House of Commons, representing the Toronto riding of Trinity. He won re-election in 1953, and he would represent the district until his death, which came shortly thereafter.

Each year, the Members of Parliament challenged the Ottawa press corps to a softball game. The game on May 26, 1954 was no different than any other: spectators cheered for both teams, politicians kibitzed with the press, and no one took the game too seriously. Conacher had intended to return to Toronto for his daughter Diane's graduation from the University of Toronto, but he cancelled the trip so that he could participate in the charity softball game. Earlier in the day he complained of a chest pain, but wrote it off as indigestion from the four hard-boiled eggs he had eaten that afternoon.

In the sixth inning, the score was 12-8 in favour of the politicians. With a teammate standing on third base, Lionel, who had been playing second base that afternoon, came to the plate. He took two pitches from George Bain of the press team, both of which were balls. On the third pitch, Lionel drove the ball deep into the crowd standing in left field. As the outfielders chased the ball, Conacher sped past first and second base, then slowed as he pulled into third with a stand-up triple. Third baseman Maurice Jefferies congratulated Conacher on his great hit. But as pitcher Bain readied a second pitch to Donald Fleming, the Progressive Conservative member for Eglinton, Lionel Conacher dropped to his knees, then fell flat out on the baseline, blood oozing from his nose and mouth. Dr. William McMillan, a Liberal member from Welland who was enjoying the game as a spectator that day, rushed to the fallen Conacher, propped his head up onto the base and tried to resuscitate him. The Ottawa Fire Department arrived almost immediately, and an ambulance followed a minute or so later. As Lionel was carried to the ambulance, the silenced spectators showed their respect by bowing their heads and saying a prayer. Lionel Conacher died en route to nearby Ottawa General Hospital.

Prime Minister Louis St. Laurent, who had thrown out the ceremonial first pitch, made this statement to the Conacher family: "The news of his passing will be met with the deepest sorrow by his colleagues in Parliament, by those whom he represented in Ottawa and by all sports-loving Canadians. No matter what task he undertook, whether in sports or in service to his community, it was typical of Lionel Conacher that he devoted his total energy to it. My wife and I wish to assure you and your children of our very deep personal sympathy in your so unexpected and so tragic bereavement."

Toronto Maple Leaf president Conn Smythe said, "I knew him all his athletic life and he was the greatest athlete I have known. He was a colourful figure and did everything with a flair."

Lionel's brother Charlie had just returned to London, England after a trip to Ireland when he was given the news. Charlie flew back to Toronto, accompanied by former NHL president Red Dutton. As a player, Dutton had been traded from the Montreal Maroons to the New York Americans in 1930, the same year that Conacher left the Americans for the Maroons. Hall of Fame goaltender Roy Worters, a longtime friend of the Conachers, was doing some work for Charlie on an island he owned in Lake Ontario, about a mile and a half off Belleville, when he heard the news. Worters had always been thankful for Lionel's convincing him to continue playing hockey at a time when he was fed up and wanted to quit.

"Like hundreds of others in Toronto, I lined up to pay my respects to Mr. Conacher at his home on Teddington Park," Gaston recalls sadly. "The body was on view there, and it was a cross-section of Toronto who came to pay their last respects. You'd be rubbing shoulders with politicians, hockey players and those of us common folk who just wanted to let the Conacher family know how much Lionel had meant to us all."

On Saturday, May 29, 1954, Lionel Pretoria Conacher was buried in the beautiful graveyard beside his home church, St. John's Anglican, near where Yonge Street meets Highway 401. The plot, occupied by Lionel and his wife Dorothy, who died in 1986, is marked by a plaque affixed to a beautiful rock. The church was built in 1863, and is an oasis of calm in the midst of the busy streetscape that lies just beyond some shrubbery.

The four surviving Conacher brothers – Dermott, Charlie, Roy and Bert – served as pallbearers, aided by friends who included Dr. Smirle Lawson. Lawson was inducted into the Canadian Football

Hall of Fame in 1963, the same year as Lionel. Honourary pallbearers included parliamentary colleagues Lester B. Pearson and Paul Martin Sr.; Mayor Allan Lamport of Toronto; hockey men Roy Worters, Red Dutton, Tommy Gorman, Harold "Baldy" Cotton and Wilfrid "Bucko" McDonald; and former heavyweight boxing champion Jack Dempsey.

Conacher was survived by his wife, Dorothy, and children Constance, Diane, Lionel Jr., David and Brian, as well as both his parents and his nine siblings: the four brothers named above, as well as sisters Dolly Henderson, Queenie Mayhue, Mary Zellers, Kay Wilson and Nora Conacher.

In the Frank Stollery Parkette, where the Conacher Brothers Service Station once stood at the corner of Davenport Road and Yonge Street, there is an Ontario historical marker – unveiled on October 5, 1985 – that commemorates Lionel Conacher's selection as Canada's finest athlete of the first half of the twentieth century. On May 31, 1992, the government of Canada unveiled a national historical marker honouring Lionel Conacher. It is located in the vast park beside Cottingham Public School, where the Conachers played hockey as children. The park, now named Lionel Conacher Park, is on Cottingham Street, east of Avenue Road, near De La Salle College.

In November 1999, debate raged over who would be named Canada's top male and female athletes of the century. Skier Nancy Greene was selected as the female athlete of the century, although many felt multi-sport athlete Bobbi Rosenfeld – whose achievements were obscured by the fact that most writers neither saw her compete nor knew much about her – deserved to win. There was much discussion over whether Lionel Conacher, Canada's athlete of the half-century, would again be honoured. Or would it be Wayne Gretzky? Milt Dunnell, the former sports editor of the Toronto Star, had the exceptional good fortune – and longevity – to cover both athletes in their prime. "These days, with all the seasons overlapping, the amount of money involved and the need to specialize," he said, "nobody will ever get a chance to do what Conacher did." Brian Conacher, Lionel's son, said: "I never saw my dad play – he retired from sports four years before I was born. But speaking objectively, the fact is that there never has been, nor probably never will be again, a more multi-talented athlete." In the end, Gretzky was chosen for the honour, with Lionel Conacher placing fourth in the voting.

THE BIG BOMBER

"They used to call Charlie Conacher 'The Big Bomber,'" Tommy Gaston smiles. "He was just like a tank. Chuck was big and strong – not many guys would mess with him. I saw him and the Kid Line play many, many times. That line just loved to play. They didn't break lines up back then like they do today. And guys would play hurt, too. I remember that Charlie played in a Stanley Cup final with a broken wrist one year.

"I loved to see him shoot. He shot the puck so hard, you thought it was going to go right through the boards. In fact, I think I remember being told that he did once break a board at the end of the rink.

"Charlie was a really nice guy. I used to run into him and Lorne Chabot at Davisville Park sometimes – I'd see them skating, and during the summer they'd often play in charity baseball games. Lorne Chabot used to live near there, and he'd have the Leafs over to his house. We didn't live very far away, so I'd often see them at the park.

"I remember that Charlie owned a dance hall up in Wasaga Beach in the early '30s. It was called the Slipper Dance Hall, and a lot of the Leafs would go up there during the summer," recalls Gaston. The Slipper was located right on the beach, at the foot of 10th Street. Today, that site is part of Wasaga Beach Provincial Park under the care of Ontario's Ministry of Natural Resources. As popular tastes changed, so did the purposes for the Slipper. When Conacher sold it to Deserya Shelton, Shelton changed the name to the Strathcona and turned the building into a very popular roller skating rink.

Helen Pavelin, a longtime Wasaga Beach resident, remembers the demise of what was the Slipper Dance Hall. "They always used to brace the roof when they closed it up in the fall so it would withstand the winter snow. But in 1951, they didn't bother because we'd only had light snow for a couple of years and I guess it didn't seem worthwhile. Well, one day in the winter, we heard a terrible crashing sound and my father got in the car and drove around to find out what had happened. He came back and said the Strathcona's roof had collapsed. It was torn down after that." Marilyn Myers, granddaughter of the man who bought the dance hall from Charlie Conacher, finishes the story. "When my dad operated the business, he turned it into the Strathcona and it was a roller skating rink. The rink fell down about 1952 from such heavy snowfalls that year. The insurance company referred to it as an act of God, so no insurance money was collected. Eventually, the government bought up these properties."

Charlie was also one of the owners of Wasaga Beach's first golf course. At the time, it was a nine-hole course, but today is part of Marlwood Golf and Country Club.

"Charlie and Lionel had a gas station, too," recalls Tom Gaston. "It was built and opened up in the summer of 1935, and it was called Conacher Brothers Service Station and Garage. It was on that triangle of land at Yonge and Davenport, right across from the old Masonic Temple. You would enter the gas station from either Davenport or Scollard Street. They were a B-A [British American] gas station, and the boys had their office upstairs over the gas station. It was really well kept up, and there was a big picture of Charlie – you know, that famous one of him with one leg raised and backhanding the puck – right on Yonge Street. I used to drop by there just to see if I could see the Conachers. Quite often, I'd see them there and chat with them for a few minutes. I remember talking with Lionel about the Maroons and lacrosse, and told Charlie my Mom had got his and Hap Day's autograph on a hockey stick in the sporting goods department at Simpson's. Lionel and Charlie were a big deal in the city."

On the day of the service station's grand opening, the Globe and Mail reported that, "For more than two hours, cars in a steady line were driven into the station. Hundreds of men and boys attended, and before the evening closed, the Conachers, in spite of their winter training, had their arms stiffened in 'writer's cramp' from slinging down their autographs."

"Charlie played hard," Gaston says. "He'd take a beating out there, and he wasn't hesitant to fight. In some ways, he reminds me of Wendel Clark. When you play that aggressively, you get hurt, and just like Wendel, Charlie's career ended too soon. By the late '30s, he was out of the Leafs' lineup a lot more often than he was in, and they finally sold him to Detroit in 1938. He was only there a year, and then his rights came back to Toronto because the Wings couldn't sign him. So Toronto traded him to the New York Americans, and he finished off his career there. They put him back on defence a lot in New York, but he was just a shadow of himself."

After retiring in 1941, Charlie got into coaching. "In 1941, the Oshawa Generals' coach, a guy named Tracy Shaw, got suspended indefinitely for hitting a referee," Tommy says. "They brought Charlie in to be coach alongside the Oshawa manager, Matt Leyden. The Generals were a powerhouse back then. They won a couple of Memorial Cups, and had a strong lineup. In the spring of '42 they won the Eastern Canada finals but got knocked out of the Memorial Cup finals by the Portage La Prairie Terriers. In 1942-43, Conacher was the full-time coach, and the Generals reached the Memorial Cup finals again – for the fifth time in six years. But this time, they were beaten by the Winnipeg Rangers. I remember that Oshawa had Bill Ezinicki on the team, and a real good kid named Red Tilson. Tilson led the league in scoring that year, then joined the army and never came back. He was killed in action."

Nineteen forty-four was the year that Conacher's Generals finally won the Memorial Cup, in a sweep of the Trail Smoke Eaters. "Back then, you could add players to your team for the playoffs," Tommy points out, "and Oshawa added Ted Lindsay, Gus Mortson and David Bauer from St. Mike's. Bauer went on to become a priest, and he ran Canada's national program for years. Both Mortson and Lindsay had great NHL careers. Oshawa whipped Trail [by scores of 9-2, 5-2, 15-4 and 11-4] and won the Memorial Cup with Charlie Conacher behind the bench.

"A couple of years later, Charlie coached the Blackhawks in Chicago. Whenever he returned to Maple Leaf Gardens, nobody made much of a fuss the way they would today. He got hired partway through the 1947-48 season, then coached them for two years after that. But Chicago had a terrible team and they didn't make the playoffs any of the years he was there. Charlie coached his brother Roy in Chicago – Roy and Doug Bentley were the stars on the team. Both of them finished in the top ten in scoring each of those years [in 1948-49, Roy was number one and Bentley number two in scoring], but that was about all the Blackhawks had going for them. By the end of the 1949-50 season, Charlie had had enough and returned to his other businesses.

"Charlie was a very successful businessman after he retired. He owned a couple of hotels with Roy Worters. They used to call Worters 'Shrimp' because he was so small. He couldn't have been more than five foot two or three, but he was a hell of a goalie. One of the hotels they owned together was called the Conroy Hotel – 'Con' for Conacher and 'roy' for Worters' first name. It was at Dufferin Street and Lawrence Avenue in North York. When they built it in the mid-fifties, it was right on the edge of a dry (no alcohol) area, and they did a ton of business. I remember hearing that they sold more beer than any other hotel in Ontario (8,500 glasses of draft beer per six-day week by 1966).

"They sold the Conroy to a Dr. Egan in 1966. Charlie called Worters the best goalie he ever faced. I never really knew how they became partners. They both were Toronto boys, but they never would have played together. Charlie was with the New York Americans in 1939 and '40, but Worters had retired in '37. Maybe Charlie's brother Lionel was the key – he and Worters played with the Pittsburgh Pirates in the '20s, and both played with the Americans between 1928 and 1930.

"I remember Charlie was at the opening game of the Leafs season in 1965. He went to the game with Bing Crosby, who was a friend of his, and the Blackhawks shut out the Leafs 4-0. A week later, Charlie had a heart attack. His health wasn't very good from then on.

"I felt horrible for Charlie in 1967. I remember he came back from a Florida vacation and had his larynx removed at Toronto General Hospital. He had throat cancer. When he got out of the hospital, he spent the summer up at his cottage at Bluewater Beach on Nottawasaga Bay, but he had to come back to Toronto each week to see his doctor. In May of that year, Charlie attended the wedding of his nephew, Brian, even though he was still convalescing from the major surgery. In the fall, he went fishing out in Vancouver with his friend, Max Bell. There's an arena named for Max Bell in Calgary. But Charlie was really sick, and he died on December 30, 1967.

"The funeral service took place January 3 at St. Paul's Anglican Church in Toronto. Two of the honourary pallbearers were Red Foster, who was a friend of Charlie's from when they were kids at Cottingham Square, and Lorne Duguid, who was an NHL player with the Montreal Maroons when Lionel was there. Lorne Duguid later married Charlie's widow, Sunny. Charlie was buried in Mount Pleasant Cemetery in Toronto, and has a large memorial stone on his plot. It's quite big, and it has a fish and 'Charles W. Conacher' engraved on it."

In appreciation for the treatment given Charlie Conacher by Dr. Douglas Bryce, a surgeon at Toronto General Hospital, the Charlie Conacher Research Fund was founded to raise money for laryngeal (throat) cancer research. Red Foster and Lorne Duguid were on the fund's committee, as were Red Horner, Joe Primeau, Harold Ballard,

John W. Bassett, Alan Eagleson, Charlie's son Pete Conacher and Doug Creighton, a founder of the Toronto Sun. The fund raised more than $4 million, which helped set up the Charlie Conacher Research Wing, located at 101 College Street, just a few blocks west of Maple Leaf Gardens where Conacher had starred. It was officially opened on October 2, 1985. When Harold Ballard died, his will provided for the Charlie Conacher Research Fund to receive a percentage of his estate. Steve Stavro, Donald Giffin and Donald Crump were named as trustees of the Ballard estate, but because Mr. Stavro had interest in purchasing Maple Leaf Gardens shares, the court appointed three new trustees in order to avoid a conflict of interest. The new trustees have allocated much of the estimated $44 million (including accrued interest) to charities named in Harold Ballard's will, but unfortunately, the Charlie Conacher Research Fund for Throat Cancer has not received any of that allocated money.

In an informal poll of Toronto Star readers conducted by Jim Proudfoot on February 1, 1985, Charlie Conacher was selected by fans as the Toronto Maple Leafs' all-time all-star at right wing, beating Lanny McDonald and Gordie Drillon. When the Hockey News selected its top fifty NHL players of all time in 1999, Charlie was number 36.

"Charlie Conacher – one of my all-time favourites," Tommy Gaston concludes. "I will never forget how hard his shot was. He was the picture of sheer power. You have to respect a guy like that."

ROY

"I didn't see Roy play as much as his brothers, but he was also a very good hockey player," Tom Gaston recalls. "It was probably very hard for him to play in the shadows of his older brothers, and maybe it was a good thing that he didn't play in Toronto where the fans' expectations would have been so high. But he was a different kind of player to both Lionel and Charlie, and he had his own, very successful career."

Roy Conacher was born October 5, 1916, along with twin brother Bert. "Bert was a hell of a hockey player, too," Tommy says, "but he lost the sight in one eye, so he could never play in the NHL. There were two sets of twins in the Conacher family: Roy and Bert as well as Nora and Kay. The girls were great athletes, too; they were star softball players in the Sunnyside Girls League."

Like his brothers, Roy also began his sporting career on the play-grounds of Jesse Ketchum Public School. In 1931, when Maple Leaf Gardens opened, Roy and his twin brother Bert sold concessions in the arena, while their brother Charlie starred on the ice. Roy's favourite sport was baseball, but Lionel convinced him to take a shot at hockey. In a March 16, 1957, article in Maclean's, Charlie Conacher reminisced about playing street hockey:

"I always felt that my hockey ability was helped by those shinny sessions on the street, and I think it helped my brother Roy's, too. It developed our shots and our stick-handling, as well, but it also contained a lasting note of tragedy. I was playing with Roy and his twin brother Bert one afternoon after I'd turned pro. Bert and I were jostling for the ball and my stick cracked him at the side of the left eye for a little two-stitch cut. We didn't think anything of it at the time, but about eight months later, Bert went blind in that eye. He was about sixteen then, and played junior hockey after that, but of course he was unable to play pro hockey."

Both Roy and Bert played for the West Toronto Nationals, who won the Memorial Cup in 1935-36. Harold Ballard was the team's manager, and Hap Day, who was still playing with the Toronto Maple Leafs at the time, was the coach. "Whenever Hap couldn't be there because the Leafs were playing, Mr. Ballard stepped behind the bench," Tommy remembers. Other members of the team were future NHLers Jack Crawford, Red Heron and "Peanuts" O'Flaherty. The next season, Roy played senior hockey for Dominion Breweries, and led them to a championship as well. In 1937-38, Roy was an all-star with the Kirkland Lake Hargreaves of the Northern Ontario Hockey Association.

Wearing Charlie's familiar number 9, Roy Conacher broke into the NHL with the Boston Bruins in 1938-39, and as a rookie he not only led the Bruins in goals, with 26, but the NHL as well. He finished tenth in scoring that season, and was runner-up for the Calder Trophy as the NHL's best rookie, behind teammate Frank "Mr. Zero" Brimsek, who earned 10 shutouts. The Bruins finished the regular season in first place, then won the Stanley Cup on Roy's winning goal in a 3-1 seventh-game victory over the Toronto Maple Leafs.

The next season, Boston finished first once again, but were knocked out of Stanley Cup competition in the first round by the New York Rangers. In 1940-41, the Bruins again topped the standings, and this time they were not to be denied in the postseason. They won the Cup again, in another seven-game final against the Leafs. After playing the 1941-42 season, Roy joined the Royal Canadian Air Force, and played the next three years with Air Force senior teams. Returning to the NHL with an honourable discharge, Roy played the last four games of the 1945-46 schedule with Boston, registering two goals and an assist. His nephew, Murray Henderson, also played for the Bruins that year. But Bruins general manager Art Ross was not convinced that Conacher could return to his pre-war form after missing almost four seasons, so he traded Roy to Detroit for Joe Carveth before the 1946-47 season.

With the Wings, Roy wore his familiar number 9. Coincidentally, a rookie named Gordie Howe, who would become a hockey legend as Detroit's number 9, wore number 17 that season – the same number Charlie Conacher had worn in his one season with Detroit in 1938-39. Proving the Bruins wrong, Roy scored a career-best 30 goals and was eighth in the NHL scoring race. In a 10-6 road victory over Chicago on March 16, 1947, Roy scored four goals – three of them in the third period – while Ted Lindsay added three more. This was the first time that two members of the Red Wings had ever scored hat tricks in the same game. Roy's centre, Billy Taylor, racked up an amazing seven assists that night. The Red Wings made the playoffs, but were eliminated in the quarterfinals. Roy scored four goals and four assists in the five games, which represented the last NHL playoff action Roy would see.

In 1947-48, after a lengthy contract holdout, the Wings traded Roy to the Rangers for Eddie Slowinski and future considerations. Roy refused to report to New York and the trade was voided. Instead, Conacher was sold to the Blackhawks on November 18, 1947. Roy and his twin brother Bert were inseparable and Roy refused to go to Chicago unless his brother came along. (Roy's wife Frances said, "When I married Roy, I married them both.") The Hawks gave Bert a job as an assistant trainer. The Conacher family reunion got even bigger in Chicago, as brother Charlie was hired to coach the Hawks six weeks after Roy joined the team. Roy placed tenth in the scoring race in his first season as a member of the sad-sack Hawks.

In 1948, Roy replaced Max Bentley, who had been traded to the Leafs, on the Pony Line with Doug Bentley and Bill Mosienko in 1948-49, and the trio had an outstanding season. Roy led the league in scoring with 26 goals and 42 assists for 68 points, earning the Art Ross Trophy and a selection to the NHL's First All-Star Team as a result. Linemate Doug Bentley was second in scoring.

Roy played two more full seasons, netting more than 20 goals and 50 points each time. In 1951-52, Roy played in the Hawks' first twelve games, scoring three goals, but he retired once he had eclipsed his brother Charlie's career total of 225 goals. In 490 regular-season games, Roy scored 226 goals and added 200 assists for 426 points. Jim Proudfoot, writing in the November 16, 1998, edition of the Toronto Star, noted: "Art Ross, who ran the Boston club, always confessed his biggest mistake was his assumption that four years off would have ruined Conacher. He dealt him, therefore. Yet if you could imagine a modest 25 (goals) each for those four wartime campaigns he missed, he'd have gone out as the biggest shooter in NHL history up till then. And Conacher averaged 25 goals annually over the rest of his NHL life."

Roy Conacher died December 29, 1984, in Victoria, British Columbia, after a long struggle with dystonia, a neurological muscle disorder that includes involuntary muscle spasms. His remains were returned to Toronto for a special memorial service at St. Paul's Anglican Church on January 5, 1985. "It was a sad day," recalls Tom Gaston. "I went with one of my neighbours, Snubber Scott, who had played baseball with the Conachers."

Roy Conacher was inducted posthumously into the Hockey Hall of Fame on November 16, 1998. In his induction speech on behalf of his father, Roy's son Mark stated: "As many who knew him would agree, my father would not, and in his lifetime, did not seek this honour. He was a man who was self-effacing – who believed that merit should speak for itself. My father became, at least for one season certainly, the best in the world at what he did. He was driven to that pinnacle by a deeply rooted motivation: a desire for perfection."

Brian Conacher is Lionel's youngest son and he enjoyed a successful career affiliated with the Toronto Maple Leafs, both as a player and an executive. He is now chairman of the Recreational Hockey Network. Brian offers his perspective on Tommy Gaston and his ties to the Conacher family: "No sports team has had a more loyal or dedicated fan than the Toronto Maple Leafs have in Tommy Gaston. Tommy has maple syrup in his veins.

"I first met Tommy when I was Vice President of Building Operations for Maple Leaf Gardens in the early 1990s. I was fascinated by his encyclopedic knowledge about the Gardens and the Leafs right from their origins.

"While Tommy was in and around the Gardens for a variety of events over the years, his true love and dedication was to the Leafs. He was in attendance at the first game in Maple Leaf Gardens on November 12, 1931, against the Chicago Blackhawks through to the final game, also against the Blackhawks, on February 13, 1999. He saw my Uncle Charlie score the first Leafs goal in the Gardens in their 2-1 loss to the Hawks. He has seen every Leafs Stanley Cup game and victory parade. Tommy lives for the blue and white.

"Tommy grew up in the era of the Kid Line and became a great admirer of the Conacher brothers as athletes and hockey players. Around 1992, he got my ear one day about the fact that my father, Lionel, was not in the Hockey Hall of Fame. Many people assumed that he was because he was in Canada's Sports Hall of Fame, but in fact, he was not. Tommy wanted to correct what he considered to be a huge omission by the Hockey Hall of Fame.

"While no one in our family had actively lobbied to get my father into the Hockey Hall of Fame, Tommy, with his infectious enthusiasm, made it a personal mission. He recruited my support and others, along with his good friend Jim Hughes, and the mission took wings. Tommy collected and dug up statistics and information on my father's career and prepared a package for submission to the selection committee. My father was typical of many veteran players whose great careers had been lost or forgotten. While it took some time, lobbying, and a huge personal commitment and effort by Tommy and Jim, they were not to be denied. On November 15, 1994, Lionel Conacher was inducted into the Hockey Hall of Fame. No one was prouder than Tommy Gaston.

"With my father's success under his belt, Tommy proceeded to also get my Uncle Roy inducted into the Hockey Hall of Fame. Roy had the best statistics of the three Conacher brothers in the NHL and played on two Stanley Cup teams with the Boston Bruins. With his induction in 1998, Roy, Charlie and Lionel became the only set of three brothers inducted into the Hockey Hall of Fame.

"In addition to being the ultimate Leafs fan, Tommy is a veteran NHL player's best friend, for he wants the former greats of hockey to be honoured appropriately with the players of the modern era. And he has certainly been a true friend and supporter of the Conacher clan. Tommy is family!"

CHAPTER FIVE

Maple Leaf Gardens

The city was electric. Maple Leaf Gardens, bathed in the glow of floodlights for its grand opening, was gleaming. No one seemed able to truly comprehend how Conn Smythe had become such a magician, turning a block of old shops and homes into a hockey palace in only 165 days – with no money. But dreams do come true. The new arena was everything the old Arena Gardens was not: beautiful, spacious and modern. Arena Gardens was not decrepit by any means, but it certainly wasn't glamorous. Maple Leaf Gardens was.

The first event at the new edifice would, of course, be a hockey game. On opening night, November 12, 1931, the Chicago Blackhawks were in town. Tom Gaston, his Dad and his brother Joe had tickets for that first game. "We paid ninety-five cents each for our seats. I think the most expensive seat in the house was only three bucks. Everybody was dressed up in 'soup and fish.' What I mean is, a lot of men were in tuxedos and top hats. The ladies wore gowns or their best dresses. And I don't just mean those people in the best seats – I mean everyone," recalls Tommy. "My Dad, Joe and I sat in the east side greys, four or five rows from the top. We called them the 'nosebleeds' because we were so high up. All three of us wore shirts and ties plus our fedoras. Everybody in the arena was dressed up.

"Dad knew there would be a lot of traffic that night, so we parked at a tire shop owned by one of his friends. It wasn't far to walk to the Gardens from there. The game was scheduled to start at 8:30, but we got there early so we could have a look around. The arena was beautiful. The seats were coloured – reds were the best seats, then blues, then greens, and the greys were up top. They didn't have golds back then. I remember thinking the seats were so bright. And everything smelled new – I'll never forget it. We couldn't get over the dome – there were no beams to hold it up! A lot of people were there just to see the arena that night, but then there were the guys like me who were excited about the arena, and were just as excited about seeing a hockey game.

"Two bands entertained the crowd before the game. The Royal Grenadiers played first, followed by the 48th Highlanders – both of them played right on the ice surface. The 48th Highlanders have played at every single home opener since the opening night of Maple Leaf Gardens. I remember that they played 'Road to the Isles' on opening night in 1931, then they played 'God Save the King.' After that, there were a number of speeches made by government officials, and they seemed to go on forever. The crowd was definitely anxious. Toronto Mayor William J. Stewart spoke, and so did Premier George S. Henry. I remember one smart aleck yelled out, 'Wider highways!' when Henry was introduced, and everybody laughed. The two captains, Cy Wentworth and Hap Day, were also asked to make speeches. While J.P. Bickell [a member of the Gardens board of directors] was making his speech, the crowd yelled out, 'Drop the puck!' It seemed like they would never start."

Finally, with all the preliminaries out of the way, it was time for the game between the Blackhawks and Maple Leafs to begin. "I can still remember the Leafs' starting lineup like it was yesterday," Tom says, reeling off the names and numbers with military precision. "Number 1, Lorne Chabot; number 2, Red Horner; number 3, Alex Levinsky; number 4, Hap Day; number 5, Andy Blair; number 6, Ace Bailey; number 7, King Clancy; number 8, Baldy Cotton. Number 9 was Charlie Conacher and number 10 was Joe Primeau. Number 11, Busher Jackson; number 12, Frank Finnigan; number 14, Bob Gracie; number 15, Syd Howe; number 16, Harold Darragh. And number 17 – Benny Grant!"

The ceremonial opening faceoff saw Mayor Stewart drop the puck between Toronto's Ace Bailey and Chicago's Tommy Cook. It wasn't long after the faceoff that the first goal was scored in Maple Leaf Gardens. "Little Mush March scored the first goal – boy, he could fly," says Gaston with a sigh. The goal came at the 2:30 mark of the first period. Charlie Conacher tied the score for the Leafs in the second period, but Chicago's Vic Ripley – believe it or not – scored the winner in the third period, and the first game at Maple Leaf Gardens ended in a 2-1 victory for the visiting Chicago Blackhawks.

"That was a very special Leafs team," recalls Tommy. "Lorne Chabot was called 'Old Bulwark.' He was the first hockey player I ever met – I met him at a carnival over at Davisville Park. He came to us from the Rangers. He was tall, and he always looked sad, but boy, was he a hell of a hockey player. Back then, the lighting was poor, so goaltenders wore caps to keep the big, bright lights out of their eyes. Chabot wore a black cap. After playing five seasons in Toronto, the Leafs traded Lorne to Montreal for George Hainsworth in 1933. After that, he bounced around. He went to the Blackhawks as part of the Lionel Conacher trade. After a year there, he played with the Montreal Maroons for a season, then finished his career with one season in goal for the New York Americans in 1936-37.

"After he retired, Chabot was crossing King Street at Atlantic Avenue – you know, just east of Dufferin Street – and he got hit by a car in June 1942. He broke his ankle and had cuts and bruises all over his body. He ended up moving back to Montreal, but he had some strange illness [osteoarthritis and nephritis] and was bed-ridden for a year. It ended up killing him. He died on October 10, 1946, just five days after he celebrated his forty-sixth birthday with his wife and two boys. What a sad ending to Chabot's story."

Tom remembers another story that involves Lorne Chabot. "The Leafs had an elderly fan named Edith Mitchell who always used to send apple pies to the players. They used to call her 'Apple Annie.' She died in the spring of 1946, but had left no money for a proper funeral, so Charlie Conacher asked Maple Leaf fans to donate a little something to help bury her with dignity. So many people sent money that Charlie paid for the burial and a gravestone and still had several hundred dollars left over. Because Apple Annie used to say that Lorne Chabot was her favourite, Conacher decided to send the surplus to Chabot's family to help with their medical expenses. He was fighting for his life in a Montreal hospital at the time and could really have used the money.

"By the way, Charlie Conacher, Bob Davidson, Hap Day and Harold Ballard were pallbearers at Apple Annie's funeral. She would have been so happy to have her 'boys' around her, and happier still to know that, even in death, she was able to do something to help others. That would have pleased her greatly.

"Red Horner was rough, tough and nasty. He still comes by the Hall from time to time. He's the oldest living member of the Hockey Hall of Fame. He cleared the area in front of the net like nobody's business, and he was an excellent bodychecker.

"Alex Levinsky – they used to call him 'Mine Boy.' His Dad had a thick accent, and when Alex was playing minor hockey with the Moore Park Juveniles, his Dad used to holler, 'That's mein boy!'

The kids would laugh, and he got tagged with the nickname. He was Horner's defence partner.

"Now, Hap Day was a real hockey player. He had strong hockey sense and was a great leader. He was the Leafs' captain. He graduated from the University of Toronto and became a pharmacist. When the Gardens was built, Happy Day's Pharmacy was included in the building just to the left of the main doors on Carlton Street. We'd often see Hap in there. He played with Clancy on defence.

"Andy Blair was a great stickhandler, and a really good penalty killer, too. When Toronto was a man short, they'd put Blair out there and let him rag the puck until the penalty was over. He had a moustache – the only one of the Leafs who had one.

"Number 6 was Ace Bailey. He and Hap Day were the only guys left from the St. Pats. Bailey led the league in scoring in 1928-29, but the line of Blair, Bailey and Baldy Cotton was really the Leafs' defensive line.

"Good old King Clancy. I just loved him, and so did the rest of Toronto. Always worked hard, but had a great time playing hockey. Number 8 was Baldy Cotton. His father was an Anglican preacher. He was a thorough hockey player – good and steady.

"Chuck Conacher – big and strong with a hell of a shot. Boy, oh boy, we loved to watch him on the Kid Line with Primeau and Jackson. 'Gentleman Joe' Primeau was the centre. He also got called 'Little Joe.' Busher used to love to fish and hunt up around Bobcaygeon. The Kid Line wore numbers 9, 10 and 11.

"Frankie Finnigan – they called him the 'Shawville Express.' He came to the Maple Leafs in a dispersal draft after the Ottawa Senators folded and he wore number 12 that first season in the Gardens. He returned to Ottawa for the 1932-33 season when the franchise was reactivated. One year, the Hockey Hall of Fame held their induction ceremonies in Ottawa to coincide with the return of the Senators to the NHL. Finnigan was there as an ambassador for the Senators hockey club. He took an Ottawa Senators pin and put it on my lapel. It had the original logo for the new team – the one that depicted the Peace Tower from the Parliament Buildings.

"Bob Gracie was fast – he could skate circles around most of the players in the league. He lived on Balliol Street around this time, and I had two rooms in a house next door to him. Gracie owned the Maple Leaf Gas Bar up in Wasaga Beach around this time, too. His brother had a photography studio, and he took pictures of me when I was a little boy.

"Syd Howe came to the Leafs with Frankie Finnigan in the Ottawa dispersal draft. He only played a few games with the Leafs that season, spending most of the year with Syracuse in the minor leagues. He went on to a long career with Detroit, where he won three Stanley Cups. He's in the Hall of Fame now, too.

"Number 16 was Harold Darragh. They called him 'Howl.' And Benny Grant was the spare goaltender. He was a bit of a show-off. He would make an easy save look like the most spectacular save in the world. The Leafs carried him for years, but he never made it as a number one goaltender."

After failing to qualify for the 1930 playoffs, Smythe's charges started to hit their stride in 1930-31, finishing second in the Canadian Division and losing a two-game, total goals quarterfinal series to Chicago by a score of 4-3. The team really began to peak in 1931-32. With the excitement of a new arena and the arrival Kid Line, the city was buzzing with talk about the Leafs. In fact, Canadians from coast to coast were talking about the Toronto Maple Leafs.

"A lot of that had to do with Foster Hewitt," Tommy reminds us. "He really should get a lot of credit for the Leafs' popularity. His Saturday night radio broadcasts went across the country, and he had millions of listeners. Back in the '30s and '40s, there wasn't a lot of money available for entertainment. Television hadn't arrived, and families did a lot more things together.

"My family was no different. We'd listened to Foster Hewitt on the radio every Saturday for as long as I can remember. After dinner on Saturday, Mom would give me fifteen cents and I'd run down to the corner store for a pound of brown sugar, which cost ten cents, and a nickel's worth of shelled walnuts. I'd make fudge and my Mom would pop some corn, and the whole family would gather around our old Atwater-Kent radio. The broadcasts came on at the end of the first period, and we'd sit glued to the action. I had framed pictures of Clancy and Conacher, and my Dad let me hang them in the front room where we had the radio. They stayed there for years. I'm sure my Mom probably could have thought of other pictures she would have preferred to have hanging in her house, but I was my Dad's pet. And Mom was a big Leafs fan, too, so I guess she couldn't have minded too much."

Gaston remembers the gondola from which Foster Hewitt did his play-by-play. "Through the years, I think people got the idea that the gondola was pretty glamorous, but it was just a simple booth at centre ice on the west side of the building, up under the girders.

Foster got to pick the location for his broadcasts. He went over to the Eaton's store at College and Yonge, and walked from floor to floor, looking out the windows at the people below. He was trying to find the best vantage point to see the pedestrians walking along the street. Picturing the people walking below as hockey players, he decided the best height to see them from was the fifth floor. They found out that the fifth floor was fifty-five feet above street level, so they went back to the Gardens and discovered that a main girder was at the 56-foot mark. Foster asked that his gondola be constructed under it, and that gondola stayed there until it was destroyed in the summer of 1979.

"Foster Hewitt was as popular as most of the hockey players. Wherever he went, people asked him for his autograph. All us kids thought he had just about the best job in the world," chuckles Tommy. "Foster Hewitt died on April 21, 1985. His funeral took place at Deer Park Church in Toronto. I sat with King Clancy during the service. Jim McKenny, the former Leafs defenceman, was covering the funeral for CITY-TV, and he came over to Clancy and me and asked us a couple of questions. The two of us were on the news that night. Foster Hewitt is buried in Mount Pleasant Cemetery in Toronto."

The 1931-32 season got off to a shaky start – the Maple Leafs didn't win a single game in their first five contests. "Conn Smythe had been so busy getting the Gardens built," Tommy remembers, "that he really hadn't spent much time overseeing the team. Art Duncan was the coach, and when they only had two ties to show for their first five games, Smythe fired him and put Dick Irvin behind the bench."

Irvin had coached the Blackhawks the year before, when they knocked the Leafs out of the playoffs and went on to the Stanley Cup finals. Under his guidance, the Leafs went from last place to first place in the Canadian Division within a matter of weeks.

"The first year in Maple Leaf Gardens was exciting." Tom recalls, "I didn't get the opportunity to see too many games that season, but I did get down to six or seven. The Leafs were a rough-and-tumble team that got into a lot of fights. I remember listening to one game where Baldy Cotton challenged the referee to a fight and had to be hauled to the dressing room by the NHL's president."

Gaston smirks as he thinks about some of the rules of the game in those days. "The goaltender had to serve his own penalties – he'd literally sit in the penalty box with his equipment on. When the referee called a penalty on the goalie, he'd throw his stick and gloves to a teammate who had been chosen to cover the net. And back then, players had to serve the full penalty – you weren't released after the other team scored." In a game in Boston on March 15, 1932, Leafs goalie Lorne Chabot tripped the Bruins' Cooney Weiland behind the net. Referee Bill Stewart called a penalty on Chabot, who handed his stick and gloves to Red Horner. Marty Barry for the Bruins came in and scored, so Alex Levinsky took a turn with Chabot's stick, replacing Horner. "Barry comes in again – and now it's 2-0 for the Bruins. Chabot's penalty still isn't over, so King Clancy plays goal. George Owen for the Bruins skates in, and he scores. The Bruins went up 3-0 with three different Leafs playing goal. You'd never see that today! The final score was 6-2 for Boston that night."

By the end of the 48-game regular season, the Toronto Maple Leafs had a record of 23 wins, 18 losses and 7 ties for 53 points, four behind the Montreal Canadiens, and good enough for second place in the Canadian Division. They would again face the Chicago Blackhawks in the first round of the playoffs.

"The playoff set-up was very different than today," Gaston explains. "In round one, you played a two-game, total goals series. Same with round two. If you got to the finals, it was a best-of-five series."

The Blackhawks shut out the Leafs 1-0 behind the goaltending of Charlie Gardiner in game one, but the Leafs came back with a 6-1 victory in game two, winning the series six goals to two. In the semifinals, Toronto was challenged by the Montreal Maroons, and Bob Gracie's overtime goal in game two gave the Leafs a 4-3 victory in that series.

"The finals came down to the Toronto Maple Leafs against the New York Rangers," states Tom Gaston, without hesitation. "The Rangers had topped the American Division, but Toronto had been able to handle them pretty well through the season. In the six regular-season games they played, the Leafs won four and lost two. The first game of the finals was played in Madison Square Garden, and the Leafs won, 6-4. The second game was also supposed to be played in New York, but the circus was in town and had already been booked into the arena for that date, so the game was played in Boston. The Leafs won that one, too, 6-2. The third game was in Toronto, and the Leafs won 6-4 to win the Stanley Cup. Because of the scores, this series has been dubbed the 'tennis series.' I remember that Conn Smythe named one of his racehorses 'Three Straight Games' after this Stanley Cup series.

"Nobody hoisted the Stanley Cup and skated around the arena like they do today. I remember listening to the game, and Frank Calder, the league president, presented the Cup to Hap Day, who was the Leafs captain. Hap cradled the Cup, but didn't hoist it. Everybody gathered around, and Dick Irvin and Connie Smythe were right there on the ice, too. Then they all skated off to the dressing room to celebrate. Knowing the reputations of that gang, I'll bet it was quite the celebration! The victory made front page news in Toronto, and I wouldn't have been surprised to hear it was in the headlines across Canada the next day.

"Each of the players received a gold medallion – a lifetime pass to any event in Maple Leaf Gardens. The city arranged for a parade to celebrate Toronto's Stanley Cup win. The Maple Leaf players rode the length of the parade route on the back of a fire truck."

CHAPTER SIX

A King and an Ace

Irvine "Ace" Bailey's career began in his hometown, Bracebridge, Ontario, in 1918. Four years later he joined Frank Selke's junior team, Toronto St. Mary's, for whom he put in two years before moving on to play senior hockey in Peterborough. On November 3, 1926, Bailey signed with the NHL's Toronto St. Pats, and in his rookie season, 1926-27, Ace finished sixth in the scoring race and led the Toronto franchise – which had changed names and ownership in February 1927 – in scoring. After a less-than-stellar sophomore year, Bailey returned to form in 1928-29, leading the league with 32 points. The next season, his production increased to 43 points, although he couldn't crack the league's top ten – the introduction of forward passing led to a boom in scoring leaguewide. During the 1930-31 season, Ace scored 42 points, fifth-best in the league and second on the Leafs only to Charlie Conacher. The rise of Conacher's Kid Line triggered a change in Ace's role on the team, and he became more of a defensive player over the next two seasons. His point totals dropped off substantially, to 13 points during 1931-32 and 18 points in 1932-33.

"Ace Bailey and I became pretty good friends long after he was forced to retire from hockey," Tommy Gaston says. "At Leaf home games, Ace was the timekeeper, sitting there in the penalty box. But he was also working in a furniture store at the Bayview Village shopping centre. My wife Ruth and I were shopping in the mall and we stopped for a cold drink, and Ace came in on his coffee break. That was the first of many times we would sit together and chat. Ace always had a cup of tea. And he was always dressed up – you'd never see him anywhere, anytime, when he wouldn't be wearing a jacket and tie. He was a very natty dresser.

"We wouldn't talk about his hockey career too much. It was usually just general conversation; sometimes we'd talk about the most recent Leaf game. And he always asked about my wife Ruth, except he'd never call her by her first name. It was always, 'And how is Mrs. Gaston these days?' He even referred to his wife Mabel as Mrs. Bailey. Ace was quite a gentleman."

On December 12, 1933, Ace Bailey's playing career came to an abrupt end. "The game was down in Boston," Tom Gaston recalls, "and in the second period, Eddie Shore carried the puck up the ice. King Clancy knocked him down, and Shore thought a tripping penalty should have been called. He was livid! King picked up the puck and started a rush into the Bruins' zone. Ace Bailey dropped back to cover the defence position for Clancy. When Shore picked himself up and started to skate back into Boston's end, he came up behind Ace and sent him flying. Nobody seems to know whether Shore thought Bailey was Clancy and was trying to get revenge for the hit, or whether Shore was seeing red and hit anybody in a Leafs uniform. Ace's head hit the ice with incredible force, and he just lay there on his back, with his legs twitching. It wasn't the hit that hurt Ace, it was the way he fell that did the damage. He never saw Shore coming at him.

"Red Horner immediately went over to Shore and knocked him unconscious with a punch to the jaw. There they were, Bailey and Shore, both unconscious on the ice. All the players from both teams milled about on the ice, surrounding the players. Shore was carried off and they stitched up a cut on his scalp. Ace was taken off, and the Bruins' team doctor, Dr. Kelley, examined him. He immediately called for an ambulance, suspecting Ace had a fractured skull. While they were waiting, Eddie Shore made his way into the room where Ace was laying and apologized. The Leafs were pretty shaken up, but they had to take a train to Montreal for their next game and left Ace in Boston with Connie Smythe.

"At Audubon Hospital in Boston, two surgeons worked on Ace. One was a Dr. Donald Munro. He performed two high-risk operations over the course of a week to relieve the pressure on Ace's brain by drilling two holes into his skull. The doctors didn't hold out much hope for survival, and Ace was administered the last rites a couple of times. He really was at death's door. It was front page news for weeks.

"Finally, after two weeks of high anxiety, Ace got past the critical point, but the doctors told him he would never play hockey again. He returned to Toronto on January 18, 1934, to complete his recovery. A few weeks after he came home to Toronto, the Bruins sent

Ace a cheque for almost $8,000 – the gate receipts from a game between Boston and the Montreal Maroons. Shore tried to visit Ace in the hospital in Boston, but they wouldn't let him in, thinking it would be too stressful for Ace."

NHL president Frank Calder suspended Shore until January 28, 1934, during which he missed sixteen games. Red Horner was suspended for six games for slugging Shore.

On January 24, 1934, the NHL's board of governors met and decided that a charity game would be played in Toronto, with the proceeds to go to Ace Bailey and his family. The Maple Leafs would face a group of players selected by an NHL executive committee. The game, which many consider to be hockey's first all-star game, was held on February 14. Tom Gaston, who attended the game – and every other All-Star Game played in Toronto – continues the story. "Each of the Leafs wore a special sweater with 'ACE' embroidered diagonally down the chest and the Leaf logo just above it. The players selected for the all-star team came onto the ice wearing their own team sweaters. It is amazing to think about the talent that played there that night. The all-stars included Charlie Gardiner in goal, Howie Morenz and Aurel Joliat from the Canadiens, Bill Cook and Ching Johnson from the Rangers, and Lionel Conacher represented Chicago. Red Dutton of the New York Americans, who was later the NHL president, played. And of course, Eddie Shore was there, too.

"There was a table at centre ice, and Ace Bailey was there, wearing glasses and a knee-length brown overcoat. He presented each player with a white sweater with 'NHL' running diagonally across the front. Players were introduced in numerical order, so Eddie Shore, wearing his usual number, 2, was the second player to come forward to receive his sweater from Ace. They looked at each other and clasped hands sincerely. That's what the crowd was waiting for, and they went wild! To this day, I think that was the loudest I ever heard a Toronto hockey crowd. It was incredible! As for Ace, he never held a grudge against Shore."

Next, Conn Smythe walked onto the ice and handed Ace Bailey his Leafs sweater with the familiar number 6. As a hush fell over the crowd, Smythe spoke. "No other player will ever use this number on the Maple Leaf hockey team," he promised. "The crowd erupted once again," Tom remembers. "The Toronto fans had a great deal of respect for Ace Bailey, and the ceremony was very dignified and emotional."

Ace Bailey's number 6 was the first uniform number ever retired in the NHL. The next season, the Bruins retired Lionel Hitchman's number 3 after his ten-year Boston career came to an end. In 1937, after the death of Howie Morenz, the Montreal Canadiens retired his number 7. (At the Bailey all-star game, Morenz's seven-year-old son skated in the pregame warmup with his Dad and the other stars.)

"The contest ended in a 7-3 Toronto victory, with Busher Jackson getting two goals. It was an exciting game – no one had ever seen anything like it before, and to see all that talent playing together was quite something. It was sort of like all-star games today, with lots of skill but not much bodychecking. They raised more than $20,000 for Ace Bailey and his family that night. And the funny thing was that Eddie Shore was cheered throughout the entire game – by those same fans who were cursing his name just a few weeks before. That handshake with Ace Bailey at centre ice turned the Toronto crowd right around."

According to Tommy, after Bailey was forced to retire, Smythe got him a job as the coach of the University of Toronto senior team, a club with which he himself had been closely involved. "Conn had been there as captain when U of T beat the Berlin Union Jacks for the Ontario Hockey Association junior championship in 1915. They changed the name of the city from Berlin to Kitchener after World War I. When Smythe came back from the war in 1921, he helped the University of Toronto team win the Allan Cup, and then he started to coach the Varsity junior team in 1922-23.

"When almost the entire team graduated from university, Conn Smythe formed an alumni team called the Varsity Grads. The Grads didn't lose a single game through the regular season in 1926-27, and they defeated Fort William for the Allan Cup. This same team represented Canada at the Olympic Games in St. Moritz, Switzerland, in 1928. Because Conn had just recently purchased the Toronto St. Pats and turned them into the Maple Leafs, he found he was too busy to go to the Olympics. In his place, W.A. Hewitt oversaw the team. He was secretary of the OHA, and Foster Hewitt's father. The manager of the team was a young Harold Ballard. In fact, Ballard carried the flag for Canada in the Olympic parade, and he wasn't even one of the athletes!

"Connie Smythe was replaced as coach of the senior team by Lester Pearson, who later went on to win the Nobel Peace Prize and become prime minister of Canada. Pearson coached the senior team in 1927 and 1928.

"Ace Bailey became U of T's coach in 1935. The team wasn't much to brag about at first, but Ace set out to improve the team." The University of Toronto joined the International Intercollegiate League, made up of teams from Harvard, Princeton, Yale, Dartmouth, McGill, the University of Montreal, and Queen's. A Yale alumnus named Alexis Thompson offered a trophy for the winner of the annual competition. It was the David Pearson Thompson Trophy, donated in memory of Alexis' father.

"The University of Toronto team under Ace Bailey won the Thompson Trophy in 1939-40. That season, they won twenty games. Their only loss all season was an exhibition game against the Toronto Goodyears – it was a fundraiser for Finnish Relief. Punch Imlach played for the Goodyears that year, while Bobby Copp, who later played for the Leafs and became a dentist, played on the U of T team." In a university publication called Torontonensis, it was stated, "Five years of hard work and sacrifice on the part of Ace Bailey has been finally rewarded and the handsome Thompson Trophy comes to Toronto." With the outbreak of war in Europe, intercollegiate competition ended after the 1939-40 season.

Tommy Gaston grows silent, and pauses for a moment. "The Maple Leafs had planned to honour Ace Bailey and Bill Barilko in a pregame ceremony on April 1, 1992. They were going to officially retire both Bailey and Barilko's sweater numbers. But a players' strike shut down the league for ten days, beginning on March 30. Ace Bailey died April 7, 1992. He never got to see his sweater raised to the rafters. They held the ceremony without him at the beginning of the following season.

"I went to Ace's funeral service at St. James-Bond United Church. Ron Ellis who was assigned Bailey's number 6 in 1968 at Ace's insistence spoke at the service and did a beautiful job. Ace's daughter Joyce invited me to come back to her house for the reception after the service, but I just didn't feel up to it. Ace was high up on my list of favourite people. He and Clancy were the first two Leafs I got to know."

"Let me tell you about King Clancy," Tommy Gaston says, growing animated. "He was my favourite player, forever. I knew Frank Selke's boys, Chilton and Frank Jr., from school. I played lacrosse with Chilton – we all grew up in the same neighbourhood, near Yonge Street and Eglinton Avenue. I lived on Taunton Road and the Selkes were on Hillsdale Avenue. There were a number of sisters, too, and one became a nun.

"When Mr. Selke was around the house, I liked to sit with him and talk hockey. He was always friendly that way. I guess I'd mentioned King Clancy's name quite often, because one day he said to me, 'Tommy, you really like King Clancy, don't you?' Well, of course I said, 'Yes, sir, I certainly do.' So he told me the King was going to be coming over to his house that Sunday at two o'clock in the afternoon. 'Now, Tommy," he said, "if you were to casually walk past the house around that time, we'll be sitting on the veranda and I'll invite you over to say hello.'

"I thought I'd died and gone to heaven. After church, I studied my watch and those minutes just dragged on. Finally, it was just before two o'clock. I walked slowly along Hillsdale Avenue, and then I heard Mr. Selke call out to me – 'Tom, come on up here. I'd like you to meet King Clancy!' King must have wondered what was wrong with me, because I had this huge grin painted on my face from the moment of the introduction until I left. We sat and talked about the Leafs for about half an hour. I remember King was very funny.

"King was the real star of the team until the Kid Line came along, and even then, he was still incredibly popular. On March 17, 1934, the Leafs celebrated St. Patrick's Day with a King Clancy Night. Of course, he was well known for being Irish. Connie Smythe stepped up to the microphone, but every time he went to introduce King, he'd purposely get interrupted.

What followed was a parade of giant floats, each of which was meant to symbolize Ireland in some way. "The game was against the New York Rangers," Tommy says. "One of their star defencemen, Ching Johnson, pulled a huge float that looked like a potato onto the ice, and everybody assumed Clancy would be inside it, but there were some junior players inside instead. A big shamrock got pulled out onto the ice – but it wasn't King, it was Bun Cook from the Rangers inside. The trainer, Tim Daly, was inside a float that looked like a bottle of ginger ale, Baldy Cotton was inside a huge top hat and Ken Doraty was inside a float that looked like a pipe. There was a float of a boot with the goaltender, George Hainsworth, inside, and another that looked like a boxing glove – Red Horner was in that one. And Joe Primeau was in a giant harp.

"Then the lights dimmed and Hap Day pulled a throne out onto the ice. It was on a big sleigh. Sitting on the throne was our King –

Clancy. He had on a long robe and a crown and a beard. When Hap pulled the throne to centre ice, King Clancy stepped down and the crowd went nuts! Charlie Conacher threw some charcoal dust in his face and everybody laughed. Then, King took off his robe, and he was wearing a green Maple Leaf sweater with a shamrock on the back. Well, if you think the crowd was loud earlier, you should have heard them then! Then King was presented with some gifts – I think he got a grandfather clock. That was a very fun night, and a wonderful tribute to one of the most popular athletes in Toronto at the time."

Toronto defeated the Rangers 3-2 on King Clancy Night. Clancy played the first period in his green shamrock sweater, but after the first period, Rangers coach Lester Patrick complained that the sweater was confusing his players, and King Clancy was forced to return to his familiar blue and white with the number 7 on the back.

King Clancy was a Leaf virtually his entire life. Although he was born and raised in Ottawa, and his NHL career began with the old Ottawa Senators, Clancy was a crowd favourite in Toronto, rivalling Charlie Conacher as the team's most popular player. He and Hap Day teamed made a formidable defence pair. It is seldom remembered that, when the King retired, he joined the Montreal Maroons as their coach, an experiment that ended after only eighteen games. Next came a stint as an official. "For ten years, King Clancy was a popular referee – which is likely the first time you've seen 'popular' and 'referee' in the same sentence," Tommy says. "But Clancy could lift a crowd no matter what he was doing. There's a famous hockey photo done by the Turofsky brothers here in Toronto. It shows Jimmy Orlando of Detroit holding his face after being cut in a stick fight with Gaye Stewart of the Leafs. Clancy was the referee in that game, and is right there in the picture."

King Clancy was coach of the Leafs for three seasons, between 1953 and 1956, after a stint behind the bench of the Leafs' farm club in Pittsburgh of the American Hockey League. He stayed on as assistant general manager for many years, and was twice called upon to step back behind the bench: late in the 1966-67 season, when Punch Imlach was sidelined with heart problems, and again in 1971-72 when Leaf coach John McLellan was suffering from ulcers.

But as the years went on and Clancy aged, his most important role with the Leafs was as a goodwill ambassador. He sat at the team's draft table each year to welcome the players the Leafs selected. He could be seen around town with a permanent broad grin on his face, shaking hands with fans. And perhaps his most important job was as a confidant to Leafs owner Harold Ballard. "After Mr. Ballard's wife died, he seemed lost," Tommy says, "and I think King took up the slack for Harold. They travelled out of town together with the Leafs. When Mr. Ballard bought the Hamilton Tiger-Cats football team, they went to games at Ivor Wynne Stadium together. But the way I remember the two of them best is sitting in 'Ballard's Bunker' at Maple Leaf Gardens." This was a special private box cut into the north end of the Gardens beneath the end blue seats. "Harold and King would sit in there, sometimes with special guests. They didn't duck away from the fans – you could see their faces and their arms leaning over the edge. Fans were respectful, and if someone asked for an autograph during intermission, the two of them would sign a program for them." After the two men passed on, the "Bunker" was boarded up for a while, but it was later used as an alumni box to accommodate former Leaf greats.

"Oh, I have to laugh when I think of Clancy," chuckles Tom. "He was so funny. You never really knew if he was serious or not when he told you something – then all of a sudden, he'd lean back and laugh himself silly. I remember one time when I was sitting with a friend in a coffee shop, and we were talking about our jobs. King came over and pulled up a chair. My friend said something like, 'My job is so bad. I only get $40 a week.' Then I said, 'You think that's bad – at my job, I only get paid $30 a week!' Well, King just looked at me, waited a few seconds, then said, 'Well, Tommy, did you ever consider that maybe that was all you were worth?' He just looked at me earnestly for a few seconds, then all of a sudden he laughed so hard that I just had to start laughing, too. Then my friend realized it was a joke, and he started to laugh. Before you know it, the three of us were laughing so hard that tears were streaming down our cheeks!"

Tommy shifts to a melancholy tone. "The King died on November 8, 1986. He was 83 years young. His service was at St. Michael's Cathedral in Toronto. You had to have an invitation to attend, and I was so appreciative that the Hockey Hall of Fame was able to get an invitation for me. You can't imagine how thankful I was to them. When I got to the church, they sat me in the row behind the Leaf executives. It was a lovely service for a lovely man. He's buried over in Mount Hope Cemetery on Bayview Avenue."

The Toronto Maple Leafs wore a special commemorative patch on their sweaters for the remainder of that season. It depicted a green shamrock topped with a golden crown. Although it has never been retired, King Clancy's number 7 is considered an "honoured number" by the Toronto Maple Leafs. A banner bearing Clancy's portrait hangs from the rafters of the Air Canada Centre (there's also one commemorating another top-notch defenceman who wore number 7 for the Leafs, Tim Horton).

Terry Clancy, King's son and himself a former Leaf, recalls his father talking about Tom Gaston. "My Dad called Tom a real fine gentleman. I remember they used to meet up at a donut shop at the corner of Carlton and Yonge, just a block away from the Gardens. You can imagine the Irish blarney that would have gone on there! Tom and his wife Ruth were married on September 7, 1946. Tom told me that he got married on the seventh because it was my Dad's number."

Terry came up through the Maple Leafs system, playing his junior hockey at St. Michael's College and putting in time with Leaf farm clubs in Rochester and Tulsa. In the 1967 expansion draft, he was claimed by the Oakland Seals, but he returned to the Leafs system and played 86 games for Toronto between 1968 and 1973. Today, Terry is involved with corporate insurance at the Toronto firm Moore-McLean.

"I thought so highly of King Clancy both as a hockey player and as a man," Tommy Gaston concludes. "King wore number 7 and it's been my favourite number through the years for that very reason."

CHAPTER SEVEN

The Thirties

After winning the Stanley Cup in 1932, the Toronto Maple Leafs, carried by the Kid Line, finished first in the Canadian Division in 1932-33. Busher Jackson was runner-up to the New York Rangers' Bill Cook in the scoring race, finishing with 44 points to Cook's 50, but both Joe Primeau and Charlie Conacher had tough years – Primeau was down 18 points from the year before, while Conacher's output dropped by 17. Nevertheless, the Kid Line was as popular as ever.

In the playoffs, the Leafs faced off against the first-place team in the American Division, the Boston Bruins. The best-of-five series went the distance, as four of the games – including the fifth, a scoreless tie after regulation time – went into overtime.

"Oh, that was a heck of a series," Tom Gaston declares. "Marty Barry scored in overtime for the Bruins to take game one. In game two, it was 0-0 after sixty minutes, then Busher scored for Toronto to tie up the series. The third game came to Toronto, and Eddie Shore scored in overtime to give the Bruins the lead in the series. The fourth game was in Toronto, too, and the Leafs won it to tie the series two games apiece.

"The fifth and deciding game was also in Toronto, on April 3, 1933, and in my opinion it's one of the most important games in the history of the Toronto Maple Leafs franchise. Along with the Barilko goal in the 1951 finals, I would say this is one of the major events in Leaf history. I wasn't at the game, but my Dad was.

"Red Horner, Ace Bailey and Joe Primeau were all hurt, but they played anyway. You could tell right away from the tight checking that it was going to be a close game. In the third period, the Bruins scored on a breakaway, but the goal was disallowed because the play was offside. At the end of regulation time, the score was deadlocked at 0-0, and that was still the score at the end of the first overtime.

Another twenty-minute overtime period was played, and the game was still scoreless. It was well past midnight, and my Mom told me I had to go to bed, but there was no way I was going to miss the finish of this game.

"In the fourth overtime, Clancy and Primeau broke in and Clancy scored on Tiny Thompson. But that goal was called back because a player was offside! I think that might have been Joe Primeau's first shift of the game, too. At the end of the fourth overtime period, league officials sat down with Conn Smythe of the Leafs and Art Ross of the Bruins, and they agreed to flip a coin to decide the winner. But when they told the players, I remember hearing that Baldy Cotton said something like, 'There's no way we're going to let them beat us by a coin toss!' The players agreed to play until a goal was scored. Fifth overtime – no goal. They went into a sixth overtime period. It was almost 2 a.m. and most of the crowd were still in their seats. Some of the spare players like Bill Thoms, Charlie Sands and Kenny Doraty were getting a lot of ice time because the regular players were so darned tired.

"Then Boston's Eddie Shore tried to pass the puck up the ice and Andy Blair intercepted it. He passed it over to number 15, Kenny Doraty, on the right wing, and Doraty slid the puck past Tiny Thompson – it was almost as if Thompson was asleep! The goal was scored at 4:46 of the sixth overtime – the second-longest game in NHL history to this day.

"The fans went crazy – it didn't matter that they were dead tired. The ice was littered with programs and hats and just about anything else the spectators could get their hands on." The game ended after 104 minutes and 46 seconds of overtime. The Leafs had outshot the Bruins 119-93, and Lorne Chabot earned the shutout for Toronto.

Ken Doraty, a native of Regina, Saskatchewan, had been playing for the Cleveland Indians of the International Hockey League, and Toronto traded for his rights that year. In 38 regular-season games he had scored only five goals, but in the 1932-33 playoffs he led all Leafs, scoring five goals in the nine games Toronto played. "Kagee" Ken Doraty was only five foot seven and 128 pounds, but he was an invaluable addition to the bench strength of the Maple Leafs, giving them fairly fresh legs at a point in the game when they were most needed. He would play portions of two more seasons in Toronto before being traded back to Cleveland in 1935.

Doraty's goal earned the Leafs a berth in the finals and the right to defend their Stanley Cup title, this time against the New York

Rangers. "Our boys were exhausted," Tommy recalls. "They finished the game with Boston around 2 a.m., then they had to change and catch a train that was waiting for them at Union Station. After an all-night train trip, the Leafs began the Stanley Cup final against the Rangers that same night!" In the best-of-five Stanley Cup finals, the Leafs were pushed aside by the Rangers in four games.

"Lorne Chabot, who was in the Leafs net the night of Doraty's historic goal, also played in the longest overtime game ever played in the NHL," Tom states. Playing for the Montreal Maroons in the 1936 playoffs, Mud Bruneteau of the Red Wings beat Chabot at 16:30 of the sixth overtime in a semifinal game that began March 24, 1936. The final score in that game was also 1-0.

In 1933-34, the Kid Line was at its zenith. Charlie Conacher led the league in scoring with 52 points, six more than runner-up Joe Primeau. Busher Jackson also ended the season in the top ten, with 38. Conacher's 32 goals also led the league. Only Marty Barry of the Bruins, with 27, came close.

The Kid Line's popularity could be easily measured by a clever promotion initiated that year by the St. Lawrence Starch Company of Port Credit, Ontario. Tom Gaston remembers it well. "Bee Hive Corn Syrup used to have an offer where you'd get a photo of an NHL player if you sent in a proof of purchase. There was a cardboard circle on top of the syrup container that was held in place by the cap – I think they called it a token collar. You would mail those in with your preferred player choices, and they'd mail you the photos you requested – one picture for each token collar you sent them. Except for the odd picture in the paper, we really had no idea what the hockey players looked like. They were our heroes from Foster Hewitt's radio broadcasts, but we didn't have television or books with pictures of our favourite players. So when Bee Hive started their promotion in 1934, every kid I knew was eating more corn syrup than ever before, just to be able to send away for hockey pictures. It was great for Bee Hive and great for us. I collected a ton of pictures, and I had every friend and relative eating Bee Hive Corn Syrup so I could get more pictures. As I recall, you could also send in collars from St. Lawrence Corn Oil or box tops from St. Lawrence Corn Starch to get pictures. It was a lot of fun."

St. Lawrence Starch ran the promotion between 1934 and the end of the 1966-67 season. There were a number of reasons why it was discontinued. The new National Hockey League Players Association was asking for substantial fees in return for the right to publish images of the players. The advent of expansion would double the number of players in the league, further raising costs skyward. Postage rates were increasing, too, and so a promotion that for thirty-three years was as good as any ever conceived was now prohibitively expensive to continue. Bee Hive hockey photos have subsequently become highly prized on the collectibles circuit.

Not surprisingly, the most requested photos were, in order of popularity, Conacher, Jackson and Primeau. Foster Hewitt's photo was also among the most wanted – not too surprising, since his play-by-play was heard by more than two million radio listeners every Saturday night.

The Leafs again finished first in the Canadian Division in 1933-34, a season that was marred by the end of Ace Bailey's career. In February of 1934, the entire city of Toronto, and likely most communities across Canada, hung in suspense awaiting news of whether Ace Bailey would survive Eddie Shore's vicious hit. After nearly slipping away several times, Bailey rallied and before long he was past the crisis. But his hockey career was over, and he wore a plate in his skull for the rest of his life.

In spite of the first-place finish, Toronto was knocked out of the playoffs by Detroit in the semifinals. In 1934-35, the Leafs finished atop the Canadian Division yet again. Charlie Conacher was the leading scorer for a second straight season, firing 36 goals and 21 assists for 57 points – ten more than runner-up Syd Howe. The fierce shot of Conacher earned him the goal scoring championship again, too. Both Syd Howe and Busher Jackson were second with 22 – fourteen less than the "Big Bomber." Toronto disposed of the Bruins in the 1935 semifinals, but they faced the tough Montreal Maroons in the Stanley Cup finals. The Maroons swept the Leafs in three straight games.

The Toronto Maple Leafs were still strong in 1935-36. Although they came second to the Montreal Maroons in the Canadian Division, the Leafs actually had one more win. (The Maroons had been in enough tie games to give them first place in the division.) Conacher finished in fifth in scoring, but both Jackson and Primeau were well off their previous season's totals. Busher Jackson's 22 points were half of his 1934-35 total, while Joe Primeau, with 17 points, dropped 13 from his total of the year before.

There was a change in the playoff format this season: the semifinals were now a best-of-three series. Toronto eliminated Boston in the quarterfinals – still a two-game, total goals series. In the semifinals, the Leafs edged the New York Americans. But in the finals, the Maple Leafs were put away, three games to one, by the Detroit Red Wings.

The Toronto Maple Leafs' first golden era was quickly coming to an end. On opening night of the 1936-37 season, Joe Primeau was presented with a sterling silver tea set to commemorate his retirement. Primeau was only thirty years old, but he had decided to spend more time with his young family and run his successful cement block business, a career that would make him a very wealthy businessman. After six games, on November 24, King Clancy retired from hockey. He had played fifteen seasons. Charlie Conacher, whose rambunctious style made him prone to injuries, suffered a wrist injury in training camp, and then re-injured it just before Christmas. He played only fifteen games in 1936-37. The Leafs were forced to inject new blood into the lineup, and fans were introduced to the likes of Gord Drillon, Syl Apps, Billy Taylor and Turk Broda. Toronto was knocked out of the playoffs in the first round, when the New York Rangers, on a goal by Babe Pratt, won the best-of-three series two games to none.

In 1937-38, the Leafs' offence was sparked by the scoring of Gord Drillon and Syl Apps, who finished first and second in the regular-season points race, while the defence was solidified with the emergence of Broda as a star goaltender. The Leafs finished the 1937-38 season on top of the Canadian Division. This season all but completed the changing of the guard. Charlie Conacher again sat out most of the season with injuries, and he would be traded before the next season. Before the season began, captain Hap Day had been traded to the New York Americans. From the Stanley Cup-winning team of 1931-32, only Horner, Jackson and Conacher remained. The revamped lineup took the Leafs to the Stanley Cup finals, where they lost to the Chicago Blackhawks.

"Those were some wonderful times," Tommy says, breaking into his patented elfin grin. "Connie Smythe made certain that Maple Leaf Gardens was looked on as a very special place. All the players wore shirts and ties, even to practices. Fans dressed up for the games, too. No windbreakers or t-shirts then, boy, oh boy. You wore a shirt and tie, too. You just did – no questions asked.

"After each home game, the Imperial Oil Three Stars were named. We could hardly wait for the newspaper the next day, because the three stars would have their pictures in the paper, superimposed on a star. We would cut them out and add them to our scrapbooks. You can imagine that we had a lot of pictures of Conacher, Jackson, Primeau and Clancy in there. I donated all my scrapbooks plus my Bee Hive photos to the Hockey Hall of Fame several years ago."

CHAPTER EIGHT

The Accident

Tommy Gaston remembers a day that changed his life forever.

"In 1940, I was working at Canadian Fairbanks Morse. The company was going through a bit of a slack period, so some of the employees were asked to help tidy up the shop. One of the boys and I were to spray the basement with whitewash. To spray the paint, there was a hand pump on a wheelbarrow. The nozzle on the hose was plugged, and as we kept on pumping the hose blew, spraying me right in the face with the whitewash. It was November 6, 1940 – I'll never ever forget that date.

"They rushed me over to St. Mike's Hospital. I heard the doctor say, 'His right eye's gone – work on the left one.' I had a little bit of sight – I could see a desk with a phone – but when I went to call my Dad, the room went black. 'What are you doing up?' a nurse barked. 'I want to call my Dad,' I answered, but she told me he was already at the hospital and sitting in the waiting room with my brother Bill."

The lime in the whitewash had severely burned Tom's pupils. He never would regain the sight in his right eye. He was only twenty-three years old.

"I spent three months in the hospital," Tom recalls with a sigh. "Every two hours, my eyes had to be dressed with hot pads and ointment. The doctor wanted to take my right eye out, but I said, 'No way! What if someday there's the technology to bring my sight back?' I wouldn't let him touch that eye. I've had three cornea transplants over the years, but none of them were successful.

"Then one day it was time to test the left eye. The doctor said, 'There's somebody here to see you. I'm going to take the bandage off your eye, and I want you to tell me who you see.' I was afraid to open my left eye in case I discovered I couldn't see with it, either. The visitor got really close – about a foot away – and I slowly opened my eye. 'Dad!' I choked on the word as I opened my eye. I could see! Not great, but I definitely could see.

"Then my Dad said, 'There's somebody else here to see you, Tom.' With my good eye, I strained to see who the other visitor was. A voice said, 'Who do you think it is, kid?' 'Gee,' I replied, 'that looks like Turk Broda, but he wouldn't come to the hospital to see me.' 'I am Turk Broda,' he said, 'and I did come to see you. Joe Stark told me I should come over and pick up your spirits a little.'

"I was flabbergasted. One of my Leaf heroes in the hospital to see me? It wasn't possible! 'Listen, kid,' Broda continued. 'When you get outta this hospital, I want you to come down to the Gardens, bring a buddy, and I'll leave a couple of passes for you to see a game as my guests.'

"Broda was the Leafs' goaltender at the time, but they had a practice goalie named Joe Stark," Gaston explains. "He had been one of my neighbourhood buddies – he used to protect me in the schoolyard when kids would pick on me. He heard that I was in the hospital and going through a rough time, so after practice one day he asked Turk to come with him to see me at St. Mike's. It sure raised my spirits to open my eye and see Turk Broda in the room. Over the course of my hospital stay, Joe brought Broda, Lorne Carr, Sweeney Schriner and Pete Langelle, all Leaf stars, to see me. Once, when Boston was in town, he brought Dit Clapper around, too. Joe Stark was a wonderful guy – a great friend.

"When I was released from the hospital, I was off work for six months. My disability pension was only $105 a year, and I got all depressed," Tom confessed. "But then my company decided to pay me my full wages for the time I was off. The war was on, and I couldn't serve my country, so selective services sent me to a company called Kindle to work on bandages and medical supplies. I was there for a year. After that, I went back to work at Canadian Fairbanks Morse.

"You know, losing my eye was an awful thing. But it didn't ruin my life like I thought it might at the time. I met my wife Ruth after the accident, and she went with me even though she knew I was blind in one eye. I had two beautiful daughters, and I got to see them grow up to be wonderful women with children of their own. I got to see my grandchildren. My working life continued, and I retired at the age of sixty-two. I've been a volunteer with the Hockey Hall of Fame for over twenty years. My loss of sight really didn't stop me from doing all the things I would have done with two good eyes.

"If I had had the chance, I would have liked to have had a little private chat with Bryan Berard," Tommy continues. Berard, a Toronto Maple Leaf defenceman poised on the brink of stardom, was struck by an errant stick in a game against the Ottawa Senators on March 11, 2000, and lost the sight in one eye. On February 26, 2001, he was forced to retire from hockey. "He was a really good player, and I know he must have gone through all sorts of emotions during that year between the Ottawa game and his retirement. I would have liked to have said, 'Son, you can't change what's happened. But you can live a fully productive life, even with just one eye. Look at me. Go on and make the best of the situation – find other things that you've always wanted to do. Paint, travel, read, write – whatever it is, you don't need to be held back by your injury.' I hope someday get the chance to meet Bryan – I really liked him as a hockey player. But even if I don't get the chance to talk to him, I'll give him the thumbs up and say, 'Way to go, kid!'"

CHAPTER NINE

Season Tickets

"I played a lot of sports, especially lacrosse, with the Selke boys," Tommy Gaston says. "I was living on Taunton Road, and they were just a street away on Hillsdale Avenue. We would usually end up playing in the churchyard after school because there was a lot of space. A friend of my brother Joe had season tickets for the Leafs, and I was fortunate enough to have been able to get down to a fair number of Leaf games through the years, but in 1940 I decided I'd like to get season's tickets of my own.

"Well, I got them, and I was thrilled. They were grey seats in Section 94, which was toward the north end of the rink on the same side as the penalty box. My seats were in the last row. Each seat cost fifty cents a game – back in 1940, the reds, which were the best seats, were only $2.50 each.

"When I got home, I told Mr. Selke that I'd got season tickets," Tom smiles. "He asked me where they were, so I told him, and he said, 'Tom, why don't you go down to Maple Leaf Gardens and see if we can't get you some better seats? I'll speak to them and tell them to find you a pair of greys a little better than that.' So I went to the Gardens ticket office, and sure enough, he had called. I got the same section, Section 94, but this time in Row D. They were much better seats.

"I have to mention that Mr. Selke was a very fine man. Later on, he and Conn Smythe had a falling out, and Frank Selke went to the Montreal Canadiens in 1946. There he set up an incredible farm system that ensured the Canadiens' success for years to come. But no matter what, every time Mr. Selke would come back to Toronto, he always took the time to come over to me and say hello.

"A few years later, I was able to upgrade and move into Row B in Section 94. I guess this would have been in the late 1940s. I was talking to some of the people who sat around me, and they told me that a lady who sat in our section, in the first row, was turning in her season's tickets that morning, and that I should go down to the Gardens to get them. I took advantage of my lunch hour, and rushed over to Maple Leaf Gardens. When I arrived, I walked in through that Carlton Street entrance, turned right and climbed that steep, narrow staircase that curved up to the ticket office. I asked the young lady there if I could upgrade my seats to the specific seats that had been vacated in Section 94, Row A. 'I'm sorry,' the lady said, 'but those tickets are not available,' and she went right back to her work. 'But I know those tickets are vacant,' I said. 'They were turned in earlier today.' She insisted the seats were not available.

"Now, I was a little peeved, so I walked down those steps and marched right over to Mr. Smythe's office. I asked if I could see Mr. Smythe, but his door was ajar and I guess he heard me. 'Invite the gentleman in,' I heard in a distinct voice I recognized immediately as that of Conn Smythe.

"The office was quite nice, but not nearly as elaborate as I had imagined. It had nice easy chairs, a big desk, and various Leaf pictures all over the walls. 'Excuse me, Mr. Smythe,' I said. 'I wasn't really expecting to see you today, and I'm only in my working clothes, but I wonder if I could have a word with you, sir.' I was timid as could be. But he calmed me right away. 'Son, it's your money that put me in this office,' he said. 'Now, how can I help you?'

"I explained the situation to Mr. Smythe, and he seemed to warm to my little speech. 'We can soon sort that out,' he said, and he had someone from the ticket office bring over the tickets, and right then and there he changed my seats to the ones I had requested!

"I was delighted, but then he surprised me even more. 'Thanks for coming in, Tom,' he said. 'Listen, I won't be going to the game on Saturday night – why don't you use my tickets?' If ever there was an award for the world's biggest smile, they'd have given me the trophy and retired the award! The seats were behind the Leaf bench. I don't think I ever was lucky enough to sit in better seats!

"Conn Smythe died on November 18, 1980," Tom says, his voice growing soft. "His death really spelled the end of an era in Toronto sports, because even though Conn hadn't been active with the Leafs for a number of years, he had been the heart and soul of professional hockey in Toronto since 1927. The funeral was held at St. Paul's Anglican Church in Toronto. I went with Lefty Reid from the Hockey Hall of Fame. Conn's casket was draped in a Union Jack, and his body was carried from the church by a group of former Leaf captains. He was buried in Park Lawn Cemetery in Toronto's west end.

Gaston points out that season ticket sales were handled differently fifty years ago. "Most season ticket holders didn't have enough money to pay for all the games in advance, so you paid for as many as you wanted as you went along. Everybody's season tickets were on a rack in the ticket office. At the beginning of the season, you paid for whatever games you could, plus the last three games of the season. You'd get your subscriber's card, and each game night, you'd climb up those stairs to the ticket office to get your tickets. You might even make a payment toward the next few games while you were there." A far cry from the way that today's sports teams market seat licences, club seats and private boxes.

Tommy also remembers a Leafs holiday tradition that has gone by the wayside. "The Leafs wouldn't sell any tickets for the game just before Christmas to the general public. Instead, each season ticket subscriber got one free ticket to take a child to the game. They called it Young Canada Night. Foster Hewitt used to have his young son Bill do a bit of the play-by-play on the radio that night. Later on, of course, Bill called the games for the Leafs on television, while his Dad continued do the radio broadcasts. The child's ticket was cut in half to indicate it was for a youth. The seat wouldn't be right beside you, but it would be as close to your season tickets as they could get. It was a great way for the children to learn to enjoy the Leafs, just like their parents."

With a chuckle, Tommy remembers the friends he got to know through the years in Section 94. "Oh boy, we had a lot of fun. It wasn't nearly as quiet then as it is now. Every time the Leafs stepped onto the ice to start the game or a new period, the organist would play 'The Maple Leaf Forever.' We made up our own words, and sang them proudly to the tune each time the organist played it:

The Maple Leafs, our hockey team
The Maple Leafs forever.
God bless the Leafs our hockey team
The Maple Leafs forever!
"You wouldn't hear fans singing like that today!"

TOMMY GASTON

Although only 10 years old, Tommy Gaston already knew which team had earned his hockey allegience. Wearing a Leaf cardigan like his heroes, this photo was taken at the Gaston home on Merton Street in North Toronto.

Photo courtesy – author collection

KING CLANCY

Tommy's favourite all-time player, Francis 'King' Clancy went from player to coach to executive president for the Toronto Maple Leafs through the Leafs' 75 year history. King also became a good friend to Tom Gaston through the years.

Photo courtesy of Imperial Oil – Turopfsky/Hockey Hall of Fame

THE CONACHER CLAN

The remarkable Conacher clan was recognized as the 'Royal Family of Sports.' All ten of the children excelled in sports, including three siblings who are now enshrined in the Hockey Hall of Fame.

Back row, left to right: Roy, Charlie, Benjamin (father), Lionel, Dermot and Bert. Front row, left to right: Victoria (also known as Queenie), Dorothy (Dolly), Elizabeth (mother), Mary Nora and Kay.

Roy, Charlie and Lionel excelled in the NHL. Brian Conacher is Lionel's son.

Photo courtesy – author collection

TURK BRODA

After Tom Gaston lost the sight in his right eye as a result of an industrial accident, Leaf goaltender Walter 'Turk' Broda was one of the first to visit the hospital. Turk made a lifelong fan that day.

Photo courtesy of Imperial Oil – Turopfsky/Hockey Hall of Fame

BILL BARILKO

Bill Barilko's Dramatic overtime goal won the Toronto Maple Leafs the Stanley Cup in 1951. Hoisted onto the shoulders of teammates Harry Watson and Bill Juzda, the celebration was short-lived. Barilko died that summer in a plane crash while on a fishing expedition. His body wasn't recovered until 1962.

Photo courtesy of Imperial Oil – Turopfsky/Hockey Hall of Fame

ACE BAILEY WITH RON ELLIS

After an on-ice injury ended his hockey career, 'Ace Bailey's' number 6 was retired by the Toronto Maple Leaf organization. But, while watching a young Leaf star named Ron Ellis, Bailey decided to take his number out of retirement. In a ceremony before the 1968-69 season, 'Ace' Bailey awarded his number 6 to honoured Ron Ellis.

Photo courtesy of Graphics artists/Hockey Hall of Fame

SAWCHUCK AND BOWER

During the playoff run in spring of 1967, veterans Terry Sawchuck (left) and Johnny Bower (right) helping the aging Leafs surprise the Montreal Canadiens by backstopping Toronto to the Stanley Cup. The young man on the extreme right is Bower's son John Junior, who sang with his Dad on the song 'Honky (The Christmas Goose).'

Photo courtesy of Imperial Oil – Turopfsky/Hockey Hall of Fame

TOM GASTON WITH DARRYL SITTLER

A class act both on and off the ice, Darryl Sittler thrilled fans as he captained the Toronto Maple Leafs through the turbulent 1970s. Although he had stints in both Philadelphia and Detroit, Darryl Sittler will always be remembered as a Maple Leaf.

Photo courtesy – author collection

TOM GASTON WITH LANNY McDONALD

Playing on a line with Darryl Sittler, Lanny McDonald quickly became a fan favourite in Toronto. His trade to Colorado during the 1970-80 seasons threw gasoline onto a combustable Toronto team, setting off a series of wildfires that hurt the team through much of the 1980s. Lanny won a Stanley Cup with the Calgary Flames in 1988-89.

Photo courtesy – author collection

CLARK AND GILMOUR

Two of the biggest reasons to cheer for the Toronto Maple Leafs in the early 1990s were Wendel Clark (left) and Doug Gilmour (right). Gilmour followed Clark as captain of the Toronto Maple Leafs, but during the 1992-93 and 1993-94 playoff runs, the two combined to skate, score and hit and bring newfound respect to the Toronto Maple Leafs.

Photo courtesy – Paul J. Bereswill/Hockey Hall of Fame

TOM GASTON WITH KEN DRYDEN

After a Hall of Fame career with the Montreal Canadiens, goaltender Ken Dryden retired from active hockey duty in 1979. But he was lured back and joined the Toronto Maple Leafs as president in May 1997.

Photo courtesy – author collection

TOM GASTON WITH PAT QUINN

After playing two seasons with the Toronto Maple Leafs in the 1960s. Pat Quinn joined the Toronto Maple Leafs management as head coach for the 1998-99 season. He added the general manager's duties as well before the 1999-2000 season.

Photo courtesy – author collection

TOM AND RUTH GASTON

This photo was taken of Tom and Ruth Gaston at the final Toronto Maple Leaf game played at Maple Leaf Gardens, February 13th, 1999. Sadly Ruth passed away that following August.

Photo courtesy – author collection

TOM GASTON WITH PHIL PRITCHARD AND CRAIG CAMPBELL

As a volunteer with the Hockey Hall of Fame for over twenty years, Tom Gaston adds the benefit of experience to a team determined to preserve hockey history. Here, Tommy Gaston poses with the Stanley Cup and the men who keep the Resource Centre of the Hockey Hall of Fame running smoothly.

Photo courtesy – author collection

TOM GASTON WITH RON ELLIS

Retired Leaf Ron Ellis now handles public relations at the Hockey Hall of Fame. But Ron and Tom enjoy a friendship that goes beyond co-workers. Ron delivered the eulogy at Ruth Gaston's funeral in 1999.

Photo courtesy – author collection

TOM GASTON ON AIR CANADA SCOREBOARD

In tribute for his many decades of supporting the Toronto Maple Leafs, Tom Gaston's photo graced the tickets for the Leafs' home opener in 2000-2001 season. Here, he is seen waving to the Toronto fans as he appeared on the scoreboard at the Air Canada Centre.

Photo courtesy – Davie Sanford/Hockey Hall of Fame

The War Years

As the Toronto Maple Leafs wound down their first decade at Maple Leaf Gardens, new stars were coming to the fore. Names such as Clancy, Conacher, Primeau, Jackson and Horner gave way to Apps, Davidson, Drillon, McDonald and Broda, while ex-Leaf standout Hap Day replaced Dick Irvin behind the bench. As World War II took the Depression's place on the front pages, this renovated Leafs club would continue to inspire Toronto's sports fans through hard times.

"Syl Apps was the classiest player Toronto has ever had," Tommy Gaston declares. Born in Paris, Ontario, the 21-year-old Apps joined the Leafs in 1936-37 and established himself instantly as a top-flight centre. "Oh, yes, Syl Apps was pure class – and well educated, too. Smythe discovered him playing football at McMaster University in Hamilton. Then, in 1936, he went to the Olympics in Berlin as a pole vaulter. He was a gentleman through and through – the proof is that he won the Lady Byng Trophy in 1942." When Red Horner retired in 1940, Apps became the captain of the Leafs.

Since his arrival in 1935, left winger Bob Davidson had emerged as a team leader, and when Syl Apps went to war in 1943, it was Davidson who took over as the Leafs captain. "Davidson was good and sturdy," remembers Tom. "He came up through the Toronto Mercantile Hockey League. He had also played for the Toronto Marlboros and Canoe Club teams. Bob had a brother, Alex, who got invited to a Leafs training camp, but he never made the team. Gee, when I think about it, the Davidson family had pretty close ties to the Gardens – Bob's Dad was an usher in Section 96 of the greys for years. I got to know him because that was the next section over from where I sat.

"Bob lived in the Toronto suburb of Leaside, near my home, and I got to know him, too, over the years. We would meet on Bayview

Avenue and talk about the team. After his playing days were over, Bob was a Leafs scout for years and years. I'd often see him and his wife around the neighbourhood when they'd be out walking their dogs.

Gordie Drillon came from Moncton, New Brunswick, and he cracked the Leafs lineup in 1936. "The Apps-Davidson-Drillon line was an excellent trio. Davidson did the checking, Apps had the finesse and was the playmaker and Gordie Drillon added the firepower. He led the league in scoring in 1937-38 – he was the last Leaf to win the scoring championship.

"Bucko McDonald was one of the best bodycheckers ever. He was big five foot ten, 205 pounds and robust – the sportswriters used to say he had a 'barrel chest.' The story goes that Jack Adams, the coach and manager of the Detroit Red Wings, saw Bucko playing lacrosse and signed him to a hockey contract. Adams figured that, given McDonald's athletic talent, he could make him into a good hockey player. And he did. Toronto got Bucko in a trade in 1938.

As he talks about Bucko McDonald, Tommy remembers that the Leaf defenceman had a role in one of the most thrilling moments of his own athletic career. "I played lacrosse myself," Tommy says. "I was a goaltender. A charity game was being played in town – this would probably be in the late '30s – and I was put in goal for the celebrity team. My defencemen were Bucko McDonald and Lionel Conacher, two of the best lacrosse players ever to play the game. I was so excited – there were my heroes standing right in front of little me! Lionel Conacher came back to me and said, 'Hey, kid! What's wrong? You're white as a sheet!' I told him I was just excited and thrilled to be playing with him and Bucko, but I think he knew the truth – that I was more than a little bit scared.

"'Look, kid,' Lionel said, 'don't worry about anybody hitting you. If they hit you, I'll kill them. And if I miss, Bucko will get them!' I don't think I faced a single shot. I have to tell you, it was one of the thrills of my life! Years later, when Bucko was the member of Parliament for the Sundridge area [near North Bay, Ontario], I ran into him at an old-timer's luncheon. I went over and introduced myself to him. 'You won't remember this,' I told him, 'but years ago, I played on your team in a celebrity lacrosse game.' Almost before I finished the sentence, he gave me a good look and said, 'Oh! Are you the little guy who was in net?' I couldn't believe he'd remember after all those years.

"Turk Broda did a great job in the Leafs net for fifteen years. And in 1949 he gave the city a good laugh. We called it the 'Battle of the Bulge,' which was also the name of a famous battle in World War II. The Leafs were in a slump, and Conn Smythe announced that they were losing too many games because they were out of shape. He singled out Garth Boesch, Vic Lynn, Sid Smith, Harry Watson and Turk as guys who had to lose weight. They were given a week to hit their target weight. I'm sure that Smythe was serious, but the press made a big deal out of the weight-loss campaign. Every day, there'd be a picture of Broda on a scale, or with a dinner plate with only a couple of vegetables on it.

"The whole city got into the act. People sent Turk food and recipes and weight-loss schemes. When the weigh-in took place, all the players had reached the goal Smythe had set for them. It was a fun time around the arena, but Smythe must have been serious about Turk because he traded to get goalie Al Rollins from Cleveland – just in case.

"Turk Broda will forever be at the top of my list of favourite players," Tommy concludes. "Sure, he was a fun guy and a great goaltender, but the fact that he would come and visit me in the hospital when I needed cheering up the most is something that means so much to me. I'll never ever forget Turk's kindness."

Tom concentrates for a moment, grows silent, then speaks about a subject on which he is clearly uncomfortable. "I was unable to serve my country during World War II. I was going to enlist, but in 1939, I had a minor health problem – a kidney infection – and they turned me down. Then, in 1940, I lost my eye. On my enlistment papers, it said 'permanently unfit.'

"Here in Toronto, Conn Smythe really got involved in the war effort. He had served in the First World War, and insisted that he be allowed to serve again in World War II, even though he was older than most of the boys enlisting. He formed the 30th Battery, and they actively served in World War II. Sportswriter Ted Reeve – they named an arena at Main and Gerrard streets after him – was one of the members of Smythe's battery. So was Shanty MacKenzie, who was a star football player with the Argonauts. After the war, Conn set MacKenzie up with a job at the Gardens. In fact, Shanty would film Leaf games for Conn Smythe, which was revolutionary at the time – this was long before Roger Neilson, the coach they called Captain Video, started to study game tapes. Shanty filmed the games and

Conn and the coaching staff would view them to see what could be improved upon.

"Smythe wrote a letter to all of the players the Toronto Maple Leafs had under contract and asked them to enlist in the war effort. A lot of the Leafs left pro hockey temporarily to serve Canada."

In 1940, Conn Smythe began to prepare the Maple Leaf organization for the war. The Leafs had reached the Stanley Cup finals in each of the past three years (coming away empty-handed). Smythe felt his coach, Dick Irvin, wouldn't be strong enough to handle the coaching duties without his "assistance." At the same time, the Montreal Canadiens had just finished last in the seven-team league and were looking for a coach to replace Pit Lepine. Smythe put forth Irvin's name, the Habs hired him, and Smythe filled the Toronto vacancy with former Leaf captain Hap Day.

Toward the end of 1941, Smythe gathered the board of directors and laid out his wartime strategy. When he was called to active duty – which would occur only a few months later – a committee made up of Frank Selke and board members Ed Bickle and William MacBrien would run Maple Leaf Gardens while Hap Day was to run the hockey team. Day and Selke were instructed to keep Smythe abreast of developments by mail.

The Toronto Maple Leafs introduced a few new faces for the 1941-42 season. Lorne Carr arrived in a trade with the New York Americans. Tom remembers him as "a strong right winger with offensive skills. He was smooth and smart." Bob Goldham came to the Leafs from their farm system, having played for the Marlboros juniors. "Goldham was one of the better defencemen of the time," notes Gaston. "He would block shots by sliding in front of the puck."

At this early stage of the war, NHL teams had not yet been depleted of most of their key talent. The Leafs had a strong team, led by Syl Apps and Gordie Drillon, who both finished with 41 points, and Sweeney Schriner, who was the only Leaf besides Drillon to score 20 goals. Toronto finished in second place, three points behind the New York Rangers.

"Sweeney Schriner was one of the first Russian-born players to play in the NHL," Gaston points out. "Johnny Gottselig, who played with the Blackhawks, was first, but both boys moved to Canada when they were very young." Sweeney and his family moved from Saratov, Russia, to Calgary, where Schriner learned his hockey. "Sweeney was one of the Leafs Turk brought to see me in the hospital. He was a hell of a nice guy – a good goal scorer, and he played on one of the

Leafs' top lines with Lorne Carr and Billy Taylor. Sweeney was a very popular Leaf. I think the nickname 'Sweeney' helped his popularity. You sure wouldn't forget it."

In the best-of-seven semifinal series, Toronto beat the first-place Rangers four games to two. In the sixth game, only six seconds remained in regulation time when Nick Metz broke a 2-2 tie. The goal, and the victory, gave the Leafs a berth in the Stanley Cup finals, where they would face the fifth-place Detroit Red Wings (six of the league's seven teams qualified for the playoffs that season).

The first two games of the finals were played at Maple Leaf Gardens, and the upstart Wings were victorious in both, by scores of 3-2 and 4-2. Game three was played at the Olympia in Detroit, and the Wings punished the Leafs by a 5-2 margin, giving them a commanding 3-0 lead in the series. Back in Toronto, Leaf fans were merciless, heaping generous abuse on coach Hap Day for what they perceived to be a lack of ability behind the bench.

With nothing to lose, Day made a bold decision for game four. He benched Gordie Drillon and Bucko McDonald, two veterans who had made important contributions during the regular season – Drillon was the team's best scorer, while McDonald's defensive play had earned him a spot on the Second All-Star Team for 1942. In their place, Day inserted Don Metz and Ernie Dickens. Metz, the younger brother of Leaf regular Nick, had played in 25 games on the wing for Toronto that season, scoring a grand total of two goals. "Nick and Don were very different types of players," Tommy recalls. "Nick was the better all-round hockey player, and Don lived in his shadow, but both brothers did their jobs well." Ernie Dickens, a rookie defenceman, had also scored two goals in the regular season – and he'd only played in 10 games. These were drastic moves that left many wondering if Day was daft.

Just before the opening face-off of game four in Detroit, Day kept the Leafs in the dressing room a little longer than usual and read them a letter he had received from Doris Klein. Doris was a 14-year-old girl who urged the Maple Leafs not to give up and told them that they really could come back to win the Stanley Cup. Whether it was the teenager's prose or Hap Day's solemn but passionate delivery remains a moot point: the Maple Leafs flew out of the dressing room, ready to control the play from the moment the puck hit the ice.

But the plan went awry. The Wings struck first and took a 2-0 lead into the first intermission.

Then, one of the most remarkable tales in hockey history began to unfold. At 13:54 of the second, Bob Davidson beat Detroit netminder Johnny Mowers. Just two minutes later, Lorne Carr knotted the score at two. In the third period, Carl Liscombe put the Wings ahead 3-2, but Syl Apps roared back to tie the game. Next, Don Metz fed his brother a pass, and Nick scored. In the Toronto net, Turk Broda held down the fort the rest of the way, and Toronto won 4-3.

Two nights later, at Maple Leaf Gardens, Hap Day made another lineup change for game five. Rookie Gaye Stewart, who had never played an NHL game, dressed in place of veteran Hank Goldup. The 18-year-old Stewart had begun the 1941-42 season with the Toronto Marlboros juniors. When their season ended, he was called up to the Leafs' farm team, the Hershey Bears of the American Hockey League, where he played five regular-season games plus the playoffs. By the time the Indianapolis Capitols defeated Hershey in the AHL finals, there was still hockey left to be played in Toronto, and so the native of Fort William (now Thunder Bay), Ontario, native joined the Maple Leafs.

In game five, the newly awakened Leafs buried the Red Wings 9-3. Don Metz scored a hat trick, and the ice was showered with fedoras. Toronto had trimmed the Wings' series lead to three games to two.

For the sixth game, the teams returned to Detroit, where the partisan crowd desperately hoped to celebrate their first Stanley Cup championship since 1937. But Turk Broda thwarted plans for any such party, shutting out the Wings, 3-0. When the final buzzer sounded, Broda was mobbed by his teammates. Zero-turned-hero Don Metz scored another goal, and was joined on the scoresheet by Bob Goldham and Billy Taylor. The series was now tied at three games apiece.

Two nights later in Toronto, a crowd of 16,240 – the largest ever to witness a hockey game in Canada to that date – jammed into Maple Leaf Gardens. Syd Howe of the Red Wings opened the scoring at 1:45 of the second period, and the score remained 1-0 as the teams took the ice for the third period. Day's young soldiers, Goldham, Dickens and Don Metz, played extraordinary defensive hockey, turning the Wings back at every rush. Finally, at 7:47 of the third period, veteran Sweeney Schriner scored to tie the game. Two minutes later, Pete Langelle scored to put the Leafs ahead 2-1. Toronto held onto the lead, and when Schriner scored again with less than five minutes to play, Broda and the Leafs knew the game – and the Stanley Cup – was theirs.

With just over a minute left on the clock, the crowd leapt to its collective feet. Try as they might, Detroit couldn't penetrate the Leafs zone with any success. Then, the Toronto fans counted down the final seconds: "Ten... nine... eight... seven... six... five... four... three... two... one!" The buzzer sounded and pandemonium overtook the arena. Never before had a team won the Stanley Cup after trailing a series three games to none – and no team to date has equalled the feat in a Stanley Cup final. The 1941-42 Toronto Maple Leafs would forever be known as the "Miracle Team," and those who doubted Hap Day's coaching abilities were now calling him a soothsayer... an alchemist... a genius!

"NHL hockey wasn't the only popular hockey being played in the Toronto area during the war years," Gaston states. "Senior hockey was very strong and drew great crowds to see some excellent hockey. Then there was the Mercantile League, which played out of Ravina Gardens. This was a league made up of company-sponsored teams – like Tip Top Tailors and Peoples Credit Jewellers – and they played some darned good hockey, too.

"The Mercantile League was a very tough league. There were some former NHL players – like Red Heron, who had been with the Leafs – and some upcoming NHL players like Moe Morris and Jackie McLean.

"Senior hockey was really big – not quite as big as the NHL, but they drew a lot of fans to their games. One of those teams was the Toronto Goodyears – I think they may have had some loose association with the Toronto Maple Leafs, but the team was run by the Goodyear Tire Company and played at the OHA Senior A level. A Goodyear employee named 'Moose' Ecclestone, coached and managed the team. His real name was Robert, but everyone knew him as Moose. He was good friends with the sportswriters, so he was in the newspapers all the time.

"Moose put together some great teams for the Goodyears. Peanuts O'Flaherty, who went on to play for the New York Americans, played with them. Punch Imlach, too. In fact, it was while he was with the Goodyears that Imlach got his nickname. His name is really George, but he was playing with the Goodyears in Windsor one evening, and he got into a fight. The other guy licked him pretty good, and one of the sportswriters wrote that Imlach was dazed and looked like he was 'punch drunk.' His teammates started to call him 'Punchy,' but then that got shortened to 'Punch.'

"Just before Christmas 1941, Moose Ecclestone was in a terrible car accident. He clung to life for a while, but he didn't pull through. He wasn't very old – maybe his early thirties – when he died. The Maple Leafs put together a benefit for him on January 30, 1942, and held it at Maple Leaf Gardens. It was a whole evening of entertainment. In the main attraction, the Senior Marlboros played a game. After the first period, the Toronto Skating Club put on a display of figure skating. Next there was a competition to see who was the fastest skater. I really enjoyed that! One player from each of the NHL teams competed. Syl Apps represented the Leafs, Flash Hollett was there from Boston, Tommy Anderson from the New York Americans – actually, they were the Brooklyn Americans that year. Sid Abel represented Detroit, Lynn Patrick was there from the Rangers, Jack Portland from Montreal and Max Bentley from Chicago. They had to skate around the ice while stickhandling a puck. After the first round, Syl Apps and Lynn Patrick were tied, so they had a lap between just the two of them and Apps won by a hair. It was great fun!

"After the second period of the Marlies game, some of the Leafs played a team of retired NHL stars. It was a short game and really fun. Joe Primeau and Busher Jackson played for the Leafs and Nels Stewart and Dit Clapper for the NHL Stars. As I recall, it ended in a tie. After that game, they called out lucky seat numbers to win prizes –Jess Applegath, who sold hats in his store on Yonge Street, had put up the prizes. When they announced the seat number over the loudspeaker, I was surprised – it was my seat! I won a Biltmore hat – a fedora – from Jess Applegath just for being in the right seat. Through all my years of going to the Leaf games, we were only lucky enough to win something one other time – on that occasion, Ruth had her seat chosen in a draw, and she won a bag and a t-shirt."

As the war intensified, Tommy remembers that there was some doubt as to whether hockey would continue. "At one point before the 1942-43 season, the board of governors discussed whether the National Hockey League should go on while the war was in progress. Thankfully for everybody, they decided that the league should carry on because it kept the populations of Canada and the U.S. entertained during a dark period of history."

But with players enlisting, a lot of teams were hurt significantly. The New York Rangers were hit particularly hard. "Oh, boy, did they ever have goaltending problems!" Tommy recalls. "'Sugar Jim' Henry had been their goalie in 1941-42, but they went through a bunch of them the next year. They started the season with a guy from Saskatchewan named Steve Buzinski. They used to call him 'The Puck Goes In-ski' Buzinski.' Geez, he leaked like a fork!" Buzinski played only nine NHL games in his career – all of them with the 1942-43 Rangers. The team won only two of those games, during which Buzinski allowed 55 goals.

Buzinski's replacements were little better. Jimmy Franks had been property of the Detroit Red Wings for several years, but had appeared in only one regular-season game and one playoff contest. The Wings loaned Franks to the New York Rangers after Steve Buzinski faltered, and Franks played 23 games, winning only five. When Franks was injured partway through the season – "Maybe he faked an injury to get out of playing goal for such an awful team," Tom snickers – Bill Beveridge was secured on loan from the Cleveland Barons. Beveridge had been a capable goaltender for several teams in the 1930s, including the Montreal Maroons, but hadn't played in the NHL in more than four seasons. He won only four of his 17 games as a Ranger. Next, the Montreal Canadiens loaned New York a goalie from their affiliate in Quebec City by the name of Lionel Bouvrette. In the only NHL game of his career, Bouvrette allowed six goals.

In 1943-44, it was Ken "Tubby" McAuley's turn. He played all 50 games, posting a goals-against average of 6.24. Suprisingly, he was brought back the next season, when he posted a 4.93 average in 46 games.

At the other end of the spectrum, the Canadiens were hurt the least by wartime talent shortages. "Few of their players enlisted," Tommy says, "so they kept a strong roster. The Leafs had a lot of players enlist, but they were deep enough in talent that they were able to maintain a high calibre of hockey." But they did so without a lot of key personnel: Syl Apps, Turk Broda, Bingo Kampman, Pete Langelle, Bud Poile, Sweeney Schriner, Wally Stanowski, Gaye Stewart and Billy Taylor joined the Canadian Army; Don Metz served in the Royal Canadian Air Force; and Bob Goldham, Joe Klukay and Normie Mann were among those who joined the Royal Canadian Navy.

Three hockey players – all of whom had ties to the Leafs – were killed in action. "Jack Fox, who was in the Leafs system, was the first player to die in World War II," recalls Gaston, wistfully. "In the newspaper, they said he was 'the first professional hockey player to make the supreme sacrifice in the present war.' Another was Red Tilson, who was also in the Leafs system. The third was Red Garrett. He had been traded by the Leafs with Hank Goldup in return for Babe Pratt in November 1942."

Because so many regulars were away preparing for the war, the Leafs employed a number of young players to fill their spots. "Oh, yes," says Tommy, "a number of players were given opportunities because of the war. In 1942, there were some university students, like Bobby Copp and Jackie McLean. Both of them were still at the University of Toronto, and because of that, the Canadian government wouldn't allow them to cross the border as long as the war was on. So Copp and McLean played only at home and in Montreal. Bobby Copp became a dentist. He was a good defensive defenceman and had played with the U of T team under Ace Bailey. Jackie McLean was a little fireplug. He was a great skater, and could score, too, but even though he wasn't very big, he never backed away from a fight. Oh, he and Murph Chamberlain of the Canadiens used to get into some dandy scraps!" Both young Leafs would begin their non-hockey careers in Ottawa: Dr. Bobby Copp began his dental practice there, while Jack McLean graduated with an engineering degree, and his contracts took him to the capital as well. Both were recruited by the Ottawa Senators of the Quebec Senior Hockey League, for whom Copp played ten years beginning in 1945-46. McLean was a Senator for two seasons, 1946-47 and 1947-48. In 1948, the Senators won the Allan Cup with Copp, McLean and future Leafs Frank Mathers and Larry Regan on the team.

The 1942-43 edition of the Maple Leafs finished in third place, and the semifinals pitted them against the first-place Detroit Red Wings. Game one, at Detroit's Olympia, saw the Wings double the Leafs 4-2. But the next game, begun on March 23, adds mystery to the history. After three periods of play, the score was knotted at two. After one overtime period, the score was still tied. A second overtime was played, and the score was still deadlocked. The game went into a third and then a fourth overtime, and at the 10:18 mark referee King Clancy indicated a Leaf goal. The puck had clearly entered the net behind Wings goaltender Johnny Mowers, but there was a question as to who had scored it. Bud Poile shot the puck and felt he had scored – many of the Wings concurred. Jack McLean felt he had tipped the puck past Mowers, and that is the way referee

Clancy saw it. As the teams skated off the ice, no official goal scorer had been announced. Two of the three daily newspapers in Detroit credited Poile with the winning goal.

Finally, on March 27, almost four days after the goal was actually scored, acting NHL president Red Dutton announced that the mystery goal scorer was, indeed, Jack McLean. "The situation is now closed, and I'm glad of it, particularly for the sake of young McLean," stated Dutton, who had been general manager of the New York Americans before they suspended operations at the close of 1941-42. "I saw McLean Saturday, and the boy seemed greatly disturbed over all the publicity that had developed out of his goal. He told me he felt badly about the whole thing, and told me he preferred having the goal credited to Poile so the whole matter would be dispensed with. Young McLean felt he was being pictured in an unfair light as a result of the play, and wanted to have his name removed from the records as the questionable goal-getter. He told me, however, that he honestly believed he had tipped the puck after Poile's shot. Clancy insisted that's how he saw the play. And I'm closing the whole incident by declaring McLean the goal-getter." Never before had a goal taken four days to credit, and with the advent of instant replay, it is unlikely that a situation like this would ever again arise. In the end, the Wings beat Toronto four games to two, and eventually won the Stanley Cup.

With the war in Europe raging, more and more recruits were being held as active reserves in Canada, and hockey players were far from immune. In fact, their fitness level was a desirable trait for recruiters. The Toronto Maple Leafs went to their 1943 training camp missing their captain, Syl Apps, as well as forward Billy Taylor and goaltender Turk Broda. Ted Kennedy picked up the slack from Syl Apps. The young centre had been traded to Toronto from Montreal, and would step into the lineup in 1943-44. Tom Gaston remembers Kennedy as "a great leader. He loved the sport and played every game with his heart. He wasn't a great skater, but he was rugged, and got where he needed to go through sheer determination." Kennedy would finish the season with 26 goals and 23 assists for 49 points – a very strong debut for a rookie.

Ted Kennedy was an immediate fan favourite, too. Tommy recalls one particular fan who sat near him at Maple Leaf Gardens. "His name was John Arnott, and he owned Arnott's Service Station, on Eglinton just a block east of Dufferin. There's a 7-Eleven store there now. Anyway, Pete Langelle joined the Leafs in the late 1930s, and he was a really fancy skater. He visited me in the hospital, too, and the nurses all came by to see him. I recall them saying, 'Where did he come from? He's so good looking!'" Tommy laughs at the memory and continues. "The fans really liked him, especially John Arnott. When things would get quiet, usually around a face-off, you'd hear a gravelly voice from the corner green seats holler, 'C'monnnnnn Peee-terrrr!!' and everybody would applaud. I know the players heard him, too – some of them mentioned it to me over the years. Langelle was working for a brewery during the summers, and I know he would give John Arnott cases of beer to thank him for yelling his name.

"Pete Langelle joined the air force before the 1943 season, and now Arnott didn't have anyone to holler for. Then in one game, the Leafs were lining up to take the face-off and Ted Kennedy was leaning in for the draw. All of a sudden, we heard a familiar voice – 'C'monnnnnn Teee-derrrr!!' Well, we all cheered like the dickens, because John Arnott had found a new favourite!"

Arnott went far beyond being a great Leaf fan. He was invited into the Leafs dressing room, a place where spectators were rarely welcome. And when the Leafs won their Stanley Cups in the late 1940s and early '50s, Arnott rode in the parades with the team. He continued to attend Leaf games until the mid 1970s, when his fading eyesight precluded him from going to the Gardens.

Another productive Leaf who emerged during this period was Gus Bodnar. The youngster from Fort William (now Thunder Bay) joined the Leafs for the 1943-44 season, and from his very first shift he was a star. "My, oh my, what a story this is," announces Gaston. "Gus Bodnar was in the starting lineup in his first game. Fifteen seconds after the puck was dropped, he had scored! In his first game, he scored two goals and an assist, and the Leafs beat the Rangers 5-2." Bodnar finished the regular season with 22 goals and 40 assists for 62 points, good for tenth place in the scoring race. As the NHL's best rookie, Bodnar was awarded the Calder Trophy that year.

In spite of the Leafs' depth on the forward lines and on defence, the club faced uncertainty in goal. Turk Broda left before the 1943 training camp to join the active reserves. His replacement: Benny Grant.

"Benny had been the Leafs' reserve goaltender forever," observes Gaston. "He never made it as a front-line netminder in the NHL." The 35-year-old native of Owen Sound, Ontario, had seen his first

NHL action in 1928-29, but he hadn't played in the NHL since 1933-34 – nor had he played hockey anywhere in 1942-43. Broda's absence meant that Grant was getting his big chance. Unfortunately, he was injured before Christmas 1943 and did not play with the Leafs after that. Jean Marois, called up from the St. Michael's junior team, filled in for one game before the Maple Leafs were able to acquire Paul Bibeault on loan from the Montreal Canadiens.

Bibeault had been the Habs' starting goalie the previous two seasons, but when Montreal was able to convince Bill Durnan to join the team in 1943, Bibeault was left without a job. Seizing the opportunity in Toronto, Bibeault was more than satisfactory as a stand-in for Broda. He also met his future wife while a Leaf. Frank Selke Jr. tells that story: "My second-oldest sister, Evelyn, was a public relations assistant and switchboard operator at Maple Leaf Gardens. I'll bet I can still remember the phone number – WAverly 1645! Evelyn met Paul while he was playing goal for the Leafs in 1943. Paul went on to play for Boston, then returned to Montreal for a while before finishing his NHL career in Chicago in 1947. Evelyn and Paul got married, and they worked together for the Buffalo Bisons of the AHL, and later with the Cincinnati Mohawks. Then Evelyn got a job with the Olympics in Montreal, and she and Paul returned to Montreal. Paul managed the Pointe Claire Arena for a while before he died of cancer in 1970."

Bill Durnan, a 27-year-old rookie, played exceptional hockey for the Canadiens during the regular season, posting a record of 38-5-7. In the semifinals, the Leafs were pushed aside four games to one by Montreal, who went on to win the Stanley Cup.

Toronto management knew changes were in order for 1944-45, starting in goal. Although they had hoped Paul Bibeault would return, Montreal refused to loan him to the Leafs for a second season. Instead, Bibeault ended up playing for Boston. Fortunately, a very good netminder was found in time for the new season. "They brought in a tall fellow from Calgary named Frank McCool," Tommy Gaston remembers. "He was a sportswriter, but a fine goaltender, too. During the season, our section would yell, 'Keep cool with McCool,' and the crowd would applaud. He was a fidgety player – very nervous. His nickname was 'Ulcers,' if you can believe that. At times during a game, McCool would have to go to the bench to get a drink of milk to calm his stomach." McCool's play in 1944-45 earned him the Calder Trophy as rookie of the year.

For the third consecutive season, the Maple Leafs finished the regular season in third place. Veterans like Bob Davidson – who had been named captain in the absence of Syl Apps – Sweeney Schriner, Lorne Carr and Babe Pratt provided plenty of leadership as well as offence, and Pratt was awarded the Hart Trophy winner as the league's most valuable player.

"Babe Pratt was quite a guy. He was big – one of the biggest players in the league at the time. And he was pretty wild, too," acknowledges Gaston. "During the playoffs in 1945, the only way the Leafs could tame him was to have Pratt share a hotel room with Hap Day, the coach. Day didn't drink or smoke, so he settled Pratt down, and Babe had a great playoff. The next season, still with Toronto, Pratt was caught gambling and was suspended by the NHL. He had never bet against the Leafs, but he had been gambling. He was suspended indefinitely, but Red Dutton, the NHL president, lifted the suspension after five games."

In the first round of the playoffs, the Leafs met first-place Montreal, and in six games they knocked the Canadiens out of the Stanley Cup race. In the finals, the second-place Red Wings provided the opposition. "This playoff series was as exciting as any ever played," enthuses Tom. "Remember the Leafs comeback victory in 1941-42, when they were down three games to none against Detroit? Well, this series was similar, except the Leafs were up three games to none this time."

The series started in Detroit, and in each of the first two games, Frank McCool posted shutouts over the Wings. Back to Toronto for game three, and again, McCool shut out Detroit. But with their backs against the wall, down three games to none, the Red Wings beat Toronto in game four at Maple Leaf Gardens. They won game five, too, with Harry Lumley recording a shutout for the Wings. In game six, Lumley again won the game with a shutout. The series was tied at three games apiece, with the deciding match to be held at Detroit's Olympia. But Babe Pratt's game-winning power-play goal gave the underdog Toronto Maple Leafs their second Stanley Cup championship of the decade.

CHAPTER ELEVEN

The Dynasty

With the end of war in Europe came the return of NHL players who had served their country, in some cases for as long as four years. As the 1945-46 season approached, Jack McLean, Pete Backor, Ross Johnstone and Windy O'Neill no longer had spots on the Toronto roster, while Gaye Stewart, Billy Taylor, Syl Apps, Bob Goldham and Turk Broda reclaimed their stalls in the Leafs dressing room.

Frank McCool was slated to begin the season as the Leafs' netminder, but his decision to hold out for a better contract kept him on the sidelines. For their first thirteen games, Toronto tried to make do with minor-leaguers Gord Bell and Baz Bastien, neither of whom proved to be an adequate replacement. By the end of November, McCool was re-signed, but the return of Turk Broda from military duty sent "Ulcers" back to his sportswriting job in Calgary. Broda's midseason homecoming came too late to reverse the Leafs' fortunes; they had dug themselves into a deep hole in the first half, posting a record of 8-17-3. Toronto boasted a powerful offence, paced by Gaye Stewart's league-leading 37 goals (just one shy of Babe Dye's 21-year-old team record), but a porous team defence, weighed down by the instability in net, caused the Leafs to allow more goals than any NHL team except the woeful New York Rangers. As a result, the defending Stanley Cup champions finished fifth in the six-team league, missing the playoffs.

Some of those who had made their NHL debuts during wartime stayed on to enjoy Hall of Fame careers. In Montreal, of course, there was Maurice "Rocket" Richard, while Toronto had Ted Kennedy, who was only 18 when he first appeared in a Leafs lineup in March 1943. In 1946-47, a dream of Teeder's came true when he was assigned sweater number 9, which had belonged to his idol, Charlie Conacher of the Kid Line. Conacher presented him with the sweater

in an informal ceremony on September 10, 1946. As much as anything, this was a sign that Kennedy had truly arrived as a Leafs
mainstay. In his two games in 1943, Kennedy wore number 20 – it
was customary in those days for rookies to wear higher numbers
(and to be assigned the less attractive berths in Pullman cars on
overnight train trips). When Syl Apps entered the military, Kennedy
inherited his number 10, but was "relegated" to number 12 when
Apps returned in 1945. Lorne Carr's retirement made number 9
available, and Kennedy requested it. "He's a good kid and a great
player," said Conacher. "You just can't disappoint a guy like that,
and it makes me feel good to give him my number 9." Kennedy
stammered, "I'll do my best to be worthy of it." Then Conacher
kidded, "You should have a great year, kid, with this number on
your back!" And he did: Ted Kennedy led the Leafs in scoring with
28 goals and 32 assists.

The 1946-47 season saw the Leafs make some substantive roster
changes. After asking Conn Smythe for a raise, centre Billy Taylor
was dealt to Detroit for winger Harry Watson. Bill Ezinicki and newcomer Howie Meeker claimed regular spots in the Leafs lineup. Sid
Smith enjoyed his first games as a Toronto Maple Leaf in part-time
duty. And Jim Thomson and Gus Mortson, dubbed the Gold Dust
Twins, made their debuts as part of a revamped blueline squad, as
did a kid from Timmins named Bill Barilko.

Tommy remembers being excited at the prospects of a great season. "Mortson and Thomson were two of the best. Gus Mortson was
a stay-at-home defenceman, while Jimmy Thomson could really move
the puck up the ice. Ezinicki wasn't very big, but he wouldn't back
away from a fight with anyone. And Howie Meeker – strong skater,
great shot. He scored five goals in one game as a rookie that season."

With a smirk, Tommy recalls watching his beloved Leafs at a practice. "I only ever saw the odd practice. I snuck in once – I think it
was a holiday. Really, you had to know somebody to get that kind of
behind-the-scenes access. There were very few people watching, but
I remember being amazed at what I saw. There was a lot of skating
and shooting, and they seemed to work on line rushes for a long
time. Hap Day had quite a few huddles with the players to go over
specific things."

The blending of veterans and youth was a tonic for the Maple
Leafs, who won 31 games (then a franchise record) and finished
second behind the Montreal Canadiens. In the semifinals of 1947,
the Leafs eliminated the Detroit Red Wings four games to one.

Advancing to the finals, the Leafs met the reigning Stanley Cup champions, the Montreal Canadiens and defeated them four games to two. For the third time in the decade, the Toronto Maple Leafs had won the Stanley Cup.

Conn Smythe had decided that the Leafs needed more strength down the middle, and his mind was set on a centre he thought would be perfect for the Leafs. "Connie Smythe always liked Max Bentley," reports Gaston. "Max was playing for the Blackhawks with his brother Doug. The Leafs had a line they called the Flyin' Forts Line – Gaye Stewart, Bud Poile and Gus Bodnar. All three of them came from Fort William (now Thunder Bay) Ontario. They really gelled as a line, really complemented each other, and they were always among the Leafs' top scorers at the end of the year." In November 1947, Smythe sent the entire Flyin' Forts Line, plus Bob Goldham and a defenceman named Ernie Dickens, to Chicago for Max Bentley and a prospect named Cy Thomas.

"Bentley – boy, could he skate! He was really quick, and could turn on a dime. They called him the Dipsy Doodle Dandy because he could really stickhandle, too. This trade gave the Leafs three all-star centres in Apps, Kennedy and Bentley. They were the Leafs' top three scorers that year. I thought the fans were going to be up in arms because Toronto had traded away so many fan favourites. But as long as the team kept winning, it seemed that the fans didn't mind anything that the Leafs did."

The 1947-48 edition of the Maple Leafs finished first in the league, breaking their year-old club record with 32 wins, while Turk Broda won the second Vezina Trophy of his career. The Toronto power-house won its second Stanley Cup in a row, and they seemed to do it with ease. In the semifinals, the Leafs dispatched the Boston Bruins in only five games – their one loss coming on April Fools' Day – while they swept the Red Wings in four straight games in the finals. Ted Kennedy led all playoff scorers with 8 goals and 14 points in 9 games.

After that championship, longtime captain Syl Apps retired to pursue a political career. Kennedy filled the vacancy. Tom Gaston hides his eyes as he recalls a poignant tale about "Teeder." "Ted Kennedy was always a class act. Two or three months after my wife Ruth died, Ted came to the Hockey Hall of Fame and looked for me. He said, 'Tom, I liked Ruth. She was a wonderful woman. I was out golfing and one of the guys told me Ruth had passed away. I wish I had known when it happened – I would have been there at the funeral, Tom. I owe it to you as a friend.'

"Isn't that something? Here's one of the greatest Leafs of all time, paying his respects to a little guy like me. I'll always remember him as a hockey player, but as long as I live, I'll never forget him as a man."

Cal Gardner and Bill Juzda were added to the roster in 1948. Both had come to Toronto from New York in exchange for defencemen Wally Stanowski and Moe Morris. "Gardner and Juzda added extra grit," Tommy says. "Gardner lives in the same neighbourhood as I do today. He could score and he added aggressiveness. Bill Juzda – they called him 'The Beast' – could score a little, too, but he certainly wasn't afraid to mix it up in the corners."

Another player who made his NHL debut in 1948 was Les Costello. "Les had been playing with St. Mike's when they won the Memorial Cup in 1947. He spent the next year with the farm team in Pittsburgh, and was called up to play in the 1948 playoffs for Toronto. He was a fine hockey player, but the Leafs were so strong that it was tough to crack the lineup. They used to say the Pittsburgh Hornets could play in the NHL and be a winning team. Les played for a couple of seasons, then he entered the seminary in 1950 and became a priest. But he didn't give up on hockey! He formed a team called the Flying Fathers, and they played hockey games for fun to raise money for charities." Tommy smiles at the memory.

Father Les Costello and a friend, Father Brian McKee from Sault Ste. Marie, Ontario, formed the Flying Fathers in 1962. Both were excellent hockey players, and they realized there was a great deal of talent within the ranks of the priesthood. The team has since played around the world, entertaining millions while raising more than $4 million for a variety of charities. The team combines solid hockey with the novel antics of teams like basketball's Harlem Globetrotters. Father Les figures the Flying Fathers have only lost about six games of the thousand they've played. "When we play these games, everyone wins" says Costello, who still plays today at the age of 73. "Families are together, charities are supported and laughter soothes the body and soul."

The Leafs endured a relatively disappointing regular season, placing fourth with a record of 22-25-13, but they found a renewed vigour in the playoffs, defeating the Boston Bruins in the semifinals in five games. Finding themselves in the finals once again, Toronto made short work of the first-place Detroit Red Wings, sweeping them for the second year in a row. The championship was the Leafs' third in a row and their fifth in eight years.

A pall was cast over the NHL on March 9, 1948, when the league assessed lifetime suspensions against former Leaf Billy Taylor and Don Gallinger of the Bruins for gambling. Both had bet against their own team at various times. "Billy Taylor should have been a superstar," Tommy Gaston sighs. "When he was nine or ten years old, they used to dress him up in a miniature Toronto Maple Leafs uniform and he would entertain the fans between periods at the old Arena Gardens. For a little guy, he could really skate. He'd stickhandle like a pro from one end of the ice to the other and shoot the puck into the net. The Toronto crowds really loved him. Later on, he starred with the Oshawa Generals junior team."

Taylor joined the Generals in 1937-38 as a 19-year-old, and led Oshawa to the Ontario Hockey Association championship. They went on to face the St. Boniface Seals in the Memorial Cup finals, played at Maple Leaf Gardens. Although Taylor earned points on eleven of the Generals' twelve goals, it was Wally Stanowski and the Seals who won the Memorial Cup.

In 1938-39, Billy Taylor scored 53 points in 14 games for Oshawa. This time, after winning the OHA championship for a third consecutive season (they would extend the string to seven in a row between 1938 and 1944), the Generals faced the Edmonton Athletic Club Roamers for the Memorial Cup. Billy Taylor scored nine goals and added six assists in the final series, which Oshawa won three games to one. Lester Patrick, the general manager of the New York Rangers, declared Billy Taylor "the greatest junior I have seen in twenty years. He should have a great career."

Unfortunately, Taylor's NHL career was disappointing. In five seasons with the Maple Leafs, interrupted by two years of war service, he reached the 20-goal plateau only once. Traded to Detroit in September 1946, he led the league in assists, but was traded to Boston for Bep Guidolin before the start of the 1947-48 campaign. Taylor struggled in Boston, and was traded to the Rangers in February 1948. After playing only two games in New York, Billy Taylor's NHL career came to a screeching halt.

NHL president Clarence Campbell issued a statement that said Billy Taylor and former Bruin teammate Don Gallinger had been suspended for life for "conduct detrimental to hockey and for asso-

TOM GASTON

ciating with a known gambler." Gallinger was only 22 years old, but had already played five seasons with the Bruins. During an investigation of Michigan gambler James Tamer, it was discovered that both Taylor and Gallinger had been identified as clients. No other players were involved, and neither player had attempted to alter the final result of a game in which they played, even though they had occasionally bet against the Bruins. Neither ever played another NHL game. On August 25, 1970, the league's board of governors lifted the lifetime bans. Taylor went on to hold scouting positions with the Philadelphia Flyers, Washington Capitals and Pittsburgh Penguins. Don Gallinger was never able to find another position in hockey. His life was clouded by further tragedy over the years: his marriage crumbled and a daughter died from bone cancer.

The Toronto Maple Leafs' reign as Stanley Cup champions ended in 1949-50. Although young Sid Smith emerged as an offensive force, and such names as George Armstrong and Tim Horton made their first appearances, the third-place Leafs were unable to stop the powerful Detroit Red Wings in the semifinals. Detroit had finished the season in first place, 11 points ahead of Montreal and 14 ahead of Toronto.

Game one, played in Detroit, saw the Leafs earn a decisive 5-0 victory, but at 8:46 of the third period an incident took place that stirred up the bad blood between the two clubs. Gordie Howe, Detroit's young star, crashed headfirst into the boards. "I don't think we'll ever know exactly what happened," Gaston says fifty years later. "Howe was about to check Ted Kennedy when he went flying into the boards. Gordie says Kennedy high-sticked him, while some of the other Wings claimed Ted Kennedy butt-ended or tripped Howe. Kennedy insists he never touched Gordie, and didn't even realize Howe was hurt until he came back down the ice and saw him lying there.

"No penalty was called on the play, but Gordie Howe was bleeding and unconscious. At one point, they thought he was going to die. A surgeon drilled into Gordie's skull to relieve the pressure, a move that saved his life. But Howe had a fractured skull, a broken nose and a damaged right eye."

The series, between two of the league's three most penalized teams during the regular season, was already a rough one, and now the violence was cranked up a notch, as fights filled the remaining games. Broda racked up three shutouts as the Leafs took a 3-2 series lead, but then the balance tipped in favour of Harry Lumley, who blanked Toronto in game six. The seventh game ended in a scoreless tie, which was broken by Wings defenceman Leo Reise at 8:39 of over-time. It was his second OT marker of the series. When his teammates called Detroit's Harper Hospital to tell Gordie the great news, he buoyed their spirits by telling them that he already knew – he had felt well enough to watch the game on television.

The Red Wings played New York in the finals, and after a goal by Pete Babando in double overtime of game seven, the Detroit Red Wings had earned the Stanley Cup. The Detroit crowd chanted, 'We want Howe! We want Howe!' and, to the amazement of the Olympia crowd and his own teammates, Gordie Howe stepped out of the player's entrance and waved to the crowd, his head still bandaged from his crash into the boards. The fans gave Howe a long standing ovation.

The arrival of a new decade brought further fine-tuning of the Maple Leafs roster. Coach Hap Day was moved up to assist Conn Smythe as general manager. Taking his place behind the bench was a name familiar to Toronto fans: Joe Primeau, who had just coached the Marlboro seniors to an Allan Cup title in 1950. He brought 19-year-old left winger Danny Lewicki, who had starred for that Marlboro squad, with him. Bill Ezinicki and Vic Lynn were traded to Boston for defenceman Fern Flaman. Rounding out the new faces was Tod Sloan, a product of the St. Mike's Majors whose 31 goals would lead the Leafs in 1950-51.

After anchoring the Toronto defence for twelve years, goalie Turk Broda considered retirement, but decided to stay on. But Conn Smythe was worried that Broda's expanding waistline would become a detriment to the Leafs, so Al Rollins, who had been acquired from the Cleveland Barons a year before, was brought in to compete for the job. Throughout training camp, Rollins and Broda were pitted against each other for the starting assignment. The battle reached its peak on October 9, 1950, the night of the annual Blue and White intra-squad game. On this occasion, the team was split in two – one side wore the Leafs' white sweaters, while the other wore the blue uniforms. Broda's team defeated the Rollins squad and, impressed by his outstanding play in the game, Primeau, Day and Smythe agreed to give Turk the job as the Leafs' regular goalie. Although rivals at first, Broda and Rollins became friends as well as the league's stingiest goaltending combination. In 70 games, the 1950-51 Leafs allowed only 138 goals, earning Rollins, who wound up playing 40 games to Broda's 31, the Vezina Trophy.

On the day of that Blue and White game, George Hainsworth was killed in a head-on collision near Gravenhurst, Ontario. Ribs broken in the crash punctured his heart, and Hainsworth died at the scene. In 1936-37, a young Turk Broda had taken the Leaf goaltending chores away from Hainsworth. Already a legend when he was traded to Toronto for Lorne Chabot in 1933, Hainsworth starred with Toronto for three full seasons. He retired with a career total of 94 NHL shutouts, a league record that stood until 1964, when it was broken by Terry Sawchuk of Detroit. At the time of his death, George Hainsworth was a city alderman in Kitchener, Ontario.

The Toronto Maple Leafs enjoyed what was perhaps their strongest season to date, finishing with 95 points. In many seasons, that mark would have been good enough to lead the league, but the Detroit Red Wings, led by the aforementioned Sawchuk, exploded for a 44-13-13 record and 101 points. For all intents and purposes, it was a two-team race during the regular season in 1950-51: the third-place Montreal Canadiens managed only 65 points.

After a 2-0 upset at the hands of the visiting Boston Bruins in game one of the semifinals, the Leafs won the series four games to one. There was a curious twist to this series, though – the teams actually played six games to get the five results. Here's why: game two took place in Toronto on Saturday night, March 31, 1951. The teams played to a 1-1 tie after sixty minutes of play, and there was still no decision after twenty minutes of overtime had been played. A local bylaw prohibited any sporting event from taking place on a Sunday, and midnight was drawing near, so the game was stopped. It went into the record books as a 1-1 tie.

Toronto would meet the Montreal Canadiens, who had upset the powerful Red Wings, in the Stanley Cup finals. This, too, was a remarkable series, as every single game went into overtime. (The Canadiens were giving the fans their money's worth in these playoffs. The first two games of the Detroit series had required 61 and 42 minutes of extra time to decide a winner.) Game one in Toronto resulted in a 3-2 overtime victory, with Sid Smith, who scored two goals including the winner, as the hero. Game two, also at Maple Leaf Gardens, saw Rocket Richard even the series with an overtime goal to give Montreal a 3-2 win. The series reverted to the Forum for game three, and at 4:47 of overtime, Ted Kennedy scored the winner to give the Leafs a 2-1 victory. The Forum hosted game four as well, and it was Harry Watson's turn to break the tie, at 5:15 of overtime.

The Leafs were ahead three games to one as the finals returned to Toronto for game five, played April 21, 1951. The first half of the game was scoreless; then the Rocket put Montreal in front at 8:56 of the second period. Three minutes later, Tod Sloan converted a pass from Ted Kennedy to tie the game. The Canadiens again pulled ahead early in the third period, and they shut the Leafs down until the final minute. Coach Primeau pulled Al Rollins in favour of a sixth attacker, and with 32 seconds left on the clock, Tod Sloan beat Gerry McNeil to tie the game. The stage was set for one of the most dramatic goals in Leaf history. At 2:53 of overtime, number 5, Bill Barilko, beat McNeil to give the Toronto Maple Leafs their sixth Stanley Cup title in ten years.

CHAPTER TWELVE

Barilko

Dr. Henry Hudson seemed destined to be tied forever to Toronto sports history. Of course, his ill-fated fishing trip with the Toronto Maple Leafs star defenceman Bill Barilko has been well chronicled. But there's more Toronto sports history – and mystery – involving Hudson.

On February 17, 1942, the Ontario Curling Bonspiel was taking place at Royals' Arena, a rink at 131 Broadview Avenue, near Queen Street. Tommy and Ruth Gaston had often gone skating there. Teams from all across the province were competing, and on this opening day a rink from the northern city of Timmins team was challenging Toronto's High Park squad. The Timmins skip was Dr. Lou Hudson, an alumnus of the University of Toronto hockey teams coached by Conn Smythe. In fact, Lou had captained the team in 1923-24 and 1925-26, and played on the Varsity Grads team that won a gold medal at the Winter Olympics in St. Moritz, Switzerland, in 1928.

The game was tied 8-8 in the 10th end, and Lou Hudson was about to play his last stone when his teammate and brother, Dr. Henry Hudson, claimed he had been shot. "I don't know how it happened," stated the 38-year-old Henry. "I was curling with the team and was leaning over with the broom. I felt a sharp pain like a sting in my thigh. I didn't know it was a bullet then. It sort of spun me around."

The other members of the Timmins team tried to stop the bleeding in Hudson's thigh, while several other curlers ran up to the arena's balcony, thinking the shot may have been fired from there. The police were called immediately, and upon their arrival every curler, locker and bag was searched, but no evidence could be found of a shot being fired.

Detective James Ledbe, as perplexed as anyone, commented, "The only answer we can see to it right now is that the gun was accidentally discharged. There were a lot of men from the north country, and many of them were wearing their north country mackinaws and windbreakers. It's quite possible that one of them forgot he had a gun in his pocket. It could have been discharged in half a dozen different ways." Another policeman, Inspector Charles Greenwood, stated, "The shot was fired by someone standing on the level of the ice; not above or below. It travelled fast enough to lodge in the thigh muscle. The course of the bullet was straight."

Dr. Henry Hudson was driven to Toronto General Hospital. "It just came out of the blue," said Hudson. As he patted his thigh, he noted, "It's still in there." The .22-calibre bullet had entered the doctor's right thigh and lodged against an artery on the inside of his leg. The bullet was removed, although not for several days, and Henry returned to his Timmins dental practice by the end of the month. No one ever solved the mystery of where the bullet came from, or why a shot was fired.

Nine years later, on August 24, 1951, Henry Hudson and Bill Barilko climbed into a Fairchild 24 plane en route to Seal River, off the northeastern corner of James Bay. By now retired, Dr. Hudson was quite a bit older than the Leaf defenceman, but they knew each other from around Timmins. Hudson was a licensed pilot, and the plan was that he would fly Barilko and his friend Allan Stanley – a New York Rangers blueliner who also called Timmins home – to Seal River. Through a miscommunication, the dentist's brother, Dr. Lou Hudson, turned up for the trip as well, and Stanley decided to stay behind. But it turned out that the combined weight of the three men would be too much for the single-engine pontoon plane to carry safely, so Lou Hudson also stayed home.

After a full weekend of fishing with exceptional results, the two Timmins pals prepared for the flight home. With over 100 pounds of trout stored in the pontoons, the plane lifted off from Seal River and made its way south to Timmins. Hudson landed the plane at Rupert House, near the southern tip of James Bay, three hours south of Seal River. Stretching their legs as the yellow Fairchild 24 was refuelled, Hudson and Barilko kibitzed with some of the locals. They recognized the Maple Leaf defenceman, whose picture and name had been all over every daily newspaper in Canada after he scored the Stanley Cup-winning goal at 2:53 of overtime in game five of the finals. The residents of Rupert House could never have known that they would be the last people to see Hudson and Barilko alive.

Late in the evening of Sunday, August 26, Dr. Hudson's plane is believed to have plummeted from the sky over Northern Ontario. When the Timmins men did not arrive home by Monday, rescue squads were deployed to find the missing plane. Their fruitless search continued on and off for months. It wasn't until June 6, 1962, that the mangled fuselage of the Fairfield 24 was discovered in the dense and swampy bush 45 miles north of Cochrane Ontario. The skeletal remains of the two friends, still strapped in their seatbelts in the seaplane, were extracted from the crash area, and on June 15, 1962, Bill Barilko was finally laid to rest in a Timmins cemetery. Allan Stanley and Harry Watson, a teammate of Barilko's on the 1951 Leaf team, were among the pallbearers. For two years, a granite memorial stone had stood over an empty grave. At last, after eleven frustrating years, the grave had an occupant.

In their song "Fifty Mission Cap," The Tragically Hip encapsulate the irony of Barilko's death:

Bill Barilko disappeared that summer – he was on a fishing trip
The last goal he ever scored, in overtime, won the Leafs the Cup
They didn't win another 'til 1962, the year he was discovered

(The Tragically Hip) Roll Music/Little Smoke Music (SOCAN)
(From the album, "Fully Completely")

Peter Worthington, one of the founders of the Toronto Sun, was a reporter with the Toronto Telegram at the time that Dr. Hudson's plane was discovered. Worthington was accompanied by Bill Masters from the Ontario Department of Lands and Forests, and Gary Field, a helicopter pilot who had discovered the plane's resting place by catching a glint of shiny metal as he flew over the dense bush. Peter Worthington reported firsthand on the grisly discovery in the June 8, 1962 Toronto Telegram. "The muskeg belches as you flounder through it, but the swamp forest and evergreens lash out to prevent your passage. Black flies regard you as fair game and you slither and slap your way along like an itchy twist dancer. Then, suddenly, you burst through a tangle of deadfall and you're on it – the wreck of a plane in which hockey player Bill Barilko and Timmins dentist Henry Hudson died eleven years ago. Poking around the wreckage seemed somehow like tampering with a grave. I found a charred 10 cent piece and saw several splintered rib bones embedded in seeping bog by the pilot's seat. I stopped looking. The plane seems to have

plummeted to the earth upside down. Tops of nearby fir trees were chopped off." Peter Worthington was the only journalist to peruse the battered remains of the plane in which Barilko and Hudson lost their lives. Today, Peter Worthington is a much-read columnist with the Toronto Sun, appearing Fridays and Sundays.

Was Dr. Henry Hudson a lightning rod for sporting tragedy, or were the separate incidents mere coincidences for a man who enjoyed his frequent visits to Toronto, shoulder to shoulder with his sporting friends? All that matters now is that the well-liked Timmins dentist died at the age of 47. Upon the discovery of his remains in 1962, he was buried in Toronto, the city to which his name has been tied as a sad and oft-forgotten footnote in the chronicles of Toronto sporting history.

"Bill Barilko was a real tough guy on the ice," snarls Tommy Gaston. "He had fire in his belly. When he hit somebody, he hammered them!"

Barilko scored the single most dramatic goal in the history of the Toronto Maple Leaf franchise. The scene: Maple Leaf Gardens, April 21, 1951. Leafs vs. Canadiens in the Stanley Cup finals. Toronto up three games to one. Score tied at two after regulation time. The teams play sudden-death overtime.

The Leafs' Harry Watson carries the puck into the Montreal zone. Passes to Howie Meeker on the right. Shot – saved by McNeil! Meeker picks up the rebound and ducks in behind the Canadiens' net. Passes out front to Gardner – he doesn't see it! Watson takes a swing. In storms Barilko from the point – he fires the loose puck... He scores!! Bill Barilko has scored to give the Toronto Maple Leafs the Stanley Cup. Bill Barilko, the hero tonight in overtime as the Toronto Maple Leafs win their seventh Stanley Cup!

Barilko would never get the opportunity to score another goal. Four months later, almost to the day, on August 26, 1951, the plane in which Barilko was a passenger crashed in the dense wooded forest of northern Ontario, killing the Leafs defenceman and the pilot, Dr. Henry Hudson.

The drama of a young hockey star scoring the winning goal to give his team the Stanley Cup championship is the stuff of Hollywood legends. And oddly enough, Hollywood is where Bill Barilko, who had the handsome look of a matinee idol, first played professional hockey. He spent 1945-46 and the better part of the 1946-47 season with the Hollywood Wolves of the Pacific Coast Hockey League. The Wolves drew a number of Hollywood actors to their games, including George Raft, Allan Ladd, William Bendix and Carmen Miranda.

During the 1946-47 season, the San Francisco Shamrocks of the same league were involved in a train wreck near Fresno, California. Although there were no fatalities, a number of the players were injured, some of them quite badly. All of the other teams in the league's Southern Division – the Wolves, the Los Angeles Monarchs, San Diego Skyhawks, Fresno Falcons and Oakland Oaks – contributed at least one player to the Shamrocks to help them play their scheduled games. Barilko's older brother Alex, playing for the Oakland Oaks that season, was his team's selection to aid the Shamrocks.

After polishing his talents under the tutelage of Tommy "Cowboy" Anderson, the Hart Trophy winner with the New York Americans in 1942, Bill Barilko was summoned to the Toronto Maple Leafs toward the end of the 1946-47 season. He was just 20 years old and played in only eighteen games, but he quickly established himself as an aggressive defensive defenceman. Seeing his first NHL playoff activity that year, Barilko helped the Maple Leafs win the Stanley Cup. In 1947-48 he was a regular fixture on the Leaf blueline and he led the NHL in penalty minutes with 147. Again, the Leafs won the Stanley Cup. The 1948-49 season was the Timmins-born defenceman's third campaign, and again, the Toronto Maple Leafs won the Cup.

In 1948-49, Toronto's dynasty looked like it might continue, but Barilko and the Blue and White were stopped in their tracks by a strong Detroit Red Wings team. The Wings not only finished the season in first place (for the second year in a row), they eliminated the Leafs from Stanley Cup contention during the semifinals. It took seven games, including overtime in the deciding match, to knock out the reigning Stanley Cup champions.

That summer, Bill and Alex opened Barilko Brothers Appliances at 167 Danforth Avenue in Toronto. The storefront is a law office today, but back then, the brothers sold radios, records and record players, kitchen appliances and sporting goods. Bill was living several blocks east in an apartment above the Eton House Tavern at 710 Danforth. On June 2, 1949, surrounded by teammates Turk

Broda, Jim Thomson and Harry Watson, Bill held one end of the ribbon, his brother Alex took the other, and coach Hap Day cut the ribbon to officially open the new store.

Anne Klisanich, the younger sister of Alex and Bill, recalls that the family was concerned that the store wouldn't be managed properly with both boys off playing hockey. Bill, of course, would play that season in Toronto, while Alex, who attended the Leafs training camp, played for the Sherbrooke Saints of the Quebec Senior Hockey League. Like his younger brother, Alex was an aggressive defenceman with a talent for bodychecking.

"The boys asked me to come manage the store," Anne remembers, "but I was still up in Timmins with my Mom, and was only eighteen at the time, so I had to say no." Barilko Brothers sponsored the Maple Leafs charity softball team in the summer of 1949, and when the hockey season arrived they offered a miniature television set – a rare new luxury – to any Leaf player who scored a hat trick or any goaltender who earned a shutout. They would have given away quite a few, as Turk Broda registered eight shutouts in 1949-50, Al Rollins earned another, and Harry Watson scored a hat trick.

Tommy Gaston remembers Barilko Brothers Appliances. "The company where I was working supplied the store with washing machines, refrigerators and stoves. My job was in shipping, and I remember getting a charge out of preparing the paperwork for the shipments to the Barilko Brothers' store. They used to call it 'the House of Champions.'"

In 1950-51, Toronto finished the season in second spot, runners-up to Detroit in the regular season. By this time, Bill Barilko was using a slapshot, an innovation later popularized by players like Andy Bathgate, Bernie "Boom Boom" Geoffrion, Stan Mikita and Bobby Hull. Bill liked the shot. "It's a deadly shot, mainly because it's low and hurried," he observed. But his coach, Joe Primeau, wasn't so sure: "The slapshot is more of a fad than anything else, and I feel it will gradually pass out."

During the first round of the playoffs, Toronto met the Boston Bruins, knocking them out in five games. The Wings were surprised by the Canadiens, who upset Detroit to advance to the finals. And at 2:53 of overtime in the fifth game, Barilko scored the goal that delivered the Stanley Cup to Toronto for the sixth time in ten years. The goal is the subject of an unforgettable Turofsky Brothers' photograph that depicts Barilko falling forward as the puck hits the twine behind Canadiens goaltender Gerry McNeil. McNeil is himself falling backward into the Habs' cage, his face frozen in a grimace as the puck narrowly evades the shaft of his goal stick.

"Bill Barilko was in the right place at the right time," Tommy smiles. "I mean, Billy wasn't known as a goal scorer at all, yet he scored a Stanley Cup-winning goal. I often wonder how well he'd be remembered today if he hadn't been right there then to score that goal. The crowd went crazy! It may very well be the loudest I ever heard Maple Leaf Gardens. And it was so dramatic – overtime in a Stanley Cup game, Bill not returning for training camp that fall. That makes it the most important goal in Toronto Maple Leaf history, doesn't it? Bill was so young when he died – only 24 years old – but he had already played five seasons with the Leafs and won four Stanley Cups!

"I was at the Canadian National Exhibition with Ruth in August 1951. We were just walking through the 'Ex' and getting a bite to eat, when we read the electronic board they used to have there that flashed the news. It said, 'Leaf hockey player Bill Barilko's plane down and missing.' That's how I found out that Billy was gone.

"The city was devastated. Everybody was talking about it. We couldn't believe it. I remember Conn Smythe was a real hero with the city. He offered a reward to help find Bill and Dr. Hudson. I know Bill's sister Anne has often told me that Conn Smythe was very good to her family through the ordeal, calling her Mom from time to time to try to reassure her that everything that could be done would be done to try to find Bill."

On October 17, 1992, just before a game against the Chicago Blackhawks, the Toronto Maple Leafs raised a pair of banners to the roof of Maple Leaf Gardens. At centre ice, Ace Bailey's daughter Joyce watched as her father's number 6 was raised to the rafters, signifying that no Maple Leaf player would ever again wear that sweater number. Then, Anne Klisanich watched tearfully as the Leafs paid tribute in similar fashion to her brother, Bill Barilko. From the moment that Dr. Hudson's plane was reported missing with Bill Barilko as a passenger, no Maple Leaf has ever worn the number 5.

CHAPTER THIRTEEN

The Fifties

"The 1950s were tough years for the Leafs," begins Tommy Gaston. "After Bill Barilko's Stanley Cup-winning goal in 1951, the team really struggled, and didn't come back to prominence until the 1960s."

Tommy puts it very matter-of-factly, but the Leafs' decade-long Stanley Cup drought is hard to account for. While it is true that the loss of Barilko would have been a shock to the team and a drain on their talent, the farm system introduced bright young defencemen like Tim Horton and Leo Boivin – both of whom are Honoured Members of the Hockey Hall of Fame. Turk Broda had reached the end of his playing career, but his replacement, Al Rollins, was a Vezina Trophy winner. In 1952, when the Leafs braintrust decided he was not the goaltender to lead them back to the Promised Land again, Rollins was traded to Chicago with Gus Mortson, Cal Gardner and Ray Hannigan for Harry Lumley. Rollins went on to win a Hart Trophy with Chicago in 1954, in spite of – or perhaps because of – the Hawks' last-place finish.

"The replacement for Al Rollins was a guy they called 'Apple Cheeks,'" recalls Gaston. "I liked Harry Lumley very much. He came from Owen Sound, and they've named the arena up there after him. I met him a few times and found him to be a very likeable guy." Lumley was a very good netminder as well. In 1952-53, the Leafs tumbled out of playoff competition, finishing fifth, but Lumley certainly couldn't be faulted for that. He led the NHL in shutouts with 10, and his goals-against average was 2.39. In 1953-54, when King Clancy replaced Joe Primeau as coach, the Leafs pulled themselves up to a third-place finish, and Lumley shone once again. His 13 shutouts and 1.86 goals-against average were both tops in the league, and he won the Vezina Trophy. But the Leafs were paired with the league-leading Detroit Red Wings in the semifinals. Detroit took the series four games to one en route to their third Cup championship in five years.

Lumley backstopped the team to another third-place finish in 1954-55 (the Leafs posted an interesting record of 24 wins, 24 losses and 22 ties). His sparkling 1.94 goals-against average was again the best in the NHL, and he missed out on another Vezina Trophy by a single goal – Detroit had allowed 134 goals to the Leafs' 135, and so their goalie, Terry Sawchuk, received the award. Finishing third sentenced the Leafs to another first-round matchup with those powerhouse Wings, who outscored them 14-6 en route to a series sweep. The Red Wings' dominance of the league cannot be fully appreciated unless it is pointed out that they finished first seven years in a row between 1948-49 and 1954-55, winning the Stanley Cup four times during that run.

The Leafs of 1954-55 may provide a clue as to what ailed the team throughout the decade: while their defence was superb, their offensive muscles had atrophied. In 1950-51, Toronto scored 212 goals in 70 games, the second-highest total in the league. Over the next four years the team's production flagged to 162, 156, 152, and finally 147 goals. Perhaps the aging of star forwards like Max Bentley and Ted Kennedy had an adverse impact on the team's fortunes. Howie Meeker's output also dropped dramatically, and in 1953-54 he retired. For every George Armstrong or Dick Duff, the Leafs' farm system – which included Pittsburgh of the American league as well as the Marlboros and St. Michael's juniors – was generating far more players with names like Hannigan, Hassard, Solinger or Timgren.

In 1955-56, the balance of power in the NHL shifted from Detroit to Montreal. The Canadiens would win a phenomenal five consecutive Stanley Cups – a record unmatched in the history of the National Hockey League. Montreal finished first in four of those years, and were fully expected to win the Stanley Cup yet again in 1960-61 after another first-place finish, only to be shocked by the upstart Chicago Blackhawks.

Meanwhile, the Toronto Maple Leafs continued to struggle. In 1955-56, they finished in fourth place, and for the fifth time in seven years they would face Detroit in the first round. That playoff appearance, lasting only five games, would be the last postseason action Toronto would see until 1959. In May 1956, Harry Lumley and Eric Nesterenko were sold to Chicago, and Ed Chadwick would take Lumley's place.

But the light at the end of the tunnel wasn't the headlight of an oncoming train, as so many thought. By mid-decade the farm system was quietly turning out some wonderful NHL players. George Armstrong emerged as an offensive force and a leader, while Dick Duff, a Toronto fan favourite, began to reach the 20-goal plateau on a regular basis. Ron Stewart and Billy Harris became dependable forwards with a knack for scoring key goals. On defence, Tim Horton was rock solid, while Bob Baun joined the big club in 1956. He was followed a year later by his future defence partner, Carl Brewer. Brewer, Baun and Harris – along with future Leaf standouts Bob Pulford and Bob Nevin – were members of the Marlboro junior team that won back-to-back Memorial Cup championships in 1955 and 1956.

The rebirth of the Toronto Maple Leafs would parallel a number of other developments in the outside world. Rock 'n' roll debuted in the mid fifties, while television became an entertainment hub for families as well. Tommy Gaston embraced the new technology. "My wife and I had a television fairly early compared to most of our friends and neighbours. I have to admit, we bought it for hockey games as much as anything. I can still remember where we got it – New Era Appliances at Main and Danforth in the east end. It was black and white, of course – a 20-inch model. We had heard about television for awhile. But what really sold us was when we stood in the showroom and watched Marilyn Bell finish her swim across Lake Ontario. It was September 9, 1954 – I remember it as clear as a bell. Oh, pardon the pun! We were so impressed. We couldn't believe how realistic the pictures were – it was just like being there. We bought the TV right then and there."

Television coverage of hockey games began with the 1952-53 season. The games at the Gardens started at 8:30 p.m., but the broadcast wouldn't begin until 9 o'clock. Tommy explains the discrepancy: "I remember hearing that the CBC didn't want to cut a popular show they had, called Juliette. She was a singer who would bring guests onto her program. The ratings must have been good, because they kept Juliette on for years and still started the telecasts at nine – by which time the first period had usually just ended. It went on that way for several years.

"Foster Hewitt stayed on the radio, while his son Bill, who sounded a great deal like Foster, did the TV play-by-play. In those days, the camera just followed the play, back and forth. Today, well – it's just marvellous how they cover all the angles, isn't it?"

It was around this time that the relationship between hockey players and team management began to change, too. "In 1957, Ted Lindsay from the Red Wings tried to start a union in the NHL. Connie Smythe was incensed! He did everything he could to bury the union. He and the NHL's board of directors used all their power to stop the idea from taking hold.

"Now, you have to remember that the six team presidents were incredibly powerful, and Smythe was probably the most powerful of them them," Gaston continues. "Smythe and Jack Adams of Detroit were so upset about the union that they decided to single out the players responsible for organizing the NHL Players Association and punish them by sending them to Chicago."

The Blackhawks were perennial losers who missed the playoffs thirteen times in the sixteen years between 1942-43 and 1957-58. In the early 1950s the club's outlook was so dim that the other five teams tried to prop up the Hawks by trading them some good prospects. Montreal sent Ed Litzenberger and Dollard St. Laurent; Ron Murphy and Jack Evans were traded from New York; Al Arbour came Chicago's way from the Red Wings; and the Leafs traded Tod Sloan, Earl Balfour and Eric Nesterenko to the Blackhawks. "This wasn't a charity situation," Tommy points out, "because the teams got money or players in return. But it was pretty darned close to charity to help the Hawks."

But the deals that saw players go to Chicago after 1957 were motivated less by philanthropy than by revenge against the union "agitators." Tommy Gaston shakes his head. "Ted Lindsay, who was leading the players' union, and Glenn Hall were traded to Chicago before the 1957-58 season. Conn Smythe was so mad at the thought that his captain, Jimmy Thomson, would be involved in a union, that he sold him to Chicago. Owners could do things like that back then, and there wasn't really anything the players could do about it." It would be ten more years before a National Hockey League Players Association got off the ground.

At the beginning of the 1954-55 season, the management of the Toronto Maple Leafs began to evolve as Conn Smythe relinquished the job of general manager to longtime Maple Leaf employee Hap Day. Day had been the first captain of the Maple Leafs, and was on the St. Patricks roster when Smythe bought the club in 1927. "He was a fine defenceman and a fine gentleman," Tommy remembers. "When the team moved into Maple Leaf Gardens, the Hap Day

Pharmacy was just to the left of the main doors on Carlton Street. We'd often see Hap in there, although I think he did more by playing hockey than he did dispensing prescriptions.

"Oh, yeah," Tommy interjects. "I just remembered – Connie Smythe made him manager of his sand and gravel business, too. The trucks used to say 'C. Smythe for Sand.' That was how much Conn Smythe liked Hap Day."

After his playing days ended, Day became coach of the Leafs. In his ten years behind the bench, from 1940-41 until 1949-50, Hap's teams won five Stanley Cup titles. Day, whose given name was Clarence, had actually been performing most of the duties of a general manager for the Leafs for several years, but without the title. He had been instrumental in hiring Joe Primeau to replace himself as coach of the Leafs in 1950, and when Primeau left the Maple Leafs, it was Day who hired King Clancy to coach the team. Three years later, Clancy was replaced by another retired Leaf, Howie Meeker. Officially, Hap Day held the position of GM for just under four years. But during that time, Conn Smythe had relinquished control of the Gardens to his son, Stafford. "Stafford pushed his father to let him run Maple Leaf Gardens and the Toronto Maple Leafs," Tommy says. "Conn agreed, and they set up a hockey commit-tee, which got to be known as the Silver Seven, to run the operation."

The Silver Seven was made up of sportsmen who had been friends for a number of years. Jack Amell was vice-president of Robert Amell and Company, a jewellery business. John W. Bassett was publisher of the Toronto Telegram and president of CFTO-TV in Toronto. George Gardiner was president of the stock brokerage firm Gardiner, Watson. William Hatch was vice president of McLaren's Food Products. George Mara was president of William Mara and Company, an alco-hol importer. Lawyer Ian Johnson had been another member of the Silver Seven, but was replaced by Harold Ballard. Both Stafford Smythe and Harold Ballard had run the Toronto Marlboros farm system for the Maple Leafs, putting together the team that had enjoyed back-to-back Memorial Cup victories in 1955 and 1956.

The hockey committee felt that Hap Day's management style was holding the Toronto Maple Leafs back. They didn't like Day's pen-chant for defensive hockey and, growing impatient, Stafford Smythe approached his father on behalf of the committee and asked that Day be replaced. The elder Smythe, resigned to the fact that he had given the hockey committee the power to better the team, felt he couldn't deny the group's request, and agreed to a change.

On March 25, 1957, Day resigned from the position, and left the Gardens for good. Tommy recalls that it was a sad day for the franchise. "Day had been great for the Leafs in various capacities for thirty years. But Smythe felt his methods were outdated, and undermined him at a press conference." In New York, Conn Smythe let the assembled media know that the Leaf system was antiquated, but that Hap Day was going to be asked if he was "still available to manage the team." With that single phrase, Smythe had, in effect, questioned Day's ability in public. Day confronted Smythe back in Toronto, livid that after thirty years of loyal service he was being asked if he was "still available." He resigned from Maple Leaf Gardens on the spot.

CHAPTER FOURTEEN

Punch

The rise of the Silver Seven to the Toronto Maple Leafs' helm coincided with one of the most tumultuous years in club history. In 1957, coach Howie Meeker was relieved of his duties – after a fifth-place finish – then was kicked upstairs into the general manager's office. Before he could get settled into his new job, however, he ran afoul of Stafford Smythe and was shown the door – perhaps mercifully, because the 1957-58 edition of the Leafs, under coach Billy Reay, placed sixth. To provide some perspective on this dubious achievement, no Toronto team had finished last overall in the NHL since the Toronto Arenas of 1918-19.

When Stafford Smythe and his hockey committee began their search for a new head coach for the Maple Leafs, there were a few candidates who stood out in particular. A top contender was Alf Pike, who had played with the New York Rangers in the 1940s, guided the Guelph Biltmores to a Memorial Cup title in 1952 and by 1958 was coaching the Winnipeg Warriors of the Western Hockey League.

On the other hand, Punch Imlach was a relative unknown outside of certain hockey circles. Imlach had been a good junior player with Ed Wildey's Toronto Young Rangers in the mid 1930s, then he impressed hockey fans around the city while playing in the senior ranks with Moose Ecclestone's Toronto Goodyears and the Marlboros. During the 1940s, he hooked up with the Quebec Aces of the Quebec Senior league, playing centre at first, then coaching, managing and even taking an ownership stake in the club. Among his charges in Quebec in the early 1950s was a young Jean Beliveau. In 1957 he took the dual role of general manager and coach of the American Hockey League's Springfield Indians, owned by Eddie Shore.

The Leafs may have been looking for a coach, but Punch Imlach wanted to be Toronto's general manager. Oddly enough, the Leafs had no general manager, although King Clancy held the title of assistant GM. The hockey committee offered Imlach the same title held by Clancy, with most of the actual duties of a fully fledged GM. After he had spent some time within the organization and earned the title, the brass reasoned, he would officially be named as general manager. Begrudgingly, Imlach agreed to the arrangement, and he joined the organization before the 1958-59 season.

The Leafs lost the first three games of the season, and five of their first eight games. The Silver Seven called Punch in to explain what was wrong with the team. Imlach stated that the problem was that Billy Reay wasn't assertive enough with the players. Imlach suggested that a coaching change needed to be executed, but because he was only the assistant GM, he lacked the authority to replace the coach. So, the hockey committee, with Conn Smythe's approval, made Punch Imlach the general manager. His first order of business was to fire Billy Reay, which Punch did at the twenty-game mark of the season, with the Leafs having gotten of to a 5-12-3 start.

While the Maple Leafs hockey committee looked for a suitable coach, Imlach stepped behind the bench. He did such a wonderful job while the search was in progress that the men in the executive suite decided that the 40-year-old Punch Imlach was the man they were looking for. He was offered the job and, upon accepting, he became the coach and general manager of the Toronto Maple Leafs.

"I watched Punch Imlach play with the Marlboro Seniors," recalls Tom Gaston. "He played the game well and he played hard. He was a real hockey brain. In fact, I think he was one of the best hockey executives that Toronto ever had."

Imlach felt the Leafs could make the 1959 playoffs, and while he may have been alone in that conviction at times, he never wavered. In early March, with five games left on the schedule, it appeared that the New York Rangers – who led Toronto by seven points – had a lock on fourth place and the final playoff berth. But Punch insisted that the Maple Leafs would be playing hockey in April, and sure enough, the Leafs went on a tear.

On the weekend of March 14-15, Toronto played the Rangers in an important home-and-home series. On Saturday night at Maple Leaf Gardens, Johnny Bower backstopped the Leafs to a 5-0 shutout. The next night in New York, Toronto edged the Rangers 6-5. In their remaining three games, the Leafs beat the Canadiens,

Blackhawks and Red Wings, ending the regular season with 65 points – one more than New York. Punch Imlach's cocky prediction was starting to look like the prophecy of a genius, and his status with the Leafs was further solidified. Toronto pushed the second-place Boston Bruins out of the playoffs in the first round, before falling to the Canadiens in the Stanley Cup finals.

A key to the Maple Leafs' renaissance was a new goaltender, Johnny Bower. Ed Chadwick had been a solid, if unspectacular, netminder for the Leafs, but the Silver Seven were convinced he was not up to the task of carrying the Leafs to a championship.

It would be an understatement to say that the NHL goaltending fraternity in the 1950s was an exclusive circle. The league had only six teams, and each club relied on a single goaltender. Teams were not required to dress a backup for each game until the mid 1960s, so it was expected that a netminder would play all 60 minutes of all 70 games. Opportunities to break into this tight-knit group were few and far between, and no one illustrated this fact more clearly than Johnny Bower.

Before he got his first shot at the NHL limelight, Bower had played eight superb seasons with the Cleveland Barons of the American Hockey League. He was twice named a First Team All-Star in the AHL, and was selected to the Second Team once. After a sixth-place finish in 1952-53, the New York Rangers elected to demote their goalie, Lorne "Gump" Worsley – an unusual move, considering that Worsley had won the Calder Trophy as rookie of the year that same season. The Rangers sent Worsley to Vancouver of the Western Hockey League and replaced him with Bower. Bower played the 1953-54 season in New York, where he posted five shutouts, cut the Rangers' goals against by almost 30, and posted a record of 29-31-10 – an improvement of 18 points in the standings. Still, the Rangers failed to make the playoffs, and so – in an interesting bit of turnaround – Worsley was recalled to replace Bower for 1954-55.

Bower had been perfectly happy in Cleveland, but his job there had been taken by former Ranger Emile "The Cat" Francis. Instead, Bower spent the next year in Vancouver, leading the Western League in shutouts and goals-against average, before returning to the AHL with the Providence Reds in 1955-56. There he won a league-leading 45 games and earned another selection to the First All-Star Team. He was also named the AHL's most valuable player of 1955-56. In fact, Bower's dominance in the American league was so complete that he was named the MVP – and the goaltender on the first All-Star team – in each of the next two seasons as well.

It was clear to the Leafs braintrust that the best goaltender outside the NHL, by far, was Johnny Bower. On June 3, 1958, Toronto claimed Bower in the inter-league draft. If NHL records are to be believed, Bower was born on November 8, 1924, which would make him 34 years old for much of the 1958-59 season. However, the question of Bower's age has always been the stuff of myth. Other sources have given different dates and, with a mischievous gleam in his eye, Bower himself claims to be unsure of his exact birth date. There is as much confusion over Johnny Bower's real name as there is over his age. He was born John Kizkan in Prince Albert, Saskatchewan, but his mother remarried. While playing in Cleveland, Johnny decided to take his stepfather's surname, Bower.

Tommy Gaston reminisces about the goalie they called the China Wall: "Johnny Bower had played so many years in Cleveland, and as I got to know him, he admitted that he didn't think he would ever get another chance in the NHL. But Punch was a smart man, and his Springfield Indians of the AHL had been beaten a number of times by Bower's Cleveland Barons. Imlach knew that the reason was Bower's goaltending, and when the Leafs needed a strong goalie, he suggested Bower.

"Johnny, to this day, is a perfect gentleman. The city adored him. Johnny played a very exciting brand of hockey. He had perfected the poke check, and would come out of his net to poke the puck away from the opposing team's forward. Johnny had a great defence in front of him, but he was a great goalie. If the other team got a goal against him, they really earned it."

Imlach and the Silver Seven made several other changes to the team in attempting to restore it to respectability. Bert Olmstead was picked up from Montreal in the intra-league draft the same day as Bower. (This was a different draft than the one that netted Bower. In the inter-league draft, NHL clubs could claim players from the rosters of minor-league clubs. In the intra-league draft, NHL teams had the chance to select cast-offs from the other five big-league teams.) Then, just before the season began, the Boston Bruins traded Allan Stanley to the Leafs for Jim Morrison. At Christmastime 1958, Toronto picked up Gerry Ehman from Detroit. Ehman had been a high-scoring veteran for Imlach's Springfield Indians the year before. Next, Larry Regan was obtained in a trade with Boston midway through the season. The acquisition of these veterans coincided beautifully with the emergence of homegrown talent nurtured through the Toronto Maple Leaf farm system that Stafford Smythe had developed: Billy Harris, Frank Mahovlich, Bob Pulford, Dick Duff, Tim Horton, Carl Brewer, Bob Baun and Bob Nevin, all of whom would play prominent roles in the Leaf dynasty of the early 1960s.

Tommy Gaston observed each one as they made their Maple Leaf debuts. "Carl Brewer and Bob Baun were like Siamese twins together – they were a perfect match. Baun was a rugged stay-at-home defenceman, and Carl had no qualms about carrying the puck down the ice. They were terrific together. Timmy Horton was graced with God-given talent. Strength was his biggest asset, wasn't it? He could give you a bear hug that would easily crush you – there was no way you'd be allowed to stand near the crease with Horton around.

"Tim started out with a hamburger stand – the donut stores came afterward. Tim Horton Donuts has turned out to be a very successful chain across Canada. I remember one time, he and Punch had a falling out. The next day, Tim brought Punch a bag of stale donuts. I had a good laugh about that one! Horton was paired up with Allan Stanley, whom the Leafs got in a trade with Boston. Stanley was slow but steady. You like to have a guy like Stanley on your team.

"Up front," notes Tommy, "the Leafs had the Big M, Frank Mahovlich. He skated with such long, graceful strides – when he was skating down the wing, he almost melted the ice. He was the NHL's rookie of the year in 1958. Then there was George Armstrong, the Chief. He lives in my neighbourhood out in Leaside. George is very quiet, but he has a dry sense of humour. He was well liked by both the fans and his teammates. Armstrong was a great team captain. Dickie Duff was a good all-around player who had a knack for scoring important goals. The Leafs had a lot of wonderful homegrown talent back then."

In 1959-60, Punch Imlach's resurgent Maple Leafs climbed all the way to second place. It had been nine years since the Leafs had finished that high in the standings. The team was basically the same as the year before, but the younger players had benefited from a year of seasoning, while Punch continued to get the most out of his veterans. The Leafs worked their way through a first-round victory over Detroit to challenge Montreal in the Stanley Cup finals, but they still weren't ready to snap the Canadiens' Stanley Cup streak. This time Montreal swept the Leafs to claim their fifth straight Cup championship.

There was a significant midseason addition to this Leaf club: Red Kelly. Tommy liked the trade that brought Kelly to the Leaf club. "It was King Clancy who really made this deal happen. Detroit had given up on Red – I don't know why – and traded him to New York with Billy McNeil for Eddie Shack and Bill Gadsby. But Red Kelly wouldn't play for New York, and he threatened to retire rather than report to the Rangers. King figured that, if Detroit wanted to get rid of Red anyway, he might convince him to come to Toronto. They snuck Kelly into Toronto for a meeting – King picked him up at the airport. They made Red wear a hat so fans wouldn't recognize him and figure out what the Leafs were up to. I think they went to a steak house, and the two Irishmen talked for hours.

"By the time they finished dinner, Red Kelly had agreed he would come to Toronto. Imlach contacted Jack Adams in Detroit and the deal was made – Red Kelly for spare defenceman Marc Reaume. It was the best trade Toronto ever made!"

Kelly had been a high-scoring, Norris Trophy-winning defenceman in Detroit, but upon his arrival in Toronto Punch Imlach turned him into a centre. He went on to help the Leafs win four Stanley Cups in the 1960s.

"The Leafs also had a player named Gerry James," Tommy adds, his memory sharp as a razor. "He was a rough-and-tumble player from Regina who had come up through the Marlboros system. He not only played hockey, he played professional football, too, for the Winnipeg Blue Bombers. Just before the Leafs' training camp in 1958, Gerry James hurt his leg badly in a football game against the Saskatchewan Roughriders and he missed that entire NHL season. He came back for the 1959-60 season, but he wasn't the same player and that was the end of his NHL career."

The Leafs finished the 1960-61 season in second place again, just two points behind the Herculean Montreal Canadiens. Red Kelly was an instant success at centre – he finished the season with 20 goals and 70 points. He was placed on a line with Frank Mahovlich, and the combination was explosive – the Big M netted a team-record 48 goals. Rookie David Keon also added 20 goals in his Calder Trophy-winning NHL debut. "Davey Keon was a great skater and a great passer," Tommy notes. "But he wasn't just smooth – he was a clean hockey player." Eddie Shack, who quickly became a favourite of Toronto hockey fans, joined the club from New York in a trade for Johnny Wilson and Pat Hannigan. "If things were quiet in the rink, Imlach would put Shack out and he would liven up the whole arena. He could skate miles, and he was a pretty good goal scorer, too. Eddie got in everybody's hair, and that's why the Toronto fans loved him so much," states Gaston. "He and I got to be pretty good friends."

In the playoffs, fourth-place Detroit surprised Toronto, and beat them four games to one. But the biggest surprise of the year came from the Chicago Blackhawks. They had finished the season in third place, but played some smart hockey and ended Montreal's Stanley Cup-winning streak at five. In the finals they defeated the Red Wings to claim their first championship since 1937-38.

Just before the 1961-62 season began, there was a power struggle between Stafford Smythe and his father, Conn. Stafford wanted control of the team, but the elder Smythe resisted. After days of arguing, Conn relented, telling Stafford that if he wanted the team so badly, he should buy his father's shares. Conn owned more than 50,000 shares, and agreed to sell 45,000 of them to Stafford at $40 each. At the time, shares in Maple Leaf Gardens were trading at $33. By November 23, 1961, Stafford Smythe and partners Harold Ballard and John Bassett had arranged the financing to give them a controlling stake in Maple Leaf Gardens. When the purchase was completed, Stafford promised his father that he would maintain the integrity of the Toronto Maple Leaf franchise. He also pledged that, just as he was now purchasing Maple Leaf Gardens from his father, Stafford's son Tom – whom Conn had singled out to one day operate the franchise – would one day get the opportunity to take over the corporation.

The headline in the Bassett-owned Toronto Telegram read, "CHANGE OF CONTROL FOR THE GARDENS." There is some doubt as to whether Conn knew that his son had partners in the purchase, or who those partners were. "Grandpa hit the roof," Tom Smythe says. "'If I had had any idea that Ballard and Bassett were involved, I'd have cancelled the sale,' Conn said. My grandfather was heartbroken. He felt deceived by his son, whom he believed to be giving away two-thirds of the Smythe legacy."

On the ice, the franchise thrived under its new ownership. Led by the offence of Mahovlich, Keon, Armstrong, Kelly, Bob Nevin and Bob Pulford, as well as the strong defence of Horton, Stanley, Baun and Brewer, the Toronto Maple Leafs again concluded the season in second place in 1961-62. A young Brian Conacher made his NHL debut during this season, while veteran Ed Litzenberger, who had captained the Stanley Cup-winning Chicago Blackhawks the year before, joined the Leafs as well.

Five years of meticulous retooling by Punch Imlach finally paid off in 1962. Facing the New York Rangers in the semifinals, Toronto turfed the Blueshirts four games to two. In the Stanley Cup finals, the Leafs were challenged by the Blackhawks and they were again victorious in six games. "It had been eleven years since our last Stanley Cup championship, and the city of Toronto was hungry," smiles Tommy. "This was Toronto's eighth championship since becoming the Maple Leafs. The city went crazy! Even though the winning game was played in Chicago, Toronto fans celebrated in the streets, especially Yonge Street.

"It wasn't until later that one of the sportswriters noted that the Leafs hadn't won since Bill Barilko's dramatic goal in 1951. Well, sure enough, Bill's remains were found just before the Leafs' Stanley Cup parade up Bay Street to City Hall."

The Toronto Maple Leaf team rode through the streets of Toronto in open convertibles. Each car held a player – dressed in shirt and tie, of course – and bore a sign indicating who was in the car. "George Armstrong carried the Cup in the car with him," Tommy says. "Once at City Hall, the Leafs lined up on the steps while speeches were made, then each of the players and executives signed the guest book inside City Hall."

The competition during the 1962-63 schedule was fierce – at season's end, only five points separated the four playoff teams. Toronto finished the campaign in first place – the first time they had done so since 1947-48.

Twenty-six-year-old rookie defenceman Kent Douglas was the only new player to crack the Leafs lineup. Asked to describe him, Tommy Gaston says, "He had played for Imlach in Springfield a few years before. The season before the Leafs traded for him, he was a First Team All-Star in the American Hockey League, and was voted best defenceman. You always knew Kent because he wore burnt cork under his eyes, like a football player. He said the TV lights gave off too much glare, so he had those black streaks under his eyes." Kent Douglas was the NHL's rookie of the year in 1963, and became a solid fifth defenceman for the Leafs.

In the '63 playoffs, the Maple Leafs met the Canadiens in the semifinals and beat them four games to one. Johnny Bower earned two shutouts in the series. Detroit was the competition in the Stanley Cup finals, and the Leafs beat the Wings handily by the same 4-1 ratio. The Stanley Cup was presented on the ice at Maple Leaf Gardens. "I remember it like it was yesterday," grins Gaston. "Armstrong was presented with the trophy and he waved all the players over to the table where it sat so they could touch it. There was no celebration like they have today. No one skated the Cup around the ice, or huddled around the Cup for a team picture."

In February 1964, the Leafs made a trade that generated shock waves among the team's fans. The popular Dick Duff was sent to New York along with Bob Nevin, Rod Seiling, Arnie Brown and Bill Collins for Ranger scoring stars Andy Bathgate and Don McKenney. As a Boston Bruin, McKenney had finished among the league's top ten scorers four years in a row, beginning in 1956-57. Andy Bathgate had been a Ranger scoring threat for years, finishing in the top ten nine straight times dating back to 1955-56. In 1961-62, Bathgate had been runner-up to Bobby Hull for the scoring championship, and in 1962-63 he placed second to Gordie Howe. Bathgate racked up 18 points in 15 games that remained on the Leafs' schedule, adding a timely spark to the team's offence.

The Leafs weren't as dominant as they had been the year before, placing third in the 1963-64 standings. Their first-round series against Montreal went the full seven games, but Toronto triumphed, winning the seventh game 3-1 in Montreal. Meanwhile, Detroit had eliminated the Rangers and were once again set to meet the Leafs in the Stanley Cup finals.

The series was a see-saw battle. The Wings pulled ahead 2-1 in game one at Maple Leaf Gardens, but Toronto came back to win with two seconds on the clock. The second game saw the Leafs spot Detroit a 3-1 lead before they rallied to tie it up, but the Wings' Larry Jeffrey scored the winner in overtime. Game three was played at the Olympia in Detroit. This time the Wings leapt to a 3-0 lead. Toronto caught up again, but Alex Delvecchio won it for Detroit with 17 seconds in regulation time. Game four, also in Motown, saw the Wings squander yet another lead, and this time the Leafs capitalized, winning 4-2. Back in Toronto, Detroit edged the Leafs 2-1 to take a 3-2 lead in the series.

Game six at the Olympia will forever be remembered as the game in which defenceman Bobby Baun, after breaking a bone in his foot during the third period, emerged from the dressing room to score the winning goal in overtime. Spurred on by these heroics, and bolstered by Johnny Bower's flawless goaltending, the Toronto Maple Leafs skated to a decisive 4-0 home-ice victory to claim their third consecutive Stanley Cup title.

The city was anything but complacent, in spite of winning the Stanley Cup for a third year in a row. "The streets flooded with fans wearing anything blue and white they could find," says Gaston. "It seemed there was no stopping our Leafs. For the third year in a row, there was a huge parade, and the Leafs were recognized on the steps of the old City Hall once again."

During the off-season, Imlach surprised the hockey world by plucking goaltender Terry Sawchuk – who had helped to give the Leafs such trouble in the 1964 Stanley Cup finals – out of the intra-league draft pool. Dickie Moore, one of the stars of Montreal's late-'50s dynasty, came out of retirement to join the Leafs roster, and Marlboro graduate Ron Ellis found a regular spot in the NHL roster. Despite the changes, 1964-65 would be a frustrating season. The Leafs sunk to fourth place, and they were no match for the Canadiens, who won the semifinal series and then the Stanley Cup. "It wasn't that the team played poorly," Tommy says. "Far from it – it's just that Montreal played so well. But I think we all felt invincible after winning the Cup the previous three seasons."

"I remember 1965-66 for a couple of reasons," Tom says, "and both have to do with music. My tastes run more toward the big bands and Lawrence Welk, but there were two songs I heard on the radio that remind me of that season. Johnny Bower had a hit record out at Christmas time, and in the spring there was one about Eddie Shack. They were both good fun, and the Toronto fans really got behind them.

A songwriter by the name of Chip Young approached Bower to record a song he had written: "Honky (the Christmas Goose)." The Leafs goaltender agreed, went into a recording studio with his son John, and they recorded "Honky" as well as a B-side, "Banjo Mule." Capitol Records pressed and released the 45-rpm single, crediting it to "Johnny Bower with Little John and the Rinky-Dinks." Listeners to the city's most influential Top 40 radio station, 1050 CHUM, began requesting the tune in droves, and it even knocked the Beatles' two-sided smash, "Day Tripper"/"We Can Work It Out," out of the station's most-requested spot for a couple of weeks. The single charted, climbing to number 29 on 1050 CHUM's chart before the novelty wore off and the holiday season ended. Various companies have tried to re-issue the recording over the years, and they have had the full blessings of Johnny Bower, but the writer of the song moved to Australia and has since died, leaving the ownership of its copyright in some dispute.

In February 1966, RCA Records released "Clear the Track, Here Comes Shack" by Douglas Rankine and the Secrets. The lyric was written by the outstanding hockey hisdtorian and former host of Hockey Night in Canada, Brian McFarlane. He asked Eddie Shack for permission to write a song about him, and was given the green light. After scratching out the words in what McFarlane remembers as "ten minutes," he asked his brother-in-law, Bill McCauley – a professional musician – to compose a tune. Now all he needed was a band. At a social event, McFarlane saw a young rock group and asked if they wanted to record a song. Douglas Rankine and the Secrets jumped at the opportunity, and they cut "Clear the Track, Here Comes Shack" as well as a B-side, "Warming the Bench." Like "Honky," this record got a giant push from CHUM radio, as Leaf fans jammed the station's request lines. On February 28, 1966, "Clear the Track, Here Comes Shack" reached the coveted number 1 spot on the CHUM chart, displacing Petula Clark's "My Love." It stayed there for two weeks before Nancy Sinatra's "These Boots are Made For Walkin'" took its place. Brian McFarlane made grand plans to have the Secrets perform the song during a Hockey Night in Canada intermission, clad in Leaf sweaters, from the ice surface of Maple Leaf Gardens, but the producer vetoed the idea. Instead, the song accompanied film footage of Eddie Shack. Nevertheless, the national exposure helped the song's popularity.

Unfortunately, the songs were about the only things to reach the top spot during the season. There was a dizzying number of off-season roster moves, none of which seemed to pay dividends. Andy Bathgate, Billy Harris and Gary Jarrett were dispatched to Detroit in return for Marcel Pronovost, Larry Jeffrey, Lowell MacDonald, Ed Joyal and Aut Erickson. Boston traded Orland Kurtenbach, Pat Stapleton and Andy Hebenton to Toronto for veteran Ron Stewart. The 37-year-old Hebenton – who at the time owned the NHL's iron-man record, having played in 630 consecutive games for the New

York Rangers and Boston Bruins between 1955 and 1964 – never played for the Leafs. He was sent straight to the Victoria Maple Leafs, Toronto's affiliate in the Western Hockey League. The next day, in the intra-league draft, Chicago grabbed Stapleton. Defenceman Carl Brewer, who was frequently at odds with Leaf management, retired at age 27. Punch also dipped into the Toronto Marlboros roster, tapping his son, Brent Imlach, to join the team for two games. Another ex-Marlie, rookie Brit Selby, was awarded the Calder Trophy that season.

The Maple Leafs came in third in 1965-66 season and faced Montreal in the semifinals. Montreal soundly defeated Toronto in a four-game sweep en route to a second consecutive Stanley Cup championship.

Tom scratches his head. "We all expected the Maple Leafs to make wholesale changes to the team during the summer of 1966, but to our amazement, Punch didn't change very much. Mike Walton had played a few games the year before, and he became a regular partway through the season.

"But nobody expected the team to win anything. They were known as the 'Over-the-Hill Gang,' because so many on the team were over 30 years old. Let me see – Bower was at least 42, Sawchuk was 37, Horton was 36, Stanley was 40, Baun was 30 and Pronovost was 36. The captain, Armstrong, was 36, Red Kelly was 39, Normie Ullman was 32 and Bobby Pulford and Eddie Shack were 30. I have to give full marks to Punch. He got the most out of those players. And I think even the players knew it might be their last shot at a Cup."

The Maple Leafs finished the season with 75 points – good enough for third place, but well behind the league champion Hawks, who finished with 94. (This was the first time in their 41-season history that Chicago had topped the standings.) In the first round of the playoffs, it was just Toronto's luck to be facing the Blackhawks. "Chicago was really at their peak that year," Tommy admits. "Hull and Mikita were about as good as anybody had seen, and Glenn Hall was in net and having a tremendous season. The Hawks wanted a Stanley Cup badly.

"But you know," Tommy continues, "there was something about that Leaf team. I think they may have wanted the Cup more than anybody. Every one of the players gave it their all. They were enjoying a second lease on life." It took six games to do it, but the Leafs defeated the Hawks, earning Toronto a visit to the Stanley Cup finals, where their competition would be the Montreal Canadiens.

"You have to remember that 1967 was Canada's Centennial year," Tommy points out. "All eyes were on Montreal because they were hosting Expo 67 that year. Montreal wanted to win the Stanley Cup to give the city one more thing to cheer about." It has even been said that the Cup would be shown off in the Quebec pavilion at Expo as a symbol of Québécois pride.

The series opened at the Montreal Forum. "Imlach raised the stakes when he called Rogie Vachon a Junior B goalie," smiles Tom. Game one, with Sawchuk in net for the Leafs and Vachon for the Canadiens, went to Montreal, 6-2. Sawchuk was injured during game one, so Bower started for Toronto in game two, a 3-0 Leaf victory. Back at Maple Leaf Gardens, the Leafs won game three on a Bob Pulford goal in the second overtime period. During the pregame warmup for game four, Bower pulled a muscle, forcing Terry Sawchuk to start. The victory went to the Canadiens, 6-2. Sawchuk bounced back from the loss to lead Toronto to a 4-1 victory in the fifth game, played in Montreal. The Leafs had taken a 3-2 lead in the series.

On May 2, the teams returned to Maple Leaf Gardens. Johnny Bower dressed for the game, but there was no way he could play, even if Sawchuk got hurt. Still, Imlach wanted the veteran goaltender in uniform because, if the Leafs won the Cup that night, he would be able to share in the team's celebration. Sawchuk started the game, and the Leafs took a 2-1 lead on goals by Pappin and Ellis. Ex-Leaf Dick Duff tallied for the Canadiens.

Tommy remembers the final minute of play. "Punch put out his veterans for the face-off. There were only 55 seconds left to play in regulation time, and Toe Blake had pulled Gump Worsley for an extra attacker. The Leafs countered with Allan Stanley at centre against Beliveau, with Pulford, Kelly, Armstrong and Horton all lined up for the Leafs. I think maybe Punch knew that this was going to be Toronto's last win with this team, so he put out the dependable guys he had gone to war with so many times."

Tommy remembers, "but he won the draw, and Armstrong scored to give Toronto a 3-1 victory and the Stanley Cup. I think the only time I've heard the Gardens louder was when Bill Barilko scored his goal in '51! The crowd went crazy! The streets around the Gardens were wild! It took us a long time to get home that night, but I didn't mind."

"That was a really memorable Cup win," Gaston sighs. "Little did we realize that it would be our last for so many years. Armstrong – such a wonderful captain – accepted the Stanley Cup from NHL president Clarence Campbell. I think back to the scene on the ice. That group had enjoyed their final hurrah. And it was the last year of 'the Original Six.'

"The next season, expansion increased the league to twelve teams and many of the Leafs regulars were gone, drafted by the new teams. But think about that 1966-67 Stanley Cup team: ten of them went on to be Hall of Famers. It's pretty phenomenal, isn't it? Bower, Sawchuk, Mahovlich, Keon, Kelly, Armstrong, Pulford, Pronovost, Horton and Stanley are all Honoured Members of the Hockey Hall of Fame. You can add Imlach and Ballard as builders, too.

"That was one hell of a team!"

CHAPTER FIFTEEN

Over the Hill and Faraway

In his wonderful book The Glory Years, former Leaf Billy Harris wrote that the Leafs "failed to exist" after the 1967 Stanley Cup victory. In his opinion, things were never again the same at Maple Leaf Gardens for a number of reasons, including NHL expansion, the rise of the National Hockey League Players Association and the absence of a Smythe directing the Gardens' affairs.

In 1967, the NHL doubled in size, adding the Los Angeles Kings, Minnesota North Stars, Oakland Seals, Philadelphia Flyers, Pittsburgh Penguins and St. Louis Blues. An expansion draft would be held to stock these clubs; the "Original Six" were allowed to protect a limited number of players, but any others they owned were up for grabs. To Los Angeles, the Leafs lost Terry Sawchuk, Ed Joyal and minor leaguers Lowell MacDonald and Bill Flett; to the North Stars, Milan Marcetta; the Oakland Seals selected Bob Baun, Kent Douglas, Aut Erickson and Gary Smith; Brit Selby became a Philadelphia Flyer; Pittsburgh claimed Larry Jeffrey; and Al Arbour, Larry Keenan and John Brenneman became St. Louis property. In addition, Red Kelly retired as a player to become coach of the Los Angeles Kings. And, within weeks of the Stanley Cup celebration, Eddie Shack was traded to Boston.

If the "Over-the-Hill Gang" was an appropriate tag for the Leafs during their Stanley Cup run, then the holdovers from that squad were positively ancient – in hockey terms – by 1967-68. In his seventeenth season with Toronto, George Armstrong continued to captain the team. Tim Horton laced up his skates for his sixteenth full year. Like Armstrong and Horton, Marcel Pronovost was a 37-year-old veteran of the hockey wars. Then there were the real greybeards: Allan Stanley, who had turned 41 in March 1967, was preparing for his twentieth NHL season; and Johnny Bower was 43 – at least. But although the Leafs' dressing room at times resembled an old-age home, Keon, Mahovlich and Pappin were in their prime, and there were a few young players – such as Ron Ellis, Mike Walton, Peter Stemkowski and Jim McKenny – who were developing into bona fide NHLers.

But the talent pipeline was bound to dry up soon. For one thing, NHL clubs were no longer allowed to sponsor junior franchises – the Leafs would not be able to rely on the Marlboros for steady injections of young players (and the St. Mike's Majors had already withdrawn from the top level of junior competition in 1961). And Stafford Smythe and Harold Ballard made a serious tactical error, selling off the Leafs' farm teams. In the sixties, the Rochester Americans of the American Hockey League had been so strong that many felt they could have competed in the NHL. And Victoria of the Western Hockey League also housed a competitive team that nurtured an exciting blend of young players with the experience of veterans who had been to the NHL. With these teams gone, the Toronto Maple Leafs would be left all but devoid of young prospects.

The lack of depth was apparent on the ice. While the other established teams feasted on their expansion cousins, the Leafs struggled: in 24 games against the "second six," Toronto's record was a sorry 10-11-3. Hardly surprising, then, that Toronto missed the playoffs for the first time since 1958.

As the 1967-68 season slipped away, Punch Imlach made the drastic decision to trade Frank Mahovlich. The Leafs had discussed deals involving the Big M before, but had always concluded he was worth keeping. "There is the famous story of the Chicago Blackhawks writing a million-dollar cheque for Mahovlich in 1962, and the Toronto newspapers announcing the deal the next day," reminds Tom. "But the deal was quashed and the Leafs kept Mahovlich for several more seasons." This time there were no second thoughts: Imlach sent Mahovlich, Peter Stemkowski and Garry Unger, plus the NHL rights to Carl Brewer, to the Detroit Red Wings in exchange for Norm Ullman, Paul Henderson and Floyd Smith. "It was a blockbuster trade, that's for sure," says Gaston. "And it rejuvenated Mahovlich. When the Leafs won the Cup in '67, the 'Big M' only scored 18 goals that year. His first full year in Detroit, 1968-69, on a line with Gordie Howe, he scored 49."

A principal in the Mahovlich trade, Carl Brewer was one of the most interesting players to wear a Toronto Maple Leaf uniform. Born in Toronto, Brewer rose through the ranks of the Marlboros system, and he was just 19 when he played his first games for the blue and white in 1958. Joining the Leafs full-time in 1958-59, Brewer was an NHL First Team All-Star in 1963, and was selected to the Second Team in both 1962 and 1965. Despite his excellent 1964-65 season, Brewer and Punch Imlach battled over contract details – and Brewer's friendship with lawyer Alan Eagleson – and Carl Brewer made good on his threat to walk away from his NHL career. Brewer returned to school, attending McMaster University in Hamilton, Ontario, and went to court to regain his amateur status. While the Maple Leafs were on their run to the Stanley Cup in 1966-67, Carl Brewer was playing for Canada's national team. The next season, Brewer became playing coach for the International Hockey League's Muskegon Mohawks – after refusing to sign his contract until Muskegon guaranteed that his brother Jack would also be signed to the team. Muskegon went from a sixth place finish in 1966-67 to first place and a league championship to which both Brewer brothers contributed extensively. But again, Carl's curiosity led him to seek out new challenges, and he went to Finland to coach and play hockey in 1968-69.

The Detroit Red Wings, who had obtained Brewer's NHL rights in the Mahovlich deal, convinced him to join the team for the 1969-70 season. Despite an absence of more than four years, Carl Brewer returned to the NHL looking as if he'd never been gone. At season's end he was named to the NHL's Second All-Star Team. While at the Wings training camp in 1970, Carl decided to retire from hockey in order to join Koho, a hockey stick and equipment manufacturing company he had discovered while playing in Helsinki. But the retirement was short-lived, as Brewer's rights were traded to St. Louis and he joined the Blues midway through the 1970-71 season.

After two years in St. Louis, Carl Brewer retired again – and again it was temporary. When the World Hockey Association set up shop in 1972, it held a mammoth draft, and the Los Angeles Sharks of the upstart league drafted the defenceman. When the Sharks traded his rights to the Toronto Toros in 1973, Brewer joined them for a season. Carl again retired after that season, joining the Toros' broadcast crew as a colour commentator.

Could there be more? Certainly! After a five-year absence from professional hockey, 42-year-old Carl Brewer was re-signed by the Toronto Maple Leafs, for whom he played 20 games in 1979-80. Tommy Gaston recalls Carl Brewer's days as a Leaf. "He could have been in the Hockey Hall of Fame if he had wanted. But Carl Brewer was not going to be dictated to by anybody – not Punch Imlach, not the NHL — nobody. He lived his hockey life the way he wanted to. I remember that he discovered one day that the Toronto Maple Leaf hockey club didn't own the rights to its own name. Brewer secured the rights to the name and made the Leafs squirm. When the case went to court to decide who owned the name 'Toronto Maple Leafs,' the team won, but it cost them hundreds of thousands of dollars to do so."

Tom carries on: "I think Carl Brewer made some major contributions to hockey through the years, but his biggest was probably initiating the court case to get the NHL to divide up millions of dollars in pension money for the veteran players. It was Brewer and his longtime companion Susan Foster who were the brains behind the investigation – it eventually brought down his old friend Alan Eagleson – and gave pension money to older players who were barely getting anything from the league."

Carl Brewer died on August 25, 2001. He had visited broadcaster and author Brian McFarlane at his farm north of Toronto the day before, and seemed to be in fine physical health, save a sleeping disorder which was being treated with the help of a machine that aided Brewer's breathing at night. McFarlane claimed he and Brewer had a wonderful afternoon visit, full of stories and fun, although ironically, the topic of death had been discussed. Brewer took home a bag of fresh vegetables and thanked McFarlane and his wife for the visit. That night, Carl Brewer went to sleep and didn't wake up. He was only 62 years old.

In 1968-69, Punch Imlach defied the youth movement, trading Jim Pappin to Chicago for former Blackhawks captain Pierre Pilote. In their prime, the Leaf blueline corps, anchored by Pilote, Tim Horton and Marcel Pronovost would have been the best ever to jump over the boards of an NHL rink; but while they still had superior hockey smarts, they had slowed down several steps. The trio was supplemented by the exuberant Jim Dorey and a young Pat Quinn.

"My, those boys were tough," exclaims Gaston. "Pat Quinn – there's a fellow I really like. Even today when I see him, he always takes time to say hello and tell a little joke or something. But back in 1969, Quinn really had something to prove. I remember that, on the opening night of the playoffs that year, Toronto was playing in Boston against the Bruins. Bobby Orr had had a super season – really stepped into superstardom. In the second period, Orr was carrying the puck up the boards. He took a look down at the puck, and just then, Quinn stepped into him and knocked him unconscious. The referee gave Quinn a penalty – I think it was for elbowing – but the Boston Garden went crazy. When Quinn entered the penalty box, fans tried to get at him – they were throwing cups and programs at him. He eventually had to be moved to the Leafs' dressing room for his own protection. Meanwhile, Orr was taken off the ice on a stretcher. They took him to the hospital and found out he'd had a slight concussion.

"But as if that wasn't tough enough, there was Jim Dorey's entry into the NHL," Tom muses. "In his first NHL game, he broke every penalty record in the book. It was at Maple Leaf Gardens – opening night 1968, in fact. Dorey fought every Pittsburgh Penguin he saw, and ended up with four minor penalties, two five-minute majors, a misconduct and a game misconduct. It was the most penalty minutes any NHL player had received in a single game.

"Welcome to the Toronto Maple Leafs, Jim Dorey!" Tommy laughs.

One of the bright lights for the Toronto Maple Leafs of the late 1960s was forward Ron Ellis. A graduate of the Marlboro system, Ron joined the Leafs for one game in 1964. The next season, Ron was assigned number 11 – Punch Imlach's lucky number. Ellis had a strong rookie season, and the superstitious Imlach was elated. In 1965-66, Ron's former Marlboro teammate, Brit Selby, was brought up to play with the Leafs. Using the rationale that number 11 had been lucky for Ron Ellis, Punch gave Selby number 11, and gave Ron Ellis number 8. Brit Selby won the Calder Trophy as the NHL's top rookie. Ron Ellis stuck with 8 for the next three seasons. But there would be yet another number change for Ellis. Tom picks up the story.

"Ronny was one of the character players. He played the game like he lived his life – dedicated and clean. He never said a bad word about anyone. And boy, did he love the game. At the time, Ace Bailey was the Leafs' penalty timekeeper. Watching Ellis game in and game out, Bailey liked what Ron Ellis brought to the Maple Leafs. Unbeknownst to Ellis, Ace talked to the Leafs' management, discussing the fact that even though his own number 6 had been retired after his injury, he was requesting that Ron Ellis was the kind of player that should wear the retired sweater.

"Ron was flattered as can be, and told Ace that he'd be honoured to wear Ace's number 6. So in a ceremony before the 1968-69 season, Ron Ellis pulled on a Leaf sweater with number 6 on the back, presented by its original wearer. Number 6 had not been worn by a Toronto player in almost 35 years. Ron Ellis wore 6 for the remainder of his career, and when he retired in mid-January 1981, the number was retired once again."

On October 17, 1992, Ace's number 6, alongside Bill Barilko's number 5, was hoisted to the rafters of Maple Leaf Gardens, retired once and for all. Ron Ellis was on the ice with Ace Bailey's daughter during that emotional ceremony. "Sadly, Ace didn't live long enough to see the actual raising of the banner," Tommy points out. "But he was aware it was going to happen before he passed away."

The Leafs made a slight bit of progress in 1968-69, finishing in fourth place in the East Division and making the playoffs, but in spite of Pat Quinn's famous bodycheck on Bobby Orr they were trounced by the Boston Bruins in four consecutive games. Within minutes of the loss to the Bruins, Stafford Smythe fired Punch Imlach.

"Over the next twenty years, the Leafs went through a lot of coaches and general managers," remembers Tom. "After Punch, Johnny McLellan was hired as coach, and Jim Gregory as general manager. McLellan had been in the Leaf system as a player, first with St. Mike's and then with the Toronto Marlboros, and he got into two games with the Leafs in 1951. In 1959, John McLellan won a world championship with the Belleville McFarlands. In 1968-69 he coached the Leafs' farm team in Tulsa to a championship. Jim Gregory had worked with Ballard and Stafford Smythe on the Marlies, too. He coached the team in 1964-65 when they won the Memorial Cup, and was general manager in 1966-67 when they repeated.

"I think the Maple Leafs were better off without Punch in some ways, although he was an excellent coach. Gregory brought some new players onto the team – guys like Jim McKenny, Ricky Ley and Terry Clancy had played a few games here and there for the Leafs, but finally got their breaks in 1969 under Gregory and McLellan."

The Punch-less Leafs of 1969-70 had trouble scoring – and trouble preventing goals. Dependable Ron Ellis scored 35 times – he had never scored fewer than 19 since he broke into the NHL. And Dave Keon, who succeeded the retired George Armstrong as captain, scored 32 goals and registered a team-leading 62 points. But aside from these two, only Mike Walton broke the 20-goal barrier.

Along with Armstrong, another of Imlach's old guard had retired prior to the '69-70 season. "When Punch Imlach was fired, Johnny

Bower told the press that he was done, too," Tom reminds us. To replace the China Wall, the Leafs juggled Bruce Gamble and Marv Edwards – picked up from Pittsburgh in the intra-league draft. Gerry McNamara, who would later become general manager of the Leafs, played two games in goal as well. He hadn't played in the NHL since 1961, when he replaced Johnny Bower for five games. The team was drastically short on talent, and the future offered precious little hope.

Terry Sawchuk, claimed by Los Angeles in the expansion draft of 1967, spent only one year on the west coast before moving on for a season each with Detroit and New York. He died on May 31, 1970. Tommy gets upset when he recalls the tragedy. "It was just rough-housing, nothing more. Apparently, Sawchuk and Ron Stewart, a Ranger teammate, got into an argument after having a few drinks at a bar on Long Island. Stewart and Sawchuk had been sharing a rented house; they were arguing over tidying the house up before they left at the end of the season.   "When they left the bar, the argument continued at their house. Nobody really knows what happened, but it seems Stewart fell on a barbecue grill, and Sawchuk stumbled on top of him, landing either on Stewart's knee or the barbecue. At any rate, he damaged his gall bladder and liver. Sawchuk was rushed to the hospital, but after two major surgeries, he died. He was only 40 years old." Sawchuk had been a fan favourite during his short stay with the Maple Leafs. His contributions to the 1967 Stanley Cup were immeasurable.

Closer to home, the Gardens was at the centre of a major scandal. Between 1969 and 1971, the Ontario Attorney General's office, suspicious about some of their business activities, investigated Harold Ballard and Stafford Smythe. Special prosecutor Clayton Powell interviewed 180 people, and his investigation discovered that cheques written between 1964 and 1969 by the Ontario Hockey Association to the Toronto Marlboro hockey club had been deposited in a separate account under the name S.H. Marlie – S for Stafford, H for Harold. Only Harold and Stafford had access to this account, and they used the money to cover personal expenses. In addition, Ballard and Smythe hired Cloke Construction, who were doing extensive remodelling work at Maple Leaf Gardens, to carry out renovations to their homes. All invoices were charged back to Maple Leaf Gardens.

In July 1969, the federal government charged both Stafford Smythe and Harold Ballard with tax evasion. Stafford was alleged to have pocketed $278,919 in undeclared income from the Toronto Marlboro money and the home renovations. Ballard was charged with failing to declare $134,685 in income from the same sources. Two years later, the Ontario Attorney General's office charged Smythe and Ballard with the theft of $146,000. Smythe was also charged with fraud worth $249,000 and Ballard with $83,000.

The Crown was set to try the pair in court when Stafford became gravely ill. On October 12, 1971, Stafford's son Tom was informed that his father had been rushed to Wellesley Hospital in downtown Toronto. The doctors treated him for a bleeding ulcer, but when Stafford took a turn for the worse, they were forced to remove much of his stomach. Just before 5 a.m. on October 13, Stafford Smythe died. Maple Leaf Gardens issued a statement: "With great sorrow, we announce the passing of our president, C. Stafford Smythe, who died this morning. The body will be resting at his home, 15 Ashley Park Road, in Etobicoke. Funeral services will be held in St. Paul's Anglican Church, Bloor and Jarvis streets, at 1 p.m., Thursday, October 14."

The pallbearers for Stafford Smythe were Harold Ballard; Leaf general manager Jim Gregory; George Mara and Terry Jeffries of the Maple Leaf Gardens board of directors; Leaf veterans George Armstrong and Bob Baun; Stafford's brother, Dr. Hugh Smythe, and his son Tom. He was buried in the yard of Christ Anglican Church in Muskoka, not far from his cottage. His tombstone, a large Muskoka rock, is inscribed with this epitaph:

Here lies Conn Stafford Smythe, Lieut. RCNVR 1940-1944.
He was dearly beloved of his wife, children and many friends.
He was persecuted to death by his enemies.
Now he sleeps in the quiet north country that loved him for
    the person he truly was.
Born Toronto March 15, 1921. Died October 13, 1971.

Stafford Smythe and Harold Ballard were to stand trial on October 25, 1971, but Stafford's death delayed Ballard's trial until May 1972. In the meantime, Ballard repaid the money he had taken from Maple Leaf Gardens, and paid the income tax as demanded by the government. As a result, the tax evasion charges were dropped, but Clayton Powell proceeded with the theft and fraud charges. After one piece of damning evidence after another had been presented, Judge Harry Deyman convicted Harold Ballard on forty-seven of the forty-nine charges of fraud or theft of money, goods and services in the amount of $205,000. Sentencing was scheduled for September 7, 1972, but Alan Eagleson interceded and asked for a postponement so Ballard could attend the 1972 Summit Series between Canada and the Soviet Union. The judge agreed.

When Harold Ballard returned to court on October 20, he was sentenced to two concurrent three-year sentences - one for theft and one for fraud. He was taken to Millhaven Correctional Institute, a minimum-security prison near Kingston Ontario.

"I certainly didn't agree with all his decisions," Tommy Gaston says, "but I have to admit that Harold always treated me nicely. I was working at the Hockey Hall of Fame at Christmas one year, and Mr. Ballard came by and brought me a gift – it was Dave Shand's stick, signed by the team. He didn't have to do that.

"One time at a banquet, I went over to say hi to King Clancy, and I got a little cocky with Harold. 'Mr. Ballard,' I said, 'I'm getting old, and I'm getting tired of waiting for the Leafs to win another Stanley Cup.' Harold looked at me long and hard and said, 'Tommy, I'm older than you are!' 'Yes,' I said, 'that may be true, but you can do something about the team and I can't!'"

Tom concludes: "I thought Stafford Smythe had the hockey brain and Harold was excellent at planning the other events that kept the Gardens, and the accountants, busy – like concerts and political events. After Smythe's death, I think Harold hurt the team for the long run. But although we may have had differing ideas about the running of the team, Harold Ballard was still a guy I could sit with over coffee and solve the problems of the world."

CHAPTER SIXTEEN

Ballard

The Smythe era at Maple Leaf Gardens drew to a close in February 1972 when, exercising a right of first refusal granted him in his partner's will, Harold Ballard sold himself Stafford Smythe's shares in the Gardens. Stafford's son Tom, with the aid of his Uncle Hugh – Stafford's brother – had tried to make an offer to keep the stock in the family, but Ballard would hear none of it. To make matters worse, Ballard asked Hugh, formerly the Leafs' team physician, to surrender his season tickets, which he did at the same time he sold his 1,200 Gardens shares to Ballard. Tom Smythe owned Doug Laurie Sports, the sporting goods store located within Maple Leaf Gardens, and was also the general manager of the Toronto Marlboros. Harold refused to renew Tom's lease for the store, and ultimately relieved Tom of his duties with the junior team.

When Ballard was released from prison – after serving nine months of his three-year sentence – he returned to Maple Leaf Gardens. Now that he had control of the corporation, he aimed to become the Conn Smythe of his generation. There would be no room for knowledgeable hockey men like Leafs general manager Jim Gregory in the organization – Ballard would undertake that responsibility himself. When he and Stafford had run the Marlboros, and later the Leafs, it was Stafford who evaluated talent, handled the roster move and negotiated trades – Harold had been in charge of booking the non-hockey events that kept Maple Leaf Gardens busy and prosperous. It had been an excellent arrangement. But now Ballard seemed to crave the spotlight occupied by the owner of one of hockey's best-loved franchises.

When fans said that Ballard ate, slept and breathed the Maple Leafs, they probably had no idea how true that statement was. Harold had an apartment built into the Gardens, right beside his office on the second floor. And he ate almost all of his meals in the Gardens'

Hot Stove Club, a members-only restaurant located on the Church Street side of the Gardens. Players would claim to be annoyed by Ballard's constant presence in the dressing room and on road trips, where he would travel with the team and stay in the same hotels.

By May 1970, having concluded that the goaltending tandem of Bruce Gamble and Marv Edwards would not lead the way to future success, the Leafs purchased Jacques Plante from the St. Louis Blues. Plante had won the Stanley Cup six times and the Vezina Trophy seven times, and had once been awarded the Hart Trophy as the NHL's most valuable player. He had also been named to the First or Second All-Star Team a combined seven times. Later on in the 1970-71 season, the Leafs traded Gamble, along with Mike Walton and a draft pick, to Philadelphia for Bernie Parent and a draft pick. The plan seemed brilliant – the older mentor tutoring the young prodigy – and the two were a very effective tandem. Plante led the league with a 1.88 goals-against average and the Leafs improved from sixth place to fourth in the East Division. They were knocked out of the quarterfinals by the New York Rangers.

Bernie Parent soaked up the nuances of goaltending from Plante. "Wow," Tommy enthuses, "Plante was definitely one of the all-time greats. He played exceptional hockey no matter where he played, including here in Toronto.

"Jacques died too early. He was living in Switzerland when he died, and is buried there. His wife came by the Hockey Hall of Fame quite often after his death, and I talked to her a great deal. She is a lovely woman."

The Leafs' defence corps in 1970-71 – Jim Dorey, Brian Glennie, Rick Ley, Jim McKenny, Mike Pelyk and Brad Selwood – had an average age of 23. To add some needed experience, and to make the goaltenders' jobs a little easier, former Leaf Bob Baun was re-acquired from Detroit, after a previous trade that would have sent "the Boomer" to St. Louis went sour.

Plante, Parent and the blueline corps were intact for the entire 1971-72 season, and they got results. The Leafs gave up 208 goals in 78 games, sixth-fewest in the 14-team NHL. Unfortunately, no other Leaf came close to Paul Henderson's 38-goal output, as the team scored only one more goal than they allowed. The predictable result: another fourth-place finish and early exit from the playoffs. This time the loss came at the hands of the powerful Boston Bruins, who went on to win the Stanley Cup.

With the arrival of the World Hockey Association in the fall of 1972, the hockey world was about to be stood on its head, but Harold Ballard and the Toronto Maple Leafs organization failed to take seriously the threat posed by the upstart league. In a bid for instant credibility, clubs in the new circuit were making audacious offers to established NHL stars. And while the experts may have scoffed at first, most of them stopped laughing once the Winnipeg Jets offered Chicago Blackhawks scoring ace Bobby Hull $1 million to jump leagues – and he accepted.

"The WHA put the players' wages out of kilter," Tommy says emphatically. "They offered so much money to lure players away, that in turn, many NHL teams had to offer competitive money to keep the player. Payrolls escalated out of control. The WHA lured Bobby Hull away from Chicago with a million dollars. The league was able to snatch Derek Sanderson and Gerry Cheevers, as well as Bernie Parent, too. Harold Ballard's position was that, if any players jumped to the new league, they would not be welcomed back."

Parent, who had made $25,000 with the Leafs in 1971-72, was offered $150,000 a year, plus a house, a boat and a car as signing bonuses, to join the Miami Screaming Eagles of the WHA. Ballard steadfastly refused to believe that any hockey player would truly be paid the kind of money that the WHA was offering. As well, he and his advisors clung to the belief – however wrong – that the WHA would never come to fruition.

Parent jumped to the WHA, and his signing further opened the floodgates. Ballard and Leafs GM Jim Gregory were livid – they had intended for Parent to be their star goaltender for the next decade – but refused to match the new league's offers, and Toronto players Rick Ley, Brad Selwood, Guy Trottier and Jim Harrison followed Parent to the WHA.

"I was sorry to see Parent leave" Gaston says. "He had all the makings of a great goaltender with Toronto, and proved it once he returned to the NHL with the Flyers. I wrote Jim Gregory a letter complaining about losing such a star player. Mr. Gregory wrote me back and was most gracious. He said, 'Nobody is more sorry to lose Bernie Parent than me. But there are decisions to be made and we have to live with them.' I always appreciated Jim Gregory taking the time to respond to my letter. I always felt he was a very knowledgeable hockey man."

In an ironic twist, the Miami Screaming Eagles never played a game. The team ended up in Philadelphia – the city from which

Bernie had come to the Leafs – as the Blazers. They raided other NHL teams for such notables as Derek Sanderson, Johnny McKenzie and Andre Lacroix, as well as young forwards who had started NHL careers such as Danny Lawson and Bryan Campbell. After appearing in one game of the 1973 playoffs, Parent claimed he hadn't been paid his full salary for the season and he quit the Blazers. During the off-season he let it be known that he wanted to return to the NHL, but that he refused to rejoin Toronto. The Maple Leafs had no choice but to trade Parent, and they sent him back to the Philadelphia Flyers for Doug Favell and a draft choice.

The WHA continued to raid NHL franchises for their stars, and members of the Leafs continued to respond to the upstart league's advances. In 1973, the Ottawa Nationals moved to Toronto, setting up shop at Varsity Arena as the Toros. Their lineup leaned strongly toward ex-Leafs, Marlboros and Leaf farm hands, including Carl Brewer, Brit Selby, Gavin Kirk, Wayne Carleton, Wayne Dillon and Guy Trottier. In 1974, owner Johnny F. Bassett – son of John W. Bassett, the former Silver Seven member – moved the team to Maple Leaf Gardens, and they added Jim Dorey and Frank Mahovlich before luring Paul Henderson to their ranks.

"I never went to a WHA game," Tommy says defiantly, "even though there were lots of opportunities for me to go see the Toronto Toros. I refused to support them as I felt they hurt hockey."

In 1975, Leaf captain Dave Keon bolted to the Minnesota Fighting Saints, a team that also included Leaf alumnus Mike Walton. The team folded halfway through the year, and Keon finished the season with the Indianapolis Racers.

Keon had been a superb player and classy representative of the Leafs for fifteen years. In 1960-61, he won the Calder Trophy. In 1967 he became the only Leaf to date to win the Conn Smythe Trophy, awarded to the most valuable player in the playoffs. When George Armstrong retired after the 1968-69 season (he would return to play two more seasons), the captain's "C" was sewn onto Keon's jersey.

None of this seemed to matter by 1975. Harold Ballard, who had no qualms about denouncing his players in the press, continually disrupted the team with his tirades. In November 1974 he was quoted in the Globe and Mail as saying that Dave Keon was a "weak captain" and insisting that he was prepared to make a major trade for a "team leader." Keon fumed all season, and the anger fuelled his leap to the WHA.

Keon never made peace with the Maple Leafs organization. When the team moved out of Maple Leaf Gardens to much fanfare in February 1999, Keon was conspicuous by his absence. When the NHL All-Star Game was held in Toronto in 2000, Dave Keon again chose not to take part in the ceremonies. There is an entire generation of Leaf admirers who would love to welcome Dave Keon back to Toronto and recognize his contributions to the Leafs. In the decade since Ballard's death, many of Keon's teammates have patched up their differences with the Toronto Maple Leafs. Not Dave Keon.

Toward the end of the 1972-73 season, John McLellan resigned as coach of the Toronto Maple Leafs. The Leafs had failed to make the playoffs, and the ulcers which had bothered McLellan so badly the season before were acting up again. When the Los Angeles Kings fired their coach, Red Kelly, Harold Ballard hired him immediately. Kelly had been a key member of the Leafs' four Stanley Cups in the 1960s as a player and was exceptionally well liked in Toronto.

Kelly inherited a team that was blossoming into a contender. Darryl Sittler had been Toronto's number one draft pick in 1970, and joined the team that autumn. Errol Thompson was the Leafs' second pick in that same draft, although he wouldn't join the Maple Leafs until 1972-73. Lanny McDonald was chosen by Toronto in the first round of the 1973 draft, and he secured a spot on the Leafs during training camp that fall. In addition, Ron Ellis, Dave Keon, Norm Ullman and Paul Henderson were putting up strong offensive numbers. The defence boasted the exciting Ian Turnbull and Jim McKenny. Doug Favell and veteran Ed Johnston would share the bulk of the goaltending duties – Jacques Plante was sent to Boston toward the end of the 1972-73 campaign.

In Sweden, Leaf scout Gerry McNamara had uncovered a couple of players who would make an immediate impact. Inge Hammarstrom scored 20 goals in 1973-74, while Borje Salming began his Hall of Fame career on defence under Red Kelly. The team improved by 22 points to 86, good enough for fourth place in the East. Slotted against a dominant Bruins squad, unfortunately, the Leafs were ousted from the quarterfinals in four straight games.

On the morning of Thursday, February 21, 1974, Toronto hockey fans awoke to tragic news: Tim Horton, the Leafs' answer to Superman for so many years, was gone. The night before, Toronto had beaten the Buffalo Sabres, 4-2. Horton, in his second year with the Sabres, was named the game's third star, despite missing much of the third period with a jaw injury. Early in the morning of the 21st, Horton was driving back to Buffalo in his Ford Pantera, a sports car that had been a signing bonus the summer before for when he re-signed with the Sabres. Travelling at a high speed on the Queen Elizabeth Way, Horton lost control of the car near St. Catharines, Ontario, and hit the centre guardrail at more than 160 kilometres per hour. The sports car rolled, throwing Tim from the wreckage, and he died instantly.

Sabres coach Joe Crozier said, "Horton brought a mature balance to the hockey club. Everyone looked up to him. It was unbelievable how the hockey players liked him." Young Sabres like Larry Carriere and Jim Schoenfeld had learned so much about playing defence from the 44-year-old veteran. Craig Ramsay, another Sabres teammate, recalls having to play the next night. "I remember having to stand there for the national anthems and the moment of silence and wondering, 'How is it we're going to play?' As a player, you play through everything. But here was a guy who had been a father figure to so many of us. Suddenly he was gone, and we had to play. To have a guy setting that kind of example for you and then be gone was a devastating blow."

Having served as a pallbearer for his friend Bill Barilko a dozen years before, Allan Stanley was now called upon to help carry an-other friend to his final resting place. Besides Stanley, the other pallbearers were George Armstrong, Bob Baun, Dick Duff, Billy Harris and Dave Keon.

By 1974-75, Sittler was regularly finishing among the NHL's top ten scorers, and in '75-76 he became the first Leaf to crack the 100-point barrier. The line of Sittler with Lanny McDonald and Errol Thompson evolved into a productive unit that was also a favour-ite among Toronto fans. Tiger Williams joined the team in 1974, and showed that he was good with the fists but had pretty good hands, too. Salming, Turnbull and McKenny were defencemen who displayed excellent offensive skills. In 1975-76, Salming scored 16 goals, Turnbull added 20 and McKenny had 10. The next season, Salming scored 12, Turnbull 22 and McKenny 14. The team was joined in 1976 by an acrobatic young goaltender named Mike Palmateer.

But Ballard couldn't be satisfied with a talented – if relatively inexperienced – team. At one point, he ridiculed Hammarstrom, telling a reporter that the young Swede could "go into the corner with six eggs in his pocket, and not break a single one." He questioned Red Kelly's coaching ability and, as documented above, Dave Keon's leadership. Still, the team flourished briefly. In 1975, the Leafs made it to the second round of the playoffs before being dumped by Philadelphia – the eventual Stanley Cup winner that year. In 1976, Toronto again went to the second round of the playoffs, and again met the Flyers. This time, Red Kelly used some pop psychology in an attempt to motivate his charges, introducing "pyramid power." The word was out in some circles that pyramids emitted positive energy waves, and so the players sat under a large pyramid that hung in the dressing room, while their sticks were placed under a smaller pyramid. Small pyramids were placed beneath the team's bench at Maple Leaf Gardens as well. If the players were skeptical, they changed their tune when the Leafs beat the Flyers 8-5 on April 22. Darryl Sittler, having reluctantly placed his sticks under Kelly's pyramid, scored five goals in the game. Although the Leafs didn't win the series against Philadelphia, they did take them to seven games in a hard-fought playoff round.

Darryl Sittler will long be remembered as one of Toronto's favourite athletes. "Oh yes, he was definitely in a class by himself," states Gaston. "On February 7, 1976, the Leafs were playing at home to Boston. The Bruins started a young goalie named Dave Reece, whom I had never heard of before. It seemed that every time Sittler touched the puck, the red light came on. It was a blowout of a game, but it wasn't until the third period that I realized what was developing. Darryl Sittler ended up scoring six goals and assisting on four more. No other NHL player has ever scored ten points in a game – neither Gretzky nor Mario ever did it. The Leafs won 11-4, and Dave Reece never played in the NHL again." Ironically, Harold Ballard had publicly chastised Sittler earlier that week for his lack of production. "Darryl Sittler is 100 percent class," Tommy affirms. "He and his wife Wendy are a charming couple. I ran into Darryl during the season in 2000, and he said, 'Tom, you're getting so well known!' Then he told me, 'Tommy, don't lose hope. We're going to win a Stanley Cup for you real soon.'"

Sittler was amply supported by a starring cast. "I never saw Lanny McDonald play a bad game," Tom begins. "He could certainly play the game, and was a great team guy. He and Sittler were close both on and off the ice. And you could never forget that big moustache that became Lanny's trademark." Tiger Williams was another favourite of Tom Gaston's. "Yes, the fans loved him from the word 'go.' If any Leaf was in trouble on the ice, he'd be standing right there to help. I remember he used to like to hunt with a bow and arrow. One time, he shot a bear and brought the bearskin to Harold Ballard. Ballard had it in his apartment at the Gardens."

Backstopped by the young Palmateer, the Leafs made the playoffs again in 1976-77. Tommy talks about the goalie with genuine zeal. "He was a real showman and an absolute wizard with the puck. He sure wasn't afraid to venture out of his crease to play the puck." The Leafs pushed Pittsburgh aside in the first round of the playoffs, then met their perennial opponents, the Philadelphia Flyers, in the quarterfinals. Red Kelly, who had long since buried the pyramid scheme, had another energy-inducing trick up his sleeve: "negative ions." The Leafs bought into this psychological ploy as well, and won the first two games of the series in Philadelphia. But returning to Toronto, the Flyers beat the Leafs in back-to-back overtimes, and went on to win the series four games to two.

That playoff defeat ended Red Kelly's tenure behind the bench. His replacement would prove to be no less unconventional. For a full decade, Roger Neilson had coached the Peterborough Petes major junior team and amassed a superb coaching record, leading the Petes to the Memorial Cup finals in 1972. He was looked upon as one of the brightest coaching prospects in the industry, and his use of videotape and statistics to prepare his teams was considered ground-breaking. Tommy remembers that the players loved the new coach. "Roger was innovative and he used modern methods of coaching, which the players appreciated. He was affectionately called Captain Video. The Toronto teams were always very well prepared under Neilson."

In 1977-78, Neilson's first season as coach of the Leafs, Sittler scored 45 goals and finished with 117 points – good for third place in the league scoring derby. The points total was a club record that would stand for fifteen years. Meanwhile, McDonald scored 47 goals and finished tenth in scoring. The team beat Los Angeles in the first round of the playoffs and the Islanders in the quarterfinals, advancing to the semifinals against Montreal. Although the Habs – the eventual winners of the Stanley Cup – swept the Leafs four straight, it was their best season in years. Neilson was being lauded as an outstanding new coach, Sittler was handed the superstar mantle he deserved, and the team was getting to be known around the league as a force to be reckoned with. All appeared to be well in the Leafs camp.

But midway through the 1978-79 season, Harold Ballard grew tired of Neilson's tactics; at the end of February he told the press that the coach was fired. The only problem was, he didn't have a replacement ready to take Neilson's place. He tried to secure Eddie Johnston, the former Leaf goalie who was now coaching the New Brunswick Hawks of the American Hockey League, but the Chicago Blackhawks, who shared the farm team with Toronto, refused to release Johnston. Gerry McNamara was approached, but he declined the offer. Meanwhile, captain Darryl Sittler and some of his teammates met with Ballard and insisted that Neilson be retained.

A regular feature of television's Gong Show was a comedian, the "Unknown Comic," who told corny jokes while wearing a paper bag over his head. The premise gave Harold an idea. He asked Neilson to stay with the team and, to make light of the firing, step behind the Leaf bench with a paper bag over his head. The crowd wouldn't know who the coach was. Then, just before the opening face-off, Neilson would remove the bag, the crowd would go berserk and the Leafs would be energized by the crowd's reaction. At first, Neilson tentatively agreed, but then he realized he would only be adding yet another sideshow to the Maple Leaf circus. On March 3, Roger Neilson was behind the bench, sans paper bag. The Leafs beat the Flyers 4-3 that night.

The Leafs again made the playoffs, but were thumped four games to none in the second round by the Montreal Canadiens. Ballard fired Roger Neilson and Jim Gregory immediately after the game.

Ballard needed a new management team, and with his next move he hoped to bring back the magic of the sixties. Punch Imlach was retained as coach and general manager. It would prove to be a recipe for disaster. The game had changed substantially since Imlach's previous sojourn with the Leafs, when players had been subservient to management. The rise of the National Hockey League Players Association had given players a voice, and contemporary attitudes would drive a wedge between Ballard and Imlach and their players.

The trouble began before the regular season. For several years, the NHLPA had endorsed a skills competition called "Showdown" which appeared between periods of the Hockey Night in Canada telecasts. Leafs Darryl Sittler and Mike Palmateer were chosen to participate in segments that would air during the 1979-80 season. But Imlach had a long-standing feud with Alan Eagleson, who was the NHLPA's executive director as well as Sittler and Palmateer's agent. Punch told the two Leaf stars that they could not participate, giving the excuse that he feared they would be injured. Both players insisted that they were going to take part, prompting Imlach to apply for a court injunction to halt them. Sittler and Palmateer competed anyway.

Further showing he was out of touch, Imlach changed the rules for the dressing room – no ping pong table, no phone calls, no alcohol. There was no communication between Imlach and the players – although he was nominally the coach, it was Floyd Smith who actually stood behind the bench for games. Despite the differences, the team promised to be competitive yet again.

But the players weren't only at odds with Imlach. Ballard was a thorn in their side as well. In December 1979, he announced that the Leafs would play an exhibition game against the Canadian Olympic team in early February. The players had not been asked, yet alone informed, and they balked at the idea. The game was to take place during the All-Star break, which meant several players – potentially Sittler, McDonald, Salming and Palmateer – would be playing seven games in nine nights. The players proposed a compromise: they would play the game if Harold Ballard allowed them to play an exhibition game the following season against a team from the Soviet Union. Ballard had never been confronted by players before, and he was aghast and angry. Not only was the game against the Soviets vetoed, but the game with the Canadian Olympic team was cancelled as well. Ballard, seething at his players' betrayal, aimed his venom at the captain, Sittler. Once treated like a son, Sittler was now called a "cancer" on the team. Ballard gave Imlach the green light to exact revenge.

The first move came the day before Christmas. Pat Boutette, a supporter of his captain, was traded to the Hartford Whalers for Bob Stephenson. Boutette had been a hard-nosed forward whose fearless play in the corners and in front of the opposing goal was a key component for the Leafs. Bob Stephenson played just fourteen games with the Leafs.

On December 29, the team took another hit. Popular winger Lanny McDonald and defenceman Joel Quenneville were traded to the Colorado Rockies for Pat Hickey and Wilf Paiement. Although both teams got fair value, it was disruptive to the team's chemistry. Paiement, who is the only Leaf to have worn number 99, was a prolific scorer in his two and a half seasons in Toronto, including a 40-goal season in 1980-81. Hickey, who quickly became a favourite of female Leaf fans, was also a serviceable forward, scoring 22 goals in the 45 games that remaining in 1979-80. But he would not be as productive the next season, and was traded away in 1981. Quenneville had been Toronto's first draft pick in 1978 after starring with the Windsor Spitfires of the Ontario Hockey Association. He went on to enjoy a long NHL career, and became a Jack Adams Award-winning coach with the St. Louis Blues.

McDonald's inclusion in the trade broke Toronto's spirit. He was a favourite of Leaf fans, who protested the trade with placards outside Maple Leaf Gardens. But more importantly, he was Darryl Sittler's winger and best friend on the team. It appeared that McDonald was traded in order to hurt Sittler, who likely would have been traded himself had he not had a no-trade clause in his contract.

Sittler reacted by cutting the captain's "C" off his Leaf sweater. But Ballard was merciless, denouncing Sittler in the press at every opportunity. Two more trades were made, both involving Sittler supporters. On January 10, defenceman Dave Hutchison was sent to Chicago for Pat Ribble. Then, on February 18, 1980, Sittler's pal and linemate Tiger Williams was dealt to Vancouver along with Jerry Butler in exchange for Bill Derlago and Rick Vaive. During the summer, another Sittler cohort, Mike Palmateer, was traded to Washington.

If the 1979-80 season wasn't enough of a disaster on the ice, Floyd Smith was in a terrible car accident near St. Catharines, Ontario that resulted in two deaths.

For better or for worse, Punch Imlach had put his stamp on the Toronto Maple Leafs, while getting back at Darryl Sittler. Then, in August 1980, Imlach suffered a heart attack. With his general manager incapacitated, Harold Ballard stepped in and assumed power. He signed Borje Salming to a huge contract – something that Imlach had been unable to do. He returned the captaincy to Sittler. And, perhaps most notably, he lost his faith in Punch Imlach. "I'm going to be the one in control of things," Ballard announced, "and if the players want to argue instead of playing hockey, they'll get an earful from me."

Ballard decided that with Floyd Smith in the hospital and Imlach recovering from a heart attack, he would hire Joe Crozier to coach the Leafs in 1980. The Leafs started strong, but began to struggle terribly, and by January 1981 Crozier was fired. Imlach, who would ordinarily hire the coach, could only watch as Harold recruited Mike Nykoluk.

Nykoluk had a long history with the Toronto Maple Leafs. As a member of the Toronto Marlboros organization, he had insisted that a friend of his from the Marlboro midget squad be invited to the Weston Dukes training camp in 1951. That friend, Bob Baun, made the team, and the two of them played on the 1955 Memorial Cup-winning Toronto Marlboros. Nykoluk made the Maple Leafs, too, but played just 32 games during the 1956-57 season. Mike's brother, Danny Nykoluk, starred with the Toronto Argonauts football team in the fifties, and was a friend of Harold Ballard's.

Mike Nykoluk had never been a head coach in the NHL, but he had been an assistant coach with the Philadelphia Flyers and New York Rangers before joining the Leafs. He'd also done colour commentary on Leafs radio broadcasts, so he wasn't a stranger to the team. Nykoluk's introduced a run-and-gun style of hockey that put the emphasis on scoring. Sittler, Paiement, Derlago and Vaive all topped the 30-goal mark, but the club's goaltending corps of Jiri Crha, Jim Rutherford and, toward the end of the season, Michel "Bunny" Larocque allowed more goals than all but two of the NHL's twenty-one teams. Toronto managed to squeak past the Washington Capitals, 71 points to 70, for the sixteenth and final playoff berth, but the Leafs were easy pickings for the first-place New York Islanders, who bombed them by scores of 9-2, 5-1 and 6-1 to sweep the best-of-five first-round series. The Isles went on to win their second consecutive Stanley Cup title.

During the summer of 1981, Darryl Sittler decided he would rescind the no-trade clause in his contract on the condition that the Leafs trade him to the Minnesota North Stars or Philadelphia Flyers. Meanwhile, Punch Imlach suffered another heart attack. While he was recuperating, Ballard "retired" Punch – leaving no doubt it wasn't Imlach's idea. As a result, the Leafs started the 1981-82 season without a general manager. Eventually, Gerry McNamara, the team's chief scout, was made acting GM.

After breaking curfew one night, Ian Turnbull was traded to Los Angeles on November 11 for Billy Harris and John Gibson. Harris played parts of three seasons at forward in Toronto, totalling 20 goals. Gibson played 27 games, but failed to score. After season-long speculation about his fate, Sittler was finally traded to the Flyers on January 20, 1982. In return, Toronto received Rich Costello, Ken Strong and a draft choice that later brought the Leafs Peter Ihnacak. Rich Costello played 12 games for Toronto over the course of two seasons. Ken Strong played 15 games over three seasons with the Leafs. Ihnacak prevented the deal from becoming a complete bust – he played seven seasons for Toronto and twice broke the 20-goal mark. The fact remains that the Maple Leafs had virtually given away two of their stars; if the intention was to do nothing more than move them out of Toronto, that was accomplished.

In 1981-82, the NHL was realigned along geographic lines. Toronto was placed in the Norris Division along with Chicago, Detroit, Minnesota, St. Louis and Winnipeg. Even among such less-than-stellar company, the Leafs finished fifth, missing the playoffs. A bright spot for the team was the prodigious scoring of Rick Vaive, who tallied 54 goals, making him the first Toronto Maple Leaf to break the 50-goal barrier. Bill Derlago and John Anderson chipped in 34 and 31, respectively. The next year, Vaive showed his offensive outburst was no fluke, netting 51 goals. The Leafs had taken some forward steps. The return of Mike Palmateer, purchased from Washington, steadied the defence markedly, as the team cut its goals-against by 50 over the year before, when Bunny Larocque stood between the pipes. Toronto improved by 12 points to 68, good for third place in the Norris Division. Their first-round playoff opponent would be the Minnesota North Stars, who had finished 28 points ahead of the Leafs. Although they were in well over their heads, the Leafs kept things close: they were beaten three games to one, but the three losses were all by scores of 5-4. After the 1983-84 season, during which the Leafs slid back to last place in their division and missed the playoffs, Mike Nykoluk was asked to "move along."

Dan Maloney, a tough winger who had played four and a half seasons for the Leafs before retiring in 1982, took over as coach. Tom remembers Maloney as being very friendly to him. "I ran into him at Eaton's one day, and he invited me to a team practice. He left my name at the gate with the security people. I was sitting in the penalty box, waiting for the practice to begin, when Dan skated over to me and said, 'Come on over to the player's bench.' He introduced me to each of the players as they skated out onto the ice. When Rick Vaive walked out, he said, 'Rick, do you have a souvenir for Tom?' Vaive went back into the dressing room and got one of his sticks and gave it to me. I've always liked Dan Maloney. And you see, there is a whole other side to some of those tough guys."

In Maloney's first season as coach, the Leafs put up a record of 20-52-8. Not only were they last in their division this year, they were dead last in the 21-team National Hockey League. If there was a silver lining to this horrible season, it was that Toronto would choose first overall in the annual entry draft. That June, Gerry McNamara stepped up to the microphone and announced, "The Toronto Maple Leafs are very proud to select, from the Saskatoon Blades, Wendel Clark." Clark was congratulated by his family and agent, and proceeded to the floor of the Metropolitan Toronto Convention Centre, where he pulled on a Maple Leaf sweater for the first time.

Tommy Gaston is amused by the memory. "I was at the draft that year – it was the first time it hadn't been held in Montreal. When the draft was over, I saw King Clancy and Harold Ballard sitting together, so I went up to them. 'Mr. Clancy, Mr. Ballard,' I said, 'I have to tell you I'm disappointed.' They looked at me and wondered what I was going to say next. 'I'm disappointed that you didn't draft me!' I told them. Well, we laughed. Here I was, almost 70 years old. Then King Clancy said, 'Y'know, Tommy, it's funny you should mention that. I was talking to Harold about that very subject, but he thought you needed another year of junior!' Well, the three of us really laughed then!"

In fact, by finishing so poorly throughout the 1980s, the Leafs were able to choose early in the draft on several occasions. In 1981, with the sixth-overall pick, they chose Jim Benning. A very good defenceman in the junior ranks, Benning was rushed into the NHL and his career very likely suffered irreparable damage as a result. In 1982, the third-overall selection gave the Leafs Gary Nylund. A big, strong defenceman, Nylund played well in Toronto before knee injuries took their toll. The Leafs' first choice in 1983, and the seventh pick overall, was the lightning-quick forward Russ Courtnall. The 1984 draft saw Toronto choose Al Iafrate with the fourth-overall selection. These players, plus such later-round draft choices as Bob McGill, Stew Gavin, Gary Leeman, Peter Ihnacak, Ken Wregget, Allan Bester and Todd Gill, would form the nucleus of the Leaf team for the rest of the decade.

In 1985-86, the Leafs managed to finish fourth – more because of the Detroit Red Wings' miserable 40-point, fifth-place showing than their own improvement. In the first round of playoffs, they surprised the hockey world, sweeping the Blackhawks in the first round and taking the St. Louis Blues to the full seven games of the divisional final. But the highlight of the year was the debut of Wendel Clark. The defenceman-turned-left-winger owned effective wrist and slapshots that enabled him to score a team-leading 34 goals in his rookie season. His bodychecking was powerful and exciting and he was fearless in front of the net – strong and all but immovable. And despite a relative lack of size – he was just under six feet and 200 pounds – he would drop his gloves with anyone, usually the opposing team's biggest, toughest player. By usually getting in the first punch, and almost always a haymaker, Wendel Clark coldcocked some of the NHL's most feared fighters. The fans of Toronto hadn't been so excited about a rookie in decades. "Boy, that Wendel was good with his dukes," notes Tom Gaston. "And he was a strong player with a great shot. If anybody touched any of his teammates, Wendel would wallop them."

Clark played on a line with right winger Gary Leeman and centre Russ Courtnall. All three had played midget hockey in Saskatchewan for the Notre Dame Hounds under Father Athol Murray, so the unit was dubbed the Hound Line. "Oh, it was an exciting line," Gaston enthuses. "Courtnall was very energetic – a great skater who could score. Gary Leeman had been a defenceman in the Western Hockey League when he was drafted. He went on to score 51 goals one season in Toronto. And Wendel – he was a defenceman when he was drafted, too – gave 100 percent every time he stepped onto the ice. His enthusiasm for the game was infectious."

The offensive performances of Vaive, Clark and Courtnall, as well as free-agent signing Steve Thomas and recent acquisition Tom Fergus, created excitement on the ice. But again, management problems would plague the team. Dan Maloney's contract had expired, and he was seeking a two-year deal. Harold Ballard and Gerry McNamara insisted they would offer no more than a one-year deal, so Maloney resigned and within a day had taken a job coaching the Winnipeg Jets.

Enter John Brophy, a career minor-league hockey player who was renowned for always playing tough – and often dirty. Brophy had spent virtually his entire playing career in the rough-and-tumble Eastern Hockey League. Rumour had it that John Brophy was the inspiration for the wild-eyed Ogie Oglethorpe character in the 1977 movie Slap Shot. Brophy was a competitor through and through, and if that meant fighting – or using his stick on an opponent – then that was what Brophy did. He brought the same spunk and moxy to the Toronto Maple Leafs when he joined the team for the 1986-87 season.

On the evening of November 5, 1986, King Clancy was watching the St. Louis-Toronto game. The Leafs had won 6-4, but King hadn't felt well during the game. The next day, he checked into Toronto's Wellesley Hospital with severe abdominal pains. A surgeon removed his gall bladder, but complications arose, and on Monday, November 10, Francis "King" Clancy died. The players wore commemorative patches on their sweaters to honour Clancy for the remainder of the season. Harold Ballard, who lost his best friend when the King died, would never be quite the same.

The 1986-87 Leaf team was exciting. The Hound Line, along with Vaive, Thomas and Vincent Damphousse, provided the bulk of the scoring, while young netminders Ken Wregget and Allan Bester shared goaltending duties. Spice was added to the mix with the addition of the wildly popular Brad Smith, a former Red Wings farm hand who'd gained the nickname "Motor City Smitty." Toronto again finished fourth in the weak Norris Division, but they upset the St. Louis Blues in the first round of the playoffs before losing to the Wings in seven games. Brophy's style found a receptive audience in Toronto, and when he wore a fedora behind the bunch during the playoffs that year, entrepreneurial fans sold facsimiles of the fedora, with a band that read "BROPHY'S BOYS."

"I had mixed feelings about Brophy's coaching style," admits Tom. "The fans loved him, but I doubted that his style would ever bring a championship to Toronto."

An off-season trade sent Rick Vaive, Steve Thomas and Bob McGill to Chicago, bringing Eddie Olczyk and Al Secord in return. Meanwhile, Brophy's blueprint called for the addition of tough guys such as Dave Semenko, Brian Curran and rookie Luke Richardson. In 1987-88, the Maple Leafs took a backward step, falling from 70 to 52 points. Only the Minnesota North Stars, with 51, turned in a poorer showing. Fortunately for the Leafs, Minnesota was in their division, so they qualified for the playoffs. Toronto was no match for the Detroit Red Wings in the first round, however, and they made an early exit from the postseason. In February 1988, Gerry McNamara had also made an early exit – from the general manager's position. The triumvirate of Brophy, Dick Duff and Gord Stellick steered the Maple Leaf ship for the rest of the season.

The question of who would be the Leafs' permanent GM was the source of much speculation. Some predicted that John Brophy would get the job, but two weeks after the club's elimination from the playoffs it was announced that the job had been given to the 31-year-old Stellick. His youth belied the fact that Stellick had been around the Maple Leafs organization for more than a decade – while still in high school, he had begun helping out in the press box, then worked his way up through the ranks until, by 1987-88, he held the post of assistant to the general manager. "I had known Gord since he was a little boy," recalls Gaston. "His mother lived near us when she was young, so I knew her family long before she got married and had children. I got to know the boys, Gord and his younger brother Bob, when they were just little. They were cute little boys. Of course, both went on to have wonderful careers with the Maple Leafs." Bob went on to become the Leafs' director of business operations and communications before starting his own public relations company.

Anyone expecting harmony in the front office would be disappointed. Stellick and Brophy disagreed on how best to run the Toronto Maple Leafs, and the players had lost faith in their coach and his lack of a regular game plan, but Harold Ballard steadfastly refused to authorize Stellick to fire Brophy.

The acquisition of defenceman Brad Marsh in the 1988 waiver draft was a rare bright spot in this dismal season. The big veteran had an unusual skating style, but he added toughness and veteran savvy to the blueline corps. "There was nothing like seeing Brad Marsh play," Tommy says. "He loved the game so much. My favourite thing about Marsh was when he was selected as one of the three stars of the game. Other guys would skate onto the ice, take a few strides, and maybe wave, but Marshy would go flying out of the gate, skate across the ice as hard as he could, stop with a big spray of ice shavings, then skate full-tilt back to the bench!"

Brophy insisted the team needed to be tougher, so on November 7, 1988, Stellick traded the popular Russ Courtnall to Montreal for slugger John Kordic and a draft choice. To say the deal would come back to haunt the Leafs would be an understatement. Stellick is currently a radio host on an all-sports station in Toronto, and listeners still needle him regularly about the Courtnall-for-Kordic deal. Courtnall continued to play consistent hockey for the Habs, contributing three more 20-goal seasons – and even leading them in scoring in 1990–91 – before being moved to Minnesota. He would enjoy several more productive years, and he retired in 1999. Kordic, on the other hand, was out of control, both on and off the ice. Rumours of drug use and heavy drinking proved to be true, and he was a wild man on the ice. His offensive talents were minimal, but he did add the toughness that Brophy had requested – to the tune of 185 penalty minutes in 46 games played in 1988-89, and 252 penalty minutes in just 55 games the next season. His ice time was minimal, his injuries frequent and his stay in Toronto mercifully short for both sides. Sadly, after bouncing from Toronto to Washington to Quebec to the Cape Breton Oilers of the AHL, John Kordic died in the summer of 1992.

John Brophy made it until Christmas 1988 before he was finally relieved of his duties. George Armstrong, the former Leaf captain and a successful junior coach who had led the Toronto Marlboros to Memorial Cup wins in 1973 and '75, was – against his best wishes – installed behind the Leafs bench on an interim basis. The Leafs finished last in the Norris Division – nineteenth overall – despite the presence of a trio of 30-goal scorers in Ed Olczyk, Gary Leeman and rookie Daniel Marois. For the second year in a row, Wendel Clark spent most of the season out of the lineup with back injuries. There was discord within the dressing room, including problems that arose when Gary Leeman began to date Al Iafrate's ex-wife.

Few Leaf observers will forget the entry draft of 1989. The Leafs held three first-round picks in that draft, having acquired the extra two in a March trade that sent Ken Wregget to Philadelphia. The Leafs opened themselves up to a considerable amount of ribbing when they proceeded to select three members of the Belleville Bulls junior team: Scott Thornton, Rob Pearson and Steve Bancroft. "The joke was that the Leafs didn't need a big scouting staff – just someone to drive a couple of hours east along Highway 401," giggles Gaston. Ironically, the Leafs would one day acquire the player chosen first overall in what was by many accounts a weak draft: Mats Sundin.

After just over a year as general manager, Gord Stellick had had enough, feeling that Harold Ballard had not seen fit to let him have the tools to do his job properly. Stellick could not hire his own coach, and he was unable to put together a coaching and scouting staff that was comparable to other teams. His every move was monitored, and then often undermined, by the owner. On August 11, 1989, Stellick resigned.

The Leafs prepared to close out the decade with a new general manager, Floyd Smith, and a new coach, Doug Carpenter. In 1980, Carpenter had coached the Cornwall Royals – with a lineup that included Hall of Famer Dale Hawerchuk – to a Memorial Cup championship. More recently he had been head coach of the New Jersey Devils. The club also had something it had lacked since Rick Vaive's trade to Chicago in 1987: a captain. Harold Ballard personally awarded the "C" to defenceman Rob Ramage, who had been acquired in a trade from Calgary, where he'd just been a member of the Flames' Cup-winning squad, in June 1989. The move raised some eyebrows, considering Ramage's lack of tenure with the team.

Carpenter believed in a wide-open, offensive brand of hockey, and the team responded. Gary Leeman had a career year, scoring 51 goals. Fourth-year pro Vincent Damphousse blossomed, scoring 33 and tabulating 94 points. Ed Olczyk and Dan Marois scored 32 and 39 goals respectively. Although injured much of the season, Wendel Clark managed 18 goals in just 38 games. Overall, team offence increased from 259 goals to a robust 337, and the Leafs broke even with a record of 38-38-4 for their first .500 season since 1978-79. In the playoffs, they ran up against 72-goal scorer Brett Hull and his St. Louis Blues, who defeated Toronto four games to one. Leaf fans may be familiar with the name of a rookie goaltender on that Blues squad: Curtis Joseph.

On April 11, 1990, just one day before St. Louis brought the Leafs' season to a close, Harold Ballard died. His final years had been fraught with a number of health problems, but it was his kidneys and heart that finally ended the Toronto owner's life. "As a Leaf fan, I went to pay my respects," Tommy says solemnly. "The Toronto Maple Leafs had Mr. Ballard lying in state at Maple Leaf Gardens. A private funeral followed and Harold was ultimately buried in Park Lawn Cemetery in the west end.

Tommy summarizes the Ballard years at Maple Leaf Gardens: "During his ownership, the building was neglected a little bit and so was the team. Harold tightened the purse strings. There were a few years during his ownership when the team was just one or two good players away from winning it all. I think of the teams that Red Kelly coached with Sittler and McDonald. The Maple Leafs threw away a Stanley Cup – I truly believe that. But say what you will about Harold, he was a good man deep down."

Sadly, Harold Ballard's "reign of terror" will forever remain his legacy. Between Stafford Smythe's death in 1971 and his own in 1990, Harold employed five different general managers and twelve coaches. Team captains were routinely humiliated, and Dave Keon was released, Darryl Sittler was traded after briefly resigning his captaincy, and Rick Vaive had the "C" stripped from him before he was traded. The saddest evidence is the Leafs' record during the years Harold Ballard was president. They won no Stanley Cup champions, never went further in the playoffs than the 1978 semifinals, and missed the playoffs completely five times.

CHAPTER SEVENTEEN

Gilmour

Harold Ballard, who had grown estranged from his children in his later years, had long threatened to leave his Leafs to charity. Few believed him, but when he died it was revealed that his will indeed named a number of local charities as beneficiaries of the sale of his assets. It would fall to the three executors of his estate – Gardens' directors Donald Crump, Donald Giffin and Steve Stavro – to carry out his last wishes. This would prove to be easier said than done; there were numerous squabbles between Giffin and Stavro, not to mention lengthy legal battles, and the affairs of Maple Leaf Gardens Ltd. would not be fully wound up until late 1996, when Stavro became the sole owner.

In the meantime, there was still an arena and a hockey team to run, and Giffin, who was appointed Ballard's successor as president of Maple Leaf Gardens, put Floyd Smith in charge of hockey operations, while retaining Doug Carpenter as coach for 1990-91.

One thing upon which the executors agreed was that respectability needed to be returned to the hockey club. An area in which Giffin felt the Leafs had suffered was their neglect of their alumni. Where the Montreal Canadiens embraced their heritage, making sure that former stars always felt welcome at the Forum and employing many of them in executive positions or as goodwill ambassadors, the Maple Leafs under Ballard seemed to have little use for their past. King Clancy's longtime involvement with the club was the exception. Giffin hoped to show that that had all changed by bringing back the surviving members of the 1931-32 Stanley Cup-winning team to drop the puck for the ceremonial face-off at the Leafs' October 10 home opener. Tom remembers that night with pride: "There, at centre ice, receiving a thunderous ovation, stood Ace Bailey, Harold Darragh, Frank Finnigan and Red Horner. It was the first step made to improve the image of the Toronto Maple Leafs."

Shortly afterward, a Toronto Maple Leaf alumni association was created, and efforts were made to convince such players as Dave Keon and Frank Mahovlich, who had been driven from the Gardens and were perfectly content to stay away, that they were once again wanted at 60 Carlton Street. "Ballard's Bunker," that sad symbol of the old order, was refurbished and set aside for visiting alumni.

The team began the season on a road trip through western Canada, and they got off to a miserable start. They lost 7-1 to Winnipeg, 4-1 to Calgary and 3-2 in Edmonton. Their sixtieth home opener at the Gardens ended in an 8-5 defeat at the hands of the Quebec Nordiques. Toronto had only a win and a tie to show for their first eleven games, and so coach Carpenter was dismissed, to be replaced by his assistant, Tom Watt. Watt – who coached his first game on October 27 – had tutored the powerful University of Toronto team during the 1970s.

The Leafs won only one of Watt's first seven games, prompting Floyd Smith to launch into a wild flurry of trading. Within ten days he dispatched Brian Curran, Lou Franceschetti, John Kordic, Tom Kurvers, Ed Olczyk, Mark Osborne and Scott Pearson and brought in veterans Dave Ellett, Mike Foligno, Mike Krushelnyski, Lucien DeBlois, Aaron Broten and Michel Petit. It was another sorry finish for the Maple Leafs: 57 points, fifth in the Norris Division and 20th in the NHL. They missed the playoffs.

On June 4, 1991, the Toronto Maple Leafs announced a personnel move that would dramtically alter the course of the franchise. Cliff Fletcher was named president, general manager and chief operating officer of the Toronto Maple Leafs. Fletcher had started his career as a scout in the Montreal Canadiens organization, and he joined the St. Louis Blues as a scout when they entered the league in 1967. A couple of years later, he was their assistant GM. When Atlanta was granted an expansion franchise to begin play in 1972, Fletcher was named general manager, a post he kept when the club moved to Calgary in 1980. There he built a team that went to the Stanley Cup finals in 1986 and won the Cup in 1989. "Cliff Fletcher was a real hockey man," Tommy says. "I liked him a lot, and I liked what he did for the team. He turned the franchise around. I'd say he was the Leafs' best GM since Punch."

Fletcher had his work cut out for him, but he rolled up his sleeves and took a methodical approach to the task at hand. Wendel Clark was re-signed and made the captain of the Toronto Maple Leafs.

Mike Murphy, who once played for the Toronto Marlboros and was a consistent 20-goal scorer during a 12-year NHL career, was brought in to assist Tom Watt, and three additional scouts were hired. The club's "open-arms" policy toward its alumni continued as Darryl Sittler was enlisted to work in hockey operations and public relations.

The Leafs, scheduled to open their season on the road in Montreal on October 3, made a further nod to tradition as the players dressed in suits and fedoras and took the train to Montreal. It looked as if the team had taken a step back in time to the glory days of the 1930s or '40s. The symbolism may or may not have been intentional, but it was good fun for the fans nonetheless.

Setting out to improve the on-ice product, Fletcher's first deal was a blockbuster. On September 19, 1991, the Leafs received Grant Fuhr, Glenn Anderson and Craig Berube from Edmonton for Peter Ing, Vincent Damphousse, Luke Richardson and Scott Thornton. "I hated to see Damphousse go," Tommy attests. "I really liked his style. He was good with the puck. But to get something, you have to give something up. It was great to have a goaltender like Grant Fuhr."

The Leafs again struggled through the first half of the season, posting a 10-25-5 record by the end of December. Unlike Floyd Smith before him, Fletcher did not panic, and no trades were made – until January 2, 1992, when Fletcher and the Leafs rung in the New Year by dropping a bombshell on Toronto sports fans. Wingers Gary Leeman and Craig Berube, defencemen Michel Petit and Alexander Godynyuk plus spare netminder Jeff Reese were sent to the Calgary Flames for centre Doug Gilmour, blueliners Jamie Macoun and Rick Nattress, utility forward Kent Manderville and veteran backup goalie Rick Wamsley. It was the largest deal ever made in the NHL's history, and it would prove to be one of the biggest steals Toronto ever made.

Doug Gilmour would singlehandedly change the face of the Leaf franchise over the next two seasons, while attaining a status among Leaf fans equal to the esteem in which Darryl Sittler, Dave Keon or Frank Mahovlich had been held. "What a breath of fresh air," smiles Gaston. "Every time Dougie stepped onto the ice, he controlled the game.

"This was a real steal of a trade with the Flames. Look at the facts – Gilmour gave the Leafs several MVP-quality seasons. Macoun was steady on defence. Manderville turned out to be a good checking centre. Wamsley was a dependable back-up goaltender who became the goalie coach. But Leeman never worked out for Calgary and could never score the 50 goals he got in Toronto, Godynyuk didn't add anything and Berube didn't stay very long. Of course, Reese was a pretty good backup to Mike Vernon, and Michel Petit had a couple good seasons, but it sure was lopsided for Toronto, wasn't it?"

Although Gilmour, "the Killer," had been a top-notch player in both St. Louis and Calgary, his profile exploded in Toronto. For a smallish player (sources list him generously at five foot eleven and 175 pounds), Gilmour was fearless, and the Toronto fans adored his feistiness. He would stand up for himself, no matter who rattled his cage. He also backchecked like a fiend, spending as much time in his own end of the rink as he did in the opposing team's. And boy, could he score! In 1982-83, as part of a Cornwall Royals major junior squad that won the Memorial Cup, Gilmour led the league with 107 assists and 177 total points. His efforts earned him the Red Tilson Trophy as the Ontario Hockey League's most valuable player. Joining the St. Louis Blues in 1983-84, Gilmour demonstrated a consistent ability to score 20 goals a year over his first three seasons before cutting loose for 42 goals, 63 assists and 105 points in 1986-87. That year he was fifth in the NHL scoring derby. Traded to Calgary in 1988, Gilmour was among the Flames' scoring leaders in each of his three full seasons and was an important part of the club's 1989 Stanley Cup championship.

Toronto fans were impressed when Gilmour scored a healthy 49 points in his first 40 games as a Maple Leaf, but no one could have been prepared for the impending offensive explosion. In his first full season with the Leafs, Doug Gilmour fired 32 goals and 95 assists for 127 points – beating Darryl Sittler's club record which had stood since 1977-78 and good for eighth in league scoring.

The Gilmour trade generated fan excitement as well as an immediate improvement on the ice as Toronto went 20-18-2 during the second half – hardly a world-beating pace, but compared with the team's recent performance it was definite cause for optimism. The Leafs finished fifth in the Norris Division, with 67 points, three shy of a playoff berth. During the off-season, Cliff Fletcher made a coaching change, bringing in Pat Burns, the Jack Adams Award-winning ex-coach of the Montreal Canadiens.

By February 1993, Fletcher was satisfied that 21-year-old goalie Felix Potvin, who had been sharing the netminding duties with Grant

Fuhr, was ready for the number one job. Fuhr and a draft choice were traded to Buffalo for left winger Dave Andreychuk, goalie Daren Puppa and a first-round draft pick. Andreychuk was placed on Gilmour's line, where the big sniper's scoring ability was the perfect complement to the diminutive centre's playmaking skills. He scored 25 goals in his first 31 games in blue and white. When the dust settled on the regular season, the Leafs had improved from 57 points to a team-record 99, good for third place in the Norris Division behind powerful Chicago and Detroit clubs. Toronto's goal production was up, from 234 to 288, while goals-against were cut from 294 to 241. Potvin's 2.50 goals-against average led the league.

If there is a defining moment in Doug Gilmour's Toronto career, it would have to be the playoff run of 1993. Gilmour was a man on a mission. The lengthy playoffs took a physical toll on him, but he grabbed the team by the scruff of the neck and shook it, with marvellous results. Toronto's first-round series against Detroit went the full seven games. With the score knotted at three at the end of regulation time in the seventh game, Nikolai Borschevsky, playing with a broken cheekbone, scored in overtime to advance the Leafs to round two.

In the quarterfinals, the Leafs were matched against Curtis Joseph and the St. Louis Blues. The first game was tied at one after 60 minutes, and there was no scoring in the first overtime period. Then, early in the second additional frame, Gilmour cradled the puck behind the Blues net. He faked to his left, then to his right. He circled back to his left, then slid out beside the net on his backhand and stuck the puck behind CuJo. The Leafs had won 2-1. Gilmour had been on the ice for 42 minutes in that game, played in a hot, stuffy Maple Leaf Gardens.

The series, a real see-saw battle, had all the ingredients of exciting hockey: highlight-reel goals, in-your-face physical play and superb drama. At one point, Wendel Clark rang a shot off Joseph's mask, sending the puck flying into the corner. The series went to a seventh game, to be played at the Gardens. The crowd, already delirious, threatened to blow the roof off Conn Smythe's old barn after game seven's 6-0 Leaf victory. Revellers spilled out onto Yonge Street in droves; car horns honked incessantly; homemade placards indicated that the Stanley Cup was due to return to Toronto. The Leafs were going to the semifinals! Bring on Gretzky and the Kings!

There were any number of subplots to this series. For instance, how would Gilmour stack up against the Kings' Wayne Gretzky?

Then there was the relationship between Leaf coach Pat Burns, who had once coached the Hull Olympiques of the Quebec junior league, and Gretzky, who as the owner of that team had been Burns' boss. Burns was an ex-cop with a blue-collar background, while Los Angeles coach – and former Leaf – Barry Melrose could be described as a "pretty boy."

The tone for the series was set in game one, played at Maple Leaf Gardens. With Toronto up 4-1, Gilmour carried the puck over the Kings' blueline. As he cut toward the middle, L.A. defenceman Marty McSorley lined him up for a massive bodycheck, but Gilmour caught a glimpse of McSorley at the very last second and made a bit of a shift, apparently evading his opponent. McSorley, feeling he had no choice but to catch Gilmour any way he could, threw his arms up into the Leaf centre's face, knocking him to the ice, where he lay prone. Wendel Clark rushed over, threw off his gloves as he made his way toward McSorley, and landed punch after punch, soundly beating him. Toronto fans went wild. It was the greatest show of teammate support in recent memory, and it quickly and decisively put McSorley in his place while establishing that the Leafs would not be pushed around. Meanwhile, behind the benches, Burns struggled to free himself as policemen and his players restrained him from getting at Melrose. The Kings coach just smirked, incensing Burns that much more. The series may have been a battle before. It now was a war.

After four games, the series was tied at two games apiece. In game five, Glenn Anderson scored with just 40 seconds left in the first overtime period to give the Leafs a 3-2 win on home ice. Game six, however, was one many Leaf fans would prefer to forget. With the score tied 4-4 and 13 seconds left in regulation time, referee Kerry Fraser assessed a boarding penalty against Glenn Anderson. Toronto was forced to start the overtime period a man short – an unenviable position, as penalty killing is hard enough without the knowledge that the next goal wins the game. Early in the extra period, the puck was in Toronto's end when Gretzky accidentally high-sticked Doug Gilmour in the face. Gilmour hit the ice, cut and bleeding, in full view of referee Fraser. No penalty was called and the play continued. Thirty seconds later, Gretzky himself scored to win the game and force a seventh game. Gilmour's wound was closed up with eight stitches.

Years later, Tommy Gaston can't help but get angry all over again. "We got jobbed! Whether it was intentional or not is beside the point – that should have been a high-sticking major to Gretzky. It would have changed the game completely. If the Leafs had scored while the Kings were a man short, Toronto would have gone to the Stanley Cup finals for the first time since they won the Cup in 1967. And we could have beaten Montreal in the finals, too – no doubt about it!"

But the Leafs didn't get that opportunity. In game seven, Gretzky would ruin the day for Toronto once again. The Kings led 4-3 with less than four minutes left in the game, when number 99, stationed behind the Leaf net, passed it out in front of the net. The puck hit Leaf defenceman Dave Ellett's skate and careened into the net past Felix Potvin. Ellett redeemed himself by scoring a goal with just over a minute left, but even after pulling Potvin for an extra attacker, the Leafs couldn't score again on Kelly Hrudey. Final score: 5-4 for L.A., who would meet the Montreal Canadiens in the finals.

In recognition for a brilliant season, Pat Burns was presented with the Jack Adams Award as coach of the year. Doug Gilmour won the Frank J. Selke Trophy as best defensive forward, and was a finalist for the Hart Trophy as the NHL's most valuable player. Mario Lemieux, who had come back from cancer treatments to win the scoring title despite playing only 60 games, was awarded the Hart.

On October 13, 1993, in a ceremony prior to a game against the Washington Capitals, the Toronto Maple Leaf organization began a tradition of honouring sweater numbers with a special significance to the team's history. That night, banners with Ted Kennedy's number 9 and Syl Apps' number 10 were raised to the roof of Maple Leaf Gardens. It was not a retirement ceremony per se – the numbers would still be available to future generations of Maple Leafs – but their status as "honoured numbers" would be acknowledged by a special patch sewn to the shoulders of the current-day players' sweaters. (In 1993-94, Glenn Anderson wore number 9, while Bill Berg had 10.) It was just one more mark of Fletcher's program to restore pride to the Leafs franchise and to embrace the club's illustrious history. In subsequent seasons, other numbers would be so honoured: number 1, which belonged to Turk Broda and Johnny Bower; number 7, for King Clancy and Tim Horton; and numbers 9 and 10 were again honoured, this time for Charlie Conacher and George Armstrong respectively.

With Felix Potvin sharp as a razor, the Maple Leafs burst out of the chute, winning the first ten games of the 1993-94 season. Cliff

Fletcher made another splash at the March trading deadline when he swapped Glenn Anderson and a draft pick to the New York Rangers for Mike Gartner. Gartner ended the season with a total of 34 goals between the two teams, making it the fifteenth straight year in which Gartner had scored 30 or more goals in a season. "What a gentleman that Gartner is," Tommy Gaston says. "Even when he was nearing retirement, he was still the fastest skater on the Leafs team. I couldn't be happier that he was inducted into the Hockey Hall of Fame."

Changes were afoot in the National Hockey League. Over the past three seasons the league had been on a growth spurt and was now up to twenty-six teams. In 1991-92, the San Jose Sharks entered the NHL, while the next season saw the addition of the Tampa Bay Lightning and the return of NHL hockey to Ottawa. Another pair of new teams, the Mighty Ducks of Anaheim and the Miami-based Florida Panthers, made their debuts in 1993-94. The league also reorganized the divisions and gave them new names: out went Adams, Patrick, Norris and Smythe and in came the more prosaic Northeast, Atlantic, Central and Pacific, while the Wales and Campbell conferences were changed to the Eastern and Western. Finally, the Minnesota North Stars picked up stakes and moved to Dallas, where they became simply the Stars.

The Maple Leafs' 98 points in the regular season placed them second in the Central Division. In the first round of the playoffs they met the Chicago Blackhawks, whom they dispatched in six games – and Felix Potvin earned three shutouts in the process. "That was the first time since Frank McCool in the 40s that a Leaf goalie had earned three shutouts in a series," Tommy points out. Round two matched the Leafs with the Sharks, who had made the playoffs in only their third NHL season (and improved to 82 points from 24 the year before). With Doug Gilmour nursing a badly bruised ankle, the teams faced off. The momentum shifted back and forth, but the Leafs prevailed – although it took the full seven games. For the second year in a row, Toronto had made the semifinals – this time against the Vancouver Canucks. This time, however, the series would not be as dramatic: the Canucks outmuscled and outscored the Leafs to win the series four games to one.

What a couple of years it had been! Toronto had played 39 playoff games – more than any other team. Gilmour had scored an incredible 63 points in the two playoff years. Photos of his battle-scarred face, toothless smile and gaunt form were everywhere, including the cover of Sports Illustrated's Canadian edition. During both seasons, much had made of Gilmour's weight loss during the playoffs, and fans sent him recipes for pasta that they hoped would revitalize their captain. Gilmour had made an indelible mark on the city – he was like a rock star on skates. The fans knew where he lived – which forced him to move on two occasions. They knew about his tattoos, his affection for motorcycles, his love for daughter Madison and his budding romance with Maple Leaf Gardens' usherette Amy Cable. Tom Gaston concludes, "Although he's been gone from Toronto for several years now, each time his name gets mentioned at the Air Canada Centre, the Toronto fans still give Dougie Gilmour a great ovation."

Quinn

Early in April 1994, Steve Stavro, the chairman of the board and chief executive officer of the Maple Leaf Gardens Ltd., launched a takeover of the Gardens and the Toronto Maple Leafs. Aided by the Toronto Dominion Bank and the Ontario Teachers' Pension Plan Board, Stavro purchased the Molson Companies' 20-percent stake in the Gardens, then purchased the 60 percent held by Harold Ballard's estate – of which he was an executor. For the next two and a half years, the publicity-shy Stavro would battle behind the scenes to accumulate the 90-percent ownership stake he would need to transform the publicly traded corporation into a private company.

The hockey team that Stavro was overtaking had proven it was consistent and competitive, but it had also shown that it didn't quite have what it took to win a Stanley Cup. Club president and general manager Cliff Fletcher didn't just fine-tune the lineup, he rolled the dice on a blockbuster deal that caught Leaf fans off-guard. On June 29, 1994, Fletcher sent team captain Wendel Clark, along with defenceman Sylvain Lefebvre, prospect Landon Wilson and a first-round draft pick to the Quebec Nordiques for high-scoring forward Mats Sundin, Todd Warriner of the Canadian national team, defenceman Garth Butcher and a first-round draft choice.

The city was stunned. Wendel Clark had been the most popular Toronto Maple Leaf in years. For many seasons, he had been the only thing Leaf fans could cheer about. Sales of his number 17 jersey practically kept LeafSport, the sporting goods store at Maple Leaf Gardens, in business. Night in and night out, he sacrificed his body to play the only way he knew how: all-out. The giveaways and bad penalties had been easy to overlook in exchange for the excitement of that wrist shot, the dipsy-doodle play he'd often make behind his back while breaking into the enemy zone, and the thunderous hits he would use to splay opponents against the boards. When the trade was announced, Wendel cried, and so did many Leaf fans. There was even a Goodbye Wendel celebration at Mel Lastman Square in North York that drew thousands of diehard fans.

The good news was that, in Sundin, the Maple Leafs were acquiring a skilled forward who was only 23 years old. The first-overall pick in the 1989 entry draft, Sundin scored 114 points for the Nordiques in only his third NHL season. He stood six foot four and weighed 225 pounds, with hands as fine as his blond hair.

Clark's departure left the Leafs without a captain. On August 18, 1994, a reception was held at the Hockey Hall of Fame and, with former Leaf captains Red Horner, Bob Davidson, Sid Smith, George Armstrong, Darryl Sittler and Rob Ramage in attendance, it was announced that Doug Gilmour would be the next to wear the "C."

A labour dispute delayed the start of the 1994-95 NHL season, after the owners locked out the players in disputes over free agency and the proposed introduction of a rookie salary cap. In the meantime, Gilmour played hockey in Switzerland to play hockey. Mats Sundin and defenceman Kenny Jonsson returned to Sweden to play for their former club teams, while Nikolai Borschevsky rejoined Spartak of the Russian league. Todd Gill was chosen by Wayne Gretzky to join an entourage of friends and family playing exhibition games in Europe.

In the meantime, Fletcher made further roster adjustments. Centre Mike Ridley was acquired from the Washington Capitals. Free-agent forward Mike Craig – who had lately been with the Dallas Stars – was signed, an acquisition that forced the Leafs to give up Peter Zezel, a popular third-line centreman, to the Stars as compensation. Finally, in the autumn, the Leafs landed a couple of utility forwards, Terry Yake and Dixon Ward.

With the disputes resolved, a new collective-bargaining agreement was approved in time to salvage at least a partial season. Teams would begin playing a condensed 48-game schedule beginning on January 20, 1995. The Toronto Maple Leafs weren't the same team they had been a year ago, and the jury-rigged schedule prevented the overhauled lineup from developing any kind of team chemistry. Fletcher saw no choice but to continually tinker with the roster. He picked up Randy Wood from Buffalo, Warren Rychel from Los Angeles and Rich Sutter from Tampa Bay. As the April 7 deadline neared, there was another flurry of trades. Underperforming winger Nik Borschevsky, the team's top goal scorer only two years before, was dealt to Calgary for a sixth-round draft choice, while Benoit Hogue came over from the New York Islanders, Grant Jennings from the Pittsburgh Penguins and Tie Domi from the Winnipeg Jets.

Tie Domi had originally been drafted by the Leafs in 1988. He played for Toronto's AHL affiliate, the Newmarket Saints, in 1989-90, but saw action in just two games with the parent club, earning no points while accumulating 42 minutes in penalties. A trade sent him to the New York Rangers, for whom he played parts of two and a half seasons. Around Christmas 1992, he was dealt to the Jets, where he made a name for himself in his first complete season by leading the NHL in penalty minutes, with 347, in 1993-94. He also found time to contribute 8 goals and 19 points, suggesting he might also be able to rely upon something other than his fists.

"Tie gets a lot of ink from the press, but underneath the tough guy there's a pretty good hockey player," Tom Gaston maintains. "Tie can skate and bodycheck, and he certainly doesn't back down from anyone, either. Over the past few years, he's been much better about taking bad penalties and knows when to pick his fights, too. He doesn't have to prove anything to anybody anymore." Since his return to the Maple Leafs, replicas of Domi's number 28 sweater have been every bit as popular as Sundin's number 13 or CuJo's number 31.

Newcomer Mats Sundin led the team in goals (23) and points (47), and Dave Andreychuk chipped in another 22 goals, but Gilmour and Gartner had off years as the indifferent Leafs skated to a 21-19-8 record, giving them fourth place in the Central Division and the fifth seed in the Western Conference playoffs. Facing the Chicago Blackhawks in the first round, Toronto won the first two games, but were eventually eliminated four games to three. Again, Sundin acquitted himself well, with five goals and nine points in the series, while Gilmour racked up six assists.

It was clear to Leaf management that retooling was needed immediately. The most glaring problem they saw was on defence. Sylvain Lefebvre had been given up in the deal that put Sundin in blue and white, while Bob Rouse was lost to the Detroit Red Wings when he became a free agent. The club missed their talents more than anyone had anticipated. The remaining blueline cast of Jamie Macoun, Dmitri Mironov, Todd Gill, Dave Ellett, Kenny Jonsson and Garth

Butcher, bolstered by the likes of Drake Berehowsky, Matt Martin and Grant Jennings, just didn't seem capable of getting the job done. In '93-94, the Leafs boasted the stingiest defence in the Western Conference. Within a year they had sunk to the middle of the pack as far as goals-against were concerned.

During the summer, Fletcher worked the phones in search of blueline support and came away with Larry Murphy, acquired from Pittsburgh for Mironov and a draft choice. Murphy was a 15-year veteran, which made him seem ancient in hockey teams. But he was a member of what was becoming a dying breed in NHL circles: a defenceman who could move the puck, contribute offensively and - perhaps most importantly – take charge of a team's power-play unit. Over the past four seasons he had accumulated 273 points in 292 games. He was also an uncannily consistent performer who had never lost any significant amount of time to injury in his career, and who had stepped his game up in the playoffs to make major contributions to Pittsburgh's back-to-back Stanley Cup wins in 1991 and '92.

Unfortunately, the Leaf faithful would never give Murphy a chance, and they got to be downright merciless when his offensive contributions slipped a bit during his second season as a Leaf. Focusing on his age, high salary, defensive miscues and lack of speed, fans at the Gardens started booing Murphy every time he touched the puck. In March 1997 he was dealt to the Detroit Red Wings, with whom he would go on to win Stanley Cups in 1997 and '98. Written off as too old by Leaf fans, Murphy was still active with the Wings during the 2000-01 season.

On the same day they acquired Murphy, the Leafs picked up Rob Zettler, a hard-working defenceman with a healthy mean streak, from the Philadelphia Flyers. A month later, another deal with the Flyers landed Dimitri Yushkevich, who would develop into a solid backliner with excellent bodychecking skills and leadership abilities – especially among the younger Russian players who would come along in later seasons. On paper, the moves promised to stabilize the blueline.

Unfortunately, the Leafs did not regain the glory they sought. The team was strong enough during the first half, but the months of January and February were marked by mediocre play. More deals were made – a three-way swap sent backup goalie Damian Rhodes to Ottawa and minor-league tough guy Ken Belanger to the Islanders for Senators backup Don Beaupre and Islanders forward Kirk Muller.

As a member of the New Jersey Devils and Montreal Canadiens, Muller had not only been a consistent 30-goal scorer, he was also a team leader who wore the "C" on his sweater for both teams, earning him the nickname "Captain Kirk." A few days later, Randy Wood and Benoit Hogue were sent to Dallas for Dave Gagner, a six-time 30-goal man in the NHL. On February 29, Sergio Momesso and popular checking forward Bill Berg were sent to the New York Rangers for wingers Wayne Presley and Nick Kypreos.

On March 3, Patrick Roy and the Colorado Avalanche shut out the Leafs, 4-0, handing Toronto its eighth loss in a row. Coach Pat Burns was fired – many observers suggested the players had tired of his gruff coaching style – and team scouting director Nick Beverley took his place behind the bench on an interim basis.

Fletcher wasn't done dealing yet. On March 13, Dave Andreychuk was sent to the New Jersey Devils for a pair of draft choices. Earlier the same day, promising young defenceman Kenny Jonsson, farm hand Darby Hendrickson, junior sniper Sean Haggerty and a first-round draft choice were sent to the Islanders for Wendel Clark, defenceman Mathieu Schneider – a strong puck carrier with a great point shot – and a blueline prospect from the junior ranks, D.J. Smith.

Under Beverley, the Leafs at least pulled out of their tailspin, going 9-6-2 the rest of the way. Their 80 points left them third in the Central Division and fourth in the West. Gilmour, Sundin and Gartner all scored better than 30 goals apiece, Wendel Clark potted 8 in his 13 games, and defenceman Larry Murphy registered a healthy 61 points. But there had been too many changes carried out too quickly, and too often they weren't paying off. Forty players wore a Leafs sweater at some point during the season, and the roster was cluttered with such names as Mike Craig, Todd Warriner, Paul Di Pietro, Mark Kolesar, Wayne Presley and Mike Hudson. The St. Louis Blues eliminated the Leafs in the first round of the playoffs in six games.

More changes were in store before the Leafs took the ice for the 1996-97 season, but unfortunately for those Leaf fans who were growing more impatient by the second, none would be the kind that brought Stanley Cup championships. On June 14, Todd Gill was sent to San Jose for centreman Jamie Baker. On June 22, Mike Gartner was traded to the Phoenix Coyotes (the transplanted Winnipeg Jets), while Dave Gagner was dealt to Calgary. In both cases Toronto got draft picks in return. On July 3, assistant coach Mike

Murphy was promoted to head coach. Later in the summer, the team acquired Scott Pearson, Daniel Marois and Greg Smyth, a trio of free agents whom the organization had previously discarded – and who appeared destined to play for the farm team in St. John's, Newfoundland, which looked to be bereft of prospects ready to help the parent club.

On November 9, after the Leafs had beaten the Edmonton Oilers 7-3, their record stood at 8-7-0. It was the last time Toronto would be better than .500. By the end of December the club's record was 17-22-0, and it would get worse – they won only two of thirteen games in January. On February 25, the Leafs sent their disgruntled captain, Doug Gilmour, along with Dave Ellett and a draft choice to the New Jersey Devils. In return, Toronto got a package of promising young talent. Twenty-two-year-old Steve Sullivan was a small – five foot nine, 160 pounds – high-flying forward who had posted some good numbers for Albany of the AHL. Jason Smith was a 23-year-old stay-at-home defenceman who had been a first-round selection of the Devils. But the potential jewel of the trade was a 19-year-old centre who was having a tremendous year with the Ottawa 67s juniors: Alyn McCauley. By season's end he would be the Ontario Hockey League's player of the year and its leading goal scorer – and he was just as effective in his own end of the rink.

At the trading deadline, Larry Murphy was sent to Detroit, where he would help the Wings win their first of two consecutive Stanley Cup titles, and Kirk Muller went to the Florida Panthers in exchange for 21-year-old minor leaguer Jason Podollan.

Despite coach Mike Murphy's enthusiasm for a defensive style of play, the 1996-97 Toronto Maple Leafs were tied for twenty-second among the league's twenty-six teams in goals-against. The team lacked a reliable backup goalie, so the struggling Felix Potvin appeared in a club-record 74 games. Finishing last in the six-team Central Division with just 68 points, Toronto missed the playoffs for the first time since 1991-92, the season Cliff Fletcher took over as general manager. It seemed fitting in a way, then, that on May 30, 1997, Cliff Fletcher was relieved of his duties as general manager and president of the Toronto Maple Leafs.

Fletcher's replacement as president of the team was the former goaltending star for the Montreal Canadiens, Ken Dryden. "You have to have a lot of respect for Mr. Dryden," Gaston says solemnly. "Just think of all that he's accomplished. He's a Hall of Fame goaltender from his days with the Canadiens; he's a lawyer; he's a bestselling author. Mr. Dryden is very respected in the hockey industry. He was an excellent choice."

Dryden set out to find a replacement for Fletcher as GM, and his first choice was his former teammate Bob Gainey, who was managing the Dallas Stars. Gainey opted to remain in Dallas for personal reasons. In 1999, he and his Stars would celebrate a Stanley Cup championship. The next candidate was David Poile, but he opted instead to join the Nashville Predators, an expansion team slated to begin play in 1998-99, in the same capacity. Finally, on the eve of the '97-98 season, Dryden announced that he would assume the title of president/general manager, while decisions would be made by a four-man committee that also included assistant GMs Bill Watters and Anders Hedberg, as well as associate general manager Mike Smith, who had recently been GM of the Winnipeg Jets.

The Leafs made a splash by signing big free-agent defenceman Mattias Ohlund of the Vancouver Canucks to a five-year contract. However, Ohlund was a restricted free agent, meaning the Canucks had the right to match Toronto's offer. They did, and the Leafs missed out on a chance to make a significant improvement to their blueline.

Mike Murphy was retained as coach, and Mats Sundin was officially made the sixteenth captain in Maple Leafs history after the Leafs got his signature on a contract that put him among the highest-paid players in the NHL. There were no off-season trades, but a spate of free-agent signings included backup goalie Glenn Healy and forward Igor Korolev. At midseason, desperate for help on the power play, the Leafs sent a draft choice to the Carolina Hurricanes for defenceman Jeff Brown. In late March, he was flipped to Washington for rearguard Sylvain Cote.

There were hints of better days to come during the 1998 Winter Olympic Games at Nagano, Japan. For the first time, NHL players would appear in the Olympics – Sundin and 23-year-old second-year pro Fredrik Modin played well for Sweden, while on the Russian team, Sergei Berezin exploded for 6 goals in 6 games. At season's end, Leaf freshman Mike Johnson's 47 points tied Calder Trophy winner Sergei Samsonov of the Boston Bruins as the league's highest-scoring rookie. But as a team, the Leafs were weak on both sides of the ledger. Their output of 194 goals was the team's lowest – with the exception of the lockout-shortened 1994-95 season – since 1963-64. Meanwhile, despite the addition of the experienced Healy, who spelled Potvin in 21 games, their goals-against ranked sixth-worst in the NHL. The predictable result was a last-place finish in the Central Division and a second consecutive failure to make the playoffs.

The fans were tired of losing, the players were dissatisfied with their record, and Leaf management grew weary of defending itself. Where the front office had been timid a year ago, bold moves were about to be made to show that the Toronto Maple Leafs meant business. The addition of the Nashville Predators – and the scheduled entry of teams in Atlanta, Columbus and Minnesota – prompted the NHL to reorganize itself into six divisions, and Ken Dryden was successful in his bid to have the Leafs moved from the Western Conference to the Northeast Division of the Eastern Conference. The result was a decrease in travel for the team, which would save money and reduce wear and tear on the players. It would also provide the chance to rekindle traditional rivalries with the Montreal Canadiens and Buffalo Sabres, and to establish one with Ontario's other NHL team, the Ottawa Senators.

Then, on June 26, 1998, Pat Quinn was hired to replace Mike Murphy as coach. A former Leaf defenceman, Quinn had coached the Philadelphia Flyers, Los Angeles Kings and Vancouver Canucks and was twice named the NHL's coach of the year. He had also twice led teams to the Stanley Cup finals – in 1994, his upstart Vancouver Canucks took the heavily favoured New York Rangers to a seventh game. Like his boss Ken Dryden, Quinn also held a law degree. No less intriguing was the fact that, like Dryden, Quinn had been the president and general manager of the Canucks, although he protested that he had no interest in any role other than as coach.

With a proven winner behind the bench, the Toronto organization went to work improving the product on the ice. Their first move was a grand slam: on July 15, 1998, free-agent goaltender Curtis Joseph was signed from Edmonton. The second move was also a huge step, as Toronto signed left winger Steve Thomas, a former Marlboro and Leaf who last wore the blue and white in 1987. He rejoined the Leafs after a three-year stint with New Jersey, whose tight defensive system had cut his production to just 14 goals in 55 games in 1997-98. In Toronto, coach Quinn wanted to open things up offensively, and the club was gambling that Thomas – placed on a line with Mats Sundin – might regain his touch.

The acquisition of CuJo, as he came to be known to Toronto fans and press alike, meant the Leafs' net was getting crowded. They now had two starting goaltenders in Joseph and Potvin, as well as a reliable backup in Glenn Healy. As he commanded a larger salary than Healy, it was apparent that Potvin would be the odd man out. The player they called "the Cat" suffered in silence throughout training camp and the beginning of the 1998-99 schedule, then went home to Montreal and waited for the Leafs to trade him. After a couple of false starts, he got his wish on January 9, 1999, when he was sent to the New York Islanders in exchange for Bryan Berard, a third-year defenceman who had won the Calder Trophy in 1997. Berard, a first-overall draft pick in 1995, owned excellent offensive skills and, with his 22nd birthday still two months away, he had the potential to be the Leafs' power-play quarterback for years to come. "Felix was a really good goalkeeper," Tommy reflects, "but he had to have a good team in front of him. In '92 and '93, he had that, and he shone, but without that kind of team Felix looked pretty ordinary some nights. CuJo is one of the league's best. He enjoys playing in Toronto and is good to the community, and in return, the fans are very good to him."

On February 12, 1999, the Maple Leaf organization held a parade that led from Maple Leaf Gardens, at the corner of Church and Carlton streets, to the new Air Canada Centre near the foot of Bay Street. The next night, the Leafs ushered in a new era with a 6-2 loss to the Chicago Blackhawks. Coincidentally, the team had lost its first match at Maple Leaf Gardens to the Blackhawks, back in 1931. Over the balance of the season, the team would mount a 7-5-3 record in games at the ACC, indicating that they were taking some time to get used to their new home.

At the trade deadline, Toronto added Yanic Perreault, a centre who had begun his career in the Leafs organization. His specialties were winning face-offs and scoring timely goals, and he would rack up 15 points in 12 games the rest of the way. The Maple Leafs also dealt Jason Smith to Edmonton for a couple of draft choices. Smith was a solid defenceman whose positional play was sound but whose lack of speed meant he didn't fit in with Quinn's system, which required defencemen to make a rapid transition from defence to offence and move the puck up the ice.

Toronto made a quantum leap forward during the 1998-99 regular-season schedule. Coach Quinn placed second to Ottawa's Jacques Martin in the voting for the Jack Adams Award. The team set a club record with 45 wins and improved 28 points to 97, good for second place in the Northeast Division – also to Ottawa. Oddly, goals-against dropped by only six, but offensively the Leafs exploded for a league-leading 268 goals, an improvement of 74 over the previous year's production. Sergei Berezin emerged as a legitimate offensive force, netting 37 goals. Steve Thomas repaid the Leafs for their confidence in him, tabulating 28 goals and 73 points. Sundin was consistent as ever, leading the club with 52 assists and 83 points. Derek King, a veteran free-agent acquisition, added 24 markers, while youngsters Mike Johnson and Steve Sullivan each chipped in 20.

There were pleasant surprises on the blueline, too. Tomas Kaberle, drafted from Kladno in the Czech Republic, secured a spot on the Leafs blueline with his outstanding play in training camp. Poised far beyond his years, he supplied effective defence and showed great ability moving the puck. Daniil (Danny) Markov had been the 223rd player selected in the 1995 Entry Draft. An alumnus of Spartak Moscow, the 22-year-old showed how feisty he could be when opponents bore in on the Leafs' goal. He also owned a hard point shot.

After missing the playoffs for two years, the Leafs returned to postseason competition with a fire in their collective belly. Pitted against Philadelphia in the first round, the Leafs played hard, aggressive hockey. The defence trio of Yuskevich, Markov and Kaberle shone as the Leafs recovered from a 3-0 loss in game one to defeat the Flyers four games to two. In the second round, the upstart Leafs took on the injury-riddled Pittsburgh Penguins. They again came back from a shutout loss in game one (2-0 this time) to win the series in six games. With that victory Toronto advanced to the conference finals – this time in the Eastern Conference rather than the Western – for the first time since 1994. The Buffalo Sabres, led by the acrobatic goaltending of Dominik Hasek, would provide the opposition. Oddly, despite their geographic proximity – the cities sit 100 miles apart at opposite ends of the Queen Elizabeth Way – the clubs had never before met in the playoffs. The Sabres eliminated the Leafs, four games to one.

Associate GM Mike Smith's contract was set to expire in late June, and he let it be known that he wanted the title and responsibilities of general manager. President and GM Ken Dryden balked, and Smith left the organization, later resurfacing in the Chicago Blackhawks' front office. A couple of weeks later, on July 14, 1999, Dryden relinquished the title of GM to coach Pat Quinn, who would become the only current NHL executive with the dual role, and the first to do both jobs for Toronto since Punch Imlach.

The off-season was quiet, the only major roster move being the signing of free agent Jonas Hoglund, who would surprise Leaf fans by scoring 29 goals on Sundin's left wing. Things picked up as the season got under way. Nikolai Antropov, a 19-year-old, six-foot five-inch centre from Kazakhstan, was another surprise. Originally ticketed for the minor leagues – and maybe even the junior ranks – Antropov cracked the lineup early in the season when an injury to Mats Sundin provided an opportunity. When Dimitri Yushkevich decided to hold out, underachieving forward Fredrik Modin was traded to Tampa Bay for defenceman Cory Cross. When Yushkevich returned to the lineup about a week into the season, the displaced Sylvain Cote was dispatched to the Chicago Blackhawks. Although he had recorded a pair of 20-goal seasons for the Leafs, Derek King had become expendable and was traded to St. Louis for a minor leaguer and future considerations on October 20. A day later, Toronto took a chance on Boston right winger Dmitri Khristich, who had taken the Bruins to salary arbitration and won. But Boston still refused to meet his price, so Pat Quinn sent them a second-round draft choice for the right to sign Khristich at the salary Boston wouldn't tender. Another displaced forward, Steve Sullivan, was placed on waivers and the Blackhawks snapped him up on October 23. Sullivan would finally get the chance to play regularly in Chicago, becoming the Hawks' scoring leader in scoring in 2000-01.

In January, Wendel Clark, released by the Blackhawks, returned to Toronto for a third tour of duty. And the lineup was set when Mike Johnson and defensive prospect Marek Posmyk were sent to Tampa Bay for gritty forward Darcy Tucker. The Leafs' record of 45-27-7 was identical to the season before, but this year, the NHL had begun awarding teams a bonus point for each overtime loss; Toronto had lost three games in overtime, so under the league's new math they ended up with a team record 100 points. Perhaps even more significantly, the Leafs finished atop their division – their first regular-season title since 1962-63.

In the first round of playoffs, Toronto met the Ottawa Senators. The two clubs were already divisional and geographic rivals, but the animosity between them had intensified because Ottawa players were connected with an uncanny number of Leaf injuries. In the fourth game of the regular season, a Radek Bonk slapshot hit the instep of Mats Sundin's foot, fracturing his ankle and causing the Leafs captain to miss nine games. It was during his absence that Nik Antropov got his chance to crack the Leafs lineup and Dmitri Khristich was obtained. In November, Pittsburgh Penguins goalie Tom Barrasso struck Yanic Perreault across the arm with his goal stick, breaking the centreman's arm. By the time the playoffs arrived, Barrasso was tending goal for the Senators.

But these were trivial compared to the Bryan Berard tragedy. At 15:20 of the second period of their game on March 11, Marion Hossa shot the puck. As he followed through, his stick caught Leaf defenceman Berard in the face. Berard collapsed to the ice as a pool of blood formed around him. He was rushed to Toronto for emergency surgery. He would undergo several operations, but doctors were not able to completely restore the sight in his right eye. Hossa was assessed a double-minor penalty; Berard's career was over – he retired, reluctantly, during the 2000-01 season. In October 1999, just after he had ended a holdout and signed a two-year contract, Berard was interviewed by the Canadian Press. Pointing out that neither he nor coach Quinn wanted to rush his return to the lineup after he had missed training camp, Berard made a statement that, in retrospect, has an eerie ring: "The last thing we want is for an injury to happen."

In game one of the Ottawa-Toronto playoff series, Senators defenceman Jason York slammed Perreault into the boards, tearing the ligaments in the Leaf's left knee and ending his season. Antropov was also injured later in the series. Toronto held on to outscore Ottawa 17-10 and win the war of attrition by four games to two. Alyn McCauley and Jeff Farkas took Perreault and Antropov's places in the lineup, and the depleted Leafs managed to win game one of their second-round series against the New Jersey Devils before being eliminated in six games.

Quinn's diagnosis was that the Senators – and especially the Devils – had pushed his team around. It was time to add some grit to the lineup. In July 2000, forwards Gary Roberts and Shayne Corson were signed as free agents, and a month later, defenceman Dave Manson came aboard. Meanwhile, Wendel Clark retired, Kris King was given his release and Kevyn Adams was lost in the expansion draft.

The city was buzzing in the wake of the Roberts signing. The excitement even got to captain Mats Sundin, who vowed he would finish among the NHL's top five scorers in 2000-01. In his heyday with Calgary, Roberts, a Toronto native, could be counted on to deliver 40 goals and rack up a couple of hundred penalty minutes a year. But nerve damage in his neck reduced him to 8 games in 1994-95 and 35 in 1995-96 before sidelining him completely for a year. He returned to active duty in 1997, and while the numbers were lower than they had been, he still possessed above-average toughness and touch around the net.

The 2000-01 season would be frustrating for Leafs fans. The Maple Leafs roared out of the starting gate, posting a 12-7-3 record through the first quarter of the season. But then, on November 29, the St. Louis Blues came to the Air Canada Centre. Toronto took a 5-0 lead into the second intermission, but seemed transfixed as the Blues scored goal after goal in the third, tying the score and then winning the game, 6-5, in overtime. The Leafs seemed to shake that one off, going 5-0-1 over their next six games, but they immediately lost six of the next seven, including a 5-0 drubbing by Pittsburgh in the first game of Mario Lemieux's remarkable comeback. For the rest of the season, Toronto was unable to string together more than two wins in a row.

Quinn couldn't find any line combinations that clicked. Khristich scored only three goals in 27 games and was traded to Washington in December for a third-round draft choice. Steve Thomas lost a quarter of the season to injury and ended up with only 8 goals on the year – his worst output in a full NHL season to date. Sundin failed to average a point a game, let alone crack the top five – he finished 38th in the league scoring derby. Igor Korolev, distracted by the deaths of both of his parents during the season, netted only 10 goals. Fans grew impatient and booed the team several times through the course of the season. At Christmastime, the Leafs had been battling for first place in the division, but as the schedule wound down there was some doubt as to whether this team, which had been billed as "built for the playoffs," would even qualify for the postseason. Toronto barely hung on, finishing seventh in the Eastern Conference, just two points ahead of the Carolina Hurricanes – who made the playoffs – and the Boston Bruins, who didn't.

"It was frustrating," admits Tommy. "Here you had a team that couldn't win during the regular season, then, almost like a miracle of science, a different team showed up for the playoffs." For a second year in a row, the Leafs drew Ottawa in the first round, but this year they wouldn't even let the Senators touch the puck. Toronto won the series in four straight games. Repeating another pattern from the year before, the Leafs went on to meet the New Jersey

Devils in the second round. They won the first two games, and the city was ready to hold the Stanley Cup parade right then and there. But the Devils bore down and beat the Leafs four games to two. The New Jersey Devils would progress through the playoff rounds to challenge the Colorado Avalanche for the Stanley Cup. "Many fans in Toronto felt that if the Leafs could have beaten the Devils, it would have ended up being a Toronto-Colorado Stanley Cup final," states Gaston. "I'm not so sure that that could have happened, but it sure is great to think about, isn't it?"

CHAPTER NINETEEN

Air Canada Centre

"It came as a bit of a surprise when we heard that the Maple Leafs were going to move to the Air Canada Centre," admits Tom Gaston. "From time to time over the past few years, we had heard that there was a possibility the team might move. One story I heard said they were going to build a new arena at Yonge Street and Highway 401. Another said out by the airport in Downsview. Either of those locations would have been difficult for Ruth and me to get to, so I probably wouldn't have renewed my season tickets.

"Come to think of it, I've never really considered giving up my season tickets at any time during the past sixty years. When I had problems with my ticker in '78, the doctor knew I enjoyed hockey games, and asked me if I got overly excited watching the Leafs play. I said I get excited, but I'm not the kind of guy who jumps up and down – I'm more of a studious fan. So the doctor told me I could keep going to hockey games as long as I kept my emotions under control. The prices keep going up, and I have to think someday I may not be able to afford them anymore, but for now, I enjoy going to the games so much.

"When the announcement came that the Leafs would be moving in with the Raptors at the old postal delivery building on Bay Street at Lakeshore Boulevard, I had to laugh. Having worked just a block away for most of my life, I was already well acquainted with the building. My job had been in shipping, and if there was something special that needed to be sent out, I would run it over to that post office. Now, I'd be making the same sort of trip – at the end of the work day, I'd be leaving the Hockey Hall of Fame, which was roughly in the same spot where I worked, and walking over to the Air Canada Centre for games. It's funny how my life has been centred around that specific block of Toronto," says Tom in amazement.

"As moving day grew closer, I sat back and realized that I had very mixed emotions about it. It wasn't like 1931, when the Leafs left Arena Gardens for Maple Leaf Gardens. Arena Gardens was really a barn. There was nothing at all special about it. Maple Leaf Gardens was a palace compared to the Leafs' old home. And they needed to move the Leafs back then because of the size of the place. But in 1999, I thought Maple Leaf Gardens was still a grand old building. It had been well maintained and had so much history attached to it. But I guess it had to happen some time. The added box seats would bring a lot more money into the organization.

"Christine Simpson – one of my dear friends – was working at Sportsnet. She called and asked if she and a camera crew could follow Ruth and me for that last game at the Gardens on February 13. We thought that was wonderful, and of course we love Christine, so we said 'Yes, of course.' Ruth and I left at our usual time – about 4:00. We went downtown and had a nice dinner of fish and chips. Then, Christine and the Sportsnet crew met us at Carlton and Yonge for our final walk to Maple Leaf Gardens. The camera followed us down busy Carlton Street, through the excited crowd to the doors of Maple Leaf Gardens. We walked in through that main entrance. I don't know if you remember, but the Leafs had a huge mural painted on the wall in the lobby. It was a collection of scenes from the Leafs' history. Anyway, we took a good look at that wall. There is a part of the mural that has two tickets on it. Ruth and I were honoured when they used our seat numbers for the tickets painted in the lobby."

Tom speaks excitedly about that last game. "The camera followed us up to our seats in the greys. So many people said hi to us that night – I felt like a bit of a celebrity. In fact, I had been asked to do a fair number of interviews about the closing of the Gardens. I spoke to CFRB radio. And Joe Bowen, the Leafs' play-by-play announcer, interviewed me for a show on the FAN 590, a special called 'Farewell to the Gardens.' A TV station from Buffalo did an interview with me. The Toronto Sun had done a piece on me and MasterCard interviewed me for a commercial they would be doing. But this night, a lot of the fans made a fuss, too. Some had seen me around the Gardens through the years and just knew I was a longtime fan, and others had seen me or heard me in the interviews. Christine and the camera crew followed us right up to our seats, and then we did an interview in the seats before the game. It was fun to talk to the media about my favourite subject!

"The game itself took me back to opening night of the Maple Leaf Gardens. At the time, I didn't think of it as history, the way I do today," admits Gaston. "It was only appropriate that Toronto would take on the Chicago Blackhawks in the last game. After all, it was the Chicago Blackhawks who played the very first game at the Gardens. Now, usually when there is a ceremonial face-off, the teams send their captains to centre ice for the puck to be dropped. The Leafs sent Mats Sundin, their captain, to take the face-off, but Chicago didn't send Chris Chelios. Instead, Dougie Gilmour skated to centre ice, and the fans gave him a huge ovation. The puck was going to be dropped by two players who played in that first-ever game at Maple Leaf Gardens – Red Horner representing the Leafs and Mush March for the Blackhawks. March had scored the very first goal at Maple Leaf Gardens, the little son of a gun! The two warriors got a standing ovation from the crowd."

The smile refuses to leave Tom's lips. "One of the things I remember is the number of flash bulbs that went off throughout the night. Everybody had a camera with them. Every time something historic took place, the arena would brighten with camera flashes.

"When Paul Morris, the public-address announcer, said, 'Last minute of play in this period,' the crowd stood and gave the Leafs a standing ovation right until the game ended. The game was a bit of a stinker, and Chicago beat us 6-2. Bob Probert of the Blackhawks scored the last goal ever to be scored at Maple Leaf Gardens.

"An usher came up to our seats and got me and Ruth and took us down to the ice surface. We watched the Leaf alumni form a ring around centre ice as they were introduced and the crowd applauded. I don't think anyone will ever forget Red Horner, the oldest living Maple Leaf player – and their captain between 1938 and 1940 – handing the flag to our current Leaf captain, Mats Sundin. It was a passing of the torch, from one generation to the next.

"After the alumni celebration ended, the arena began to clear. But Ruth and I were asked to join a party on the ice surface. It was very exclusive, and we were thrilled and honoured to be asked. It was for players and their families plus special invited guests, and somehow, someone thought to ask us. We wandered around and talked to a lot of the players. The first one we spent time with was Mike Gartner – what a class act! Christine Simpson was there, too. We stayed until 12:30, and only left then because we were afraid we'd miss our bus."

Tom is asked to draw comparisons between the two buildings and the two different eras. "Well, you have to remember that I go back a very long way," says Gaston. "When I started to go to Leaf games, my ticket was around a dollar. Now I pay $35 for each seat. During intermissions in the earlier years, a band would entertain the crowd with big band music. Later, an organ replaced the bands. But now, the music is pre-recorded and I find it kind of loud. Since the '60s, the voice over the public-address system had been Paul Morris. I used to call him 'Golden Tonsils.' He had a very pleasant voice. Actually, I got to know Paul through the years – I'd frequently run into him in the corridors of the Gardens before the game, and we'd chat about this and that. The announcer they have now at the ACC, Andy Frost, is good – but very different from Mr. Morris."

"When I started going to the Gardens, they sold hot dogs, peanuts, popcorn, ice cream and cold drinks. We couldn't really afford to buy food at the game, so I'd buy a big bag of peanuts before we went and sneak it in under my jacket. They didn't start serving alcohol at MLG until the '90s. Now at the Air Canada Centre, they've got the same foods but they've also got hamburgers, submarine sandwiches, corned beef sandwiches and sushi.

"In the early days, the rink used to be flooded by hand with a big fire hose. They scraped the ice by hand between periods, but they wouldn't flood at every intermission. Then Paul Morris's dad, Doug Morris, came up with a contraption that worked beautifully to flood the ice surface. It was a sort of wagon with a barrel on the back that was pulled around the rink by a couple of guys. It would spread an even layer of water over the ice surface. It wasn't until much later that Zambonis came onto the scene. And now they use two Zambonis so that they can have contests and other forms of entertainment between periods.

"Speaking of entertainment, Conn Smythe used to have soldiers demonstrate manoeuvres on the ice during the war. I don't know what was more entertaining, though – watching the manoeuvres or seeing the soldiers slip on the ice!"

"When the Gardens first opened, the grey seats were just benches. After the war, they put in actual seats. And the seat colours, from highest price to lowest, were red, blue, green and grey. It wasn't until the '60s that the gold seats came to the Gardens. The ACC has platinum seats with special privileges, as well as gold, red, blue, green and grey. Except now the greys are called purples to tie in with the Raptors' team colours.

"In the earliest days, there were no face-off circles – they came later. There were just red dots on the ice. There was no red goal line, either, and the centre red line didn't come in until the 1940s. The Leafs always had a big maple leaf at centre ice. Now there's also advertising on the ice and on the boards. Oh yeah, and up until the 1950s there was just chicken wire above the boards surrounding the ice surface. Now they've got seamless glass. It sure is safer for the spectators, but I don't think it's half as fun. There used to be some wild feuds with fans needling the players through the chicken wire.

"The Gardens didn't get escalators until the 1950s. That was a huge deal." Tom laughs as he pulls up another image. "And do I need to remind the gentlemen about those awful troughs in the washrooms up until the 1970s?"

Tommy concludes, "When you've been going to games for as long as I have – it's more than seventy years now – everything has changed. The hockey is different, the arenas are different. Heck, the world is different! But I've enjoyed the progress and think that anything that is done to better the game is welcome."

CHAPTER TWENTY

Hockey Hall of Fame

"It's funny how small the world truly is. I had a job for the better part of my working life at Canadian Fairbanks Morse, located at 26-28 Front Street West in Toronto, and did my banking in the big, beautiful old bank at the northwest corner of Yonge and Front. Started there in 1938. Today, that branch of the Bank of Montreal is the Great Hall of the Hockey Hall of Fame, where the Stanley Cup and all the other trophies are kept, and where the Honoured Members selected for the Hall have their photos and names displayed.

"I've been volunteering at the Hockey Hall of Fame several days a week for more than 22 years. Whenever hockey players, referees or builders (those people who helped create and strengthen the game off the ice) are inducted into the Hockey Hall of Fame, they sign the huge Tom Gaston book, which is displayed in a glass case just to the left of the Stanley Cup. I was down there today, and the book was opened to the page from 1999, where you could see the signatures of the three Honoured Members inducted that year: Scotty Morrison in the Builders category, Andy Van Hellemond in the Referees category, and of course the retired player honoured that year: number 99, Wayne Gretzky."

The plaque on the case holding the "Tom Gaston" book reads:

> In Honour of Tom Gaston
> A Great Friend and Volunteer
> of the
> Hockey Hall of Fame and Museum
> Dedicated Friday, November 4, 1994

"The old office building where I worked is long gone, and is now a courtyard in BCE Place where I often sit and watch the world go by. Gee, back when I started at Fairbanks Morse, in wintertime I would park my car in the lot of a warehouse market. It cost me fifty cents a week. Yesterday I ran into Conn Smythe's grandson, Tom Smythe, and he told me it cost him $24 to park for just over two hours in a lot under the corner of Yonge and Front. My word, times sure have changed." That warehouse market is now the site of the Humming-bird Centre, a performing arts venue on the southeast corner of Yonge and Front, kitty-corner to the Hockey Hall of Fame.

"After I'd been at Fairbanks Morse a while, a couple of the guys struck out on their own and started their own company," Tom says. "It was called Upton, Bradeen & James, and was located in Don Mills at 30 Railside Road. They asked me to come join their company, so I did. And that's where I retired.

"Now, retirement wasn't exactly my decision," Tommy is quick to point out. "I was feeling lousy, so Ruth made me go to the doctor. He checked my heart and said, 'Tom, you and I have to talk. Your heart is under a lot of stress – that's why you feel the way you do. You are not going back to work.' But I said, 'Doc, I have to work. I can't afford to retire.' He said very bluntly, 'Tom, you can't afford to die, either,' and walked out of the room. That's just how frankly he put it!

"I told Ruth, and we went home. Ruth called up my work and told them we were coming over. Ruth marched me into the boss's office, and before I could say a word, she said, 'Tom has finished working here, effective immediately. The doctor has told Tom the stress on his heart is killing him, so as of today, Tom Gaston has retired.' I'll bet my jaw was on the desk, but I have to say I honestly don't think I would have been able to tell the boss if Ruth hadn't been with me.

"It's funny, but after that I felt just great. I guess stress really can make you sick. After I retired, I felt better than I had in twenty years!"

Tom explains that it wasn't long afterward that he got involved with the Hall. "I was puttering around the house and decided that I had way too much stuff cluttering the place. I got a big box and started to put my hockey stuff into it. There was fifty years' worth of Toronto Maple Leaf calendars, programs from the '30s and '40s, all kinds of scrapbooks and various artifacts. I figured, 'Why not donate all this to the Hockey Hall of Fame?'"

The idea of a Hockey Hall of Fame was initiated in 1941 by W.A. Hewitt, George Slater and Captain James Sutherland – a triumvirate appointed by the Canadian Amateur Hockey Association to uncover hockey's beginnings. The three men suggested that a hall of fame be set up in Kingston, Ontario, one of the sites often named as the location of the first hockey game. The CAHA, in tandem with the NHL, liked the idea and began to organize the Hockey Hall of Fame in 1943. Founding members of the Hall's board of governors included NHL team executives Conn Smythe of Toronto and Art Ross of Boston. Although the new organization didn't have the money needed to build a home for the Hall, a number of players were enshrined in 1945, including Dan Bain, Hobey Baker, Russell Bowie, Charlie Gardiner, Eddie Gerard, Frank McGee, Howie Morenz, Tommy Phillips, Harvey Pulford, Art Ross, Hod Stuart and Georges Vezina. Lord Stanley of Preston and Sir Montagu Allan – both of whom are immortalized on hockey championship trophies – were enshrined as builders.

The lack of funding put an end to the dream of a Hockey Hall of Fame located in Kingston. Years went by, and additions were made to the honour roll of players, builders and officials in 1945, '47, '50 and '52, but still there was no place to visit – no shrine to welcome the fans who may have wished to learn about and appreciate the exploits and ideas of the greatest athletes and their patrons. Finally, on August 26, 1961, Prime Minister John Diefenbaker of Canada and Livingston Merchant, the U.S. ambassador to Canada, cut the ribbon to officially open the Hockey Hall of Fame's new facility, located on the grounds of the Canadian National Exhibition in Toronto. Cyclone Taylor and forty-two other members of the Hall were on hand to christen the shrine.

The Hockey Hall of Fame was originally open solely during the three weeks of the Canadian National Exhibition, from mid August until the Labour Day weekend. Later, it was opened on weekends, and eventually became a full-time museum. Bobby Hewitson, who had grown up playing with the Conacher boys at Toronto's Jesse Ketchum Public School, was named the Hall's first curator. Hewitson had served as an excellent referee, and later referee-in-chief of the NHL, while writing about sports for the Toronto Telegram. After retiring from his on-ice duties, he became a member of the Hot Stove League –a feature that aired between periods of the national radio broadcasts of Toronto Maple Leaf hockey games, and one that later made the transition to television. Bobby Hewitson was inducted into the Hockey Hall of Fame as an official in 1963.

Maurice "Lefty" Reid was appointed curator of the Hockey Hall of Fame in 1968, succeeding Bobby Hewitson. Reid, who had also been a sportswriter for the Telegram, oversaw both the Hockey Hall of Fame and the Canadian Sports Hall of Fame at the time. "We were located on the Exhibition grounds," Lefty recalls. "When we first opened, it was just the caretaker and me, and we had two museums open two hours each day, seven days a week. The NHL financed the Hockey Hall of Fame, and we were working on a shoestring budget, to say the least."

Tom Gaston remembers the day he loaded the car with some of his hockey souvenirs and drove them to the Hall's location at the CNE. "Lefty Reid was a great guy, and when I asked him if he wanted my hockey collection, his eyes lit up and he said, 'Absolutely! We'd love to have your collection!'"

Lefty continues the story: "Tommy called me up one day and said he had some old hockey materials – did the Hockey Hall of Fame want them? I went up to his house, and saw all kinds of things – calendars, programs, newspaper clippings, pennants – that he wanted to give to the Hall. I was delighted! He had recently retired – I don't think he had been well – and he also asked if I could use an extra pair of hands around the Halls. Sure I could!

"We had added a couple of other people to the staff by this point, but handling all the work was a real challenge. That's why volunteers were so important. Tommy was ready to help in any way possible. At first, he would come in two or three days a week, and seemed to really be thriving on it. I truly believe that volunteering at the Hockey Hall of Fame added years to his life. He was a delightful person to have around, with a real streak of humility. He never did anything to draw attention to himself – that was just the kind of guy he was. I knew he'd always be a credit to the organization if he was representing the Hockey Hall of Fame. There just aren't enough people like Tommy Gaston in the world."

Lefty Reid worked for twenty-one years to develop the Hall, making enormous progress in establishing it as a world-class museum and resource centre. Now retired, he lives in the vicinity of Peterborough, Ontario.

In 1979 the Hockey Hall of Fame acknowledged Tom Gaston's sizeable contribution. "Ruth and I were very excited, because they held a press conference at the Hall to recognize my donations," Tommy says. "The same day I was being recognized, so was Ace Bailey for donating his scrapbooks. He was one of my favourites from the early days of the Leafs, and we actually became pretty good friends through the years. Also at the Hall that day were Andy Bathgate and Harry Howell – they were the first two players I met at the Hockey Hall of Fame. Bathgate had been inducted in 1978, and Harry Howell in 1979. Both were great New York Ranger players. I remember Ruth saying how handsome they both were, and I had to laugh."

During the CNE days, Tom was put to work in the library. "I would also sit outside the Hall and sell calendars," remembers Gaston. "And Lefty Reid used to get a lot of Honoured Members coming to the Hall to sign autographs, so I would act as host for the players, making sure they were well taken care of."

By the 1980s, it was clear that the Hockey Hall of Fame had outgrown its CNE location. After years of accumulating invaluable and irreplaceable items of historical interest from fans like Tommy Gaston, the Hall's collections had grown too large to display properly, or even to store. Ian "Scotty" Morrison was appointed to secure a new, larger location for the Hockey Hall of Fame.

Like Bobby Hewitson, Scotty Morrison had been an NHL on-ice official. After his refereeing career came to a close, Morrison was named the NHL's referee-in-chief and later the league's vice president of officiating. Scotty Morrison remembers Tom Gaston a little differently than most. "Even before I officially met Tom Gaston, I knew who he was. Before Toronto games, I would head down to Maple Leaf Gardens early and sit in the coffee shop with my wife. Every second or third game, an older gentleman would walk over to me and ask me the very same question every time: "How are you tonight, Mr. Morrison? Who's refereeing this evening?' Same routine, every single time!

"I would always answer, and I never did find out what the point of the question was. Lo and behold, ten years later, I was appointed vice president of project development for the Hockey Hall of Fame and was spending a fair bit of time at the Hall of Fame's location on the Exhibition grounds. There I would see this older man – and I knew he was familiar, but I couldn't put a finger on why. Then one day it dawned on me – 'That's the guy who always asked me who was refereeing the Leaf game!' We had a good laugh over that."

Tom speaks about Scotty Morrison in glowing terms: "I remember watching Scotty Morrison as a referee. He looked so small out there, but boy, did he ever do a great job. When Scotty became referee-in-chief, Ruth and I used to run into him in the Gardens coffee shop fairly regularly – he was always so nice. After years of approaching him, asking him who the referee would be that night, one day I went into the coffee shop on my own. 'Where's your wife?' Scotty asked. I told him she had had some troubles with her heart, which was true. But then I said, 'The trouble is, the refereeing is so darned bad, it gave her a heart attack!' Scotty just stood there and didn't know what to say, but when he saw me start to crack a smile, I think he laughed out of relief as much as anything!"

Morrison valued Tom's contributions as a volunteer at the Hockey Hall of Fame. "I used to kid him a lot," he says. "If he came in at 9:15, I'd say, 'Tommy, you're late this morning!' Or if he left midafternoon, I'd catch him leaving and joke, 'Uh, Tom – are you working a short day today? That's not the kind of behaviour we expect from a high-salaried employee!' Of course, he was volunteering his time, so we were delighted with any time he could give the Hall, but the two of us would have a good laugh over that. Everybody relates to Tom as soon as they meet him. He just has that presence about him."

Morrison also remembers Tom's work in correcting an oversight and getting Lionel Conacher inducted into the Hall. "Tom and Jim Hughes were absolutely determined to get him recognized by the Hockey Hall of Fame's selection committee. Jim Hughes was another volunteer at the Hockey Hall of Fame – his son Pat played for the Edmonton Oilers. Tommy and Jim realized that, not only was Lionel Conacher a great hockey player, he was a superb athlete. The two of them felt that Conacher had been missed by the Hall, so they put their total commitment into compiling all the relevant statistics for the selection committee. They took what could have been a fairly tedious job and did it with such passion and intensity – just as they did all their work for the Hall. When the selection committee announced that Lionel Conacher would be added to the Hockey Hall of Fame in the Veterans category, Tommy and Jim were giddy. And it made me feel wonderful, too. The Veterans category was instituted for situations exactly like that of Lionel Conacher."

"In the last year at the old Hockey Hall of Fame, we had a Christmas party at the Old Mill Restaurant in the west end," recounts Tommy. "Mr. Morrison got up and made a beautiful speech, then presented me with a bronze plaque as a lifetime member of the Hockey Hall of Fame! Well, I'm a pretty sensitive guy at the best of times, but I had to take my handkerchief and wipe away a few tears when I got that award. I would have to say it's the award that makes me most proud."

Scotty Morrison was chairman and chief executive officer of the Hockey Hall of Fame, and was instrumental in securing the Hall's current location at the corner of Yonge and Front in Toronto. He was inducted into the Hockey Hall of Fame as a builder in 1999. Today, he enjoys life in Ontario's Haliburton region. He remains on the Hall's board of directors as well as its executive committee, and he dearly cherishes his memories of his outstanding tenure.

The current president of the Hockey Hall of Fame is Jeff Denomme. Having started as an intern with the Hall when it was at its CNE location, Denomme has worked his way through the ranks, and has been piloting the Hockey Hall of Fame as it entered into the 21st century. "Tom Gaston's passion for hockey is exemplified through his longtime contributions as a volunteer of the Hockey Hall of Fame. His work in the Resource Centre has made a positive impact on the Hall's successful transition from the CNE Grounds to BCE Place in 1993, and its continued growth and development. I have always appreciated Tom's personal encouragement and his dedication to the preservation of the history of the game."

The Hockey Hall of Fame moved into its current location in the heart of downtown Toronto, reopening with much pomp and ceremony on June 18, 1993. "The city closed Yonge and Front streets," Tom comments. "All of the Honoured Members were invited back to Toronto, and they rode in open convertibles from the Royal York Hotel – a few blocks west along Front Street – to the Hall of Fame. There was a road hockey game in progress on the streets, and then the Hall held the world's biggest face-off to help launch the new location. Each of the Honoured Members had a hockey stick and they stood on the street right at the corner, and then a giant puck was dropped. It was a lot of fun! I talked to so many of the Honoured Members – guys like the Richard brothers, Frank Mahovlich, Johnny Bower and Bernie Geoffrion. I knew many of them from the old days at the CNE."

Tom Gaston gets a little melancholy: "For me, it was like going back home. That area was a significant part of my youth. I worked right beside where the Hockey Hall of Fame is located, and did my banking where the Stanley Cup sits. In the food court on the lower level, I can point out the exact spot where I lost my eye. This is where my professional life started."

"I remember it took quite a long time to prepare the new location for the move," states Gaston. "There was painting and cleaning to be done, as well as a lot of renovations. Once we moved into BCE Place, I started to bring Ruth with me to the Hockey Hall of Fame. She volunteered with me in the Resource Centre – she would collect all the mail sent to the Honoured Members in care of the Hockey Hall of Fame, and re-route it to their homes. She also sorted and filed press clippings, and she would keep all the business cards properly filed for Phil Pritchard, the director of the Resource Centre. I was doing some filing, too, but I also relieved the guys in the Hall at the exit where you leave the museum and enter the store. I would do that two to three hours a day during lunch hours."

The day-to-day operation of an organization such as the Hockey Hall of Fame relies heavily upon volunteers like Tom and Ruth Gaston. Another who brings her own charm and passion for hockey to the Hall of Fame is Anne Klisanich. Anne was just 19 years old when her brother, Bill Barilko, departed on his ill-fated fishing trip in the summer of 1951. Today she is a charming grandmother, having lost none of her zest for life nor her attractiveness. She speaks eloquently of her friends, the Gastons: "On Tuesday, September 24, 1996 – my very first day at the Hockey Hall of Fame – Craig Campbell, the manager of the Resource Centre and Archives, took me around and introduced me to all the pleasant staff members of the Hockey Hall of Fame. I was particularly intrigued in meeting Tommy and Ruth Gaston, and I was blessed in knowing dear Ruth, a most pleasant, dignified and gracious lady.

"Tommy and Ruth have been great role models with their wonderful dedication to their families, their church, their community and their commitments as volunteers at the Hockey Hall of Fame," Anne continues. "My husband Emil became a volunteer in April 2000, and he has also gotten to know Tommy. Emil says Tommy's humour transcends this magnificent building. We always find our right place at the right time, and for us, it was meeting this remarkable couple, Tommy and Ruth, at the Hockey Hall of Fame. We hit the jackpot!"

On the days they spend at the Hall, Anne and Emil Klisanich work very hard. Yet, because of the legendary proportion assumed by the Stanley Cup-winning goal her brother scored in 1951 and the subsequent tragedy of his death, it seems that Anne is always making time to squeeze in an interview about her brother.

On May 1, 2001, the Toronto Maple Leafs heralded the fiftieth anniversary of the goal Bill Barilko scored to clinch the Stanley Cup for Toronto. Anne was escorted onto the ice at the Air Canada Centre prior to the Leafs' playoff game against the New Jersey Devils, accompanied by ten members of the 1950-51 Leaf squad that shared a dressing room with Bill Barilko that night. Four members of The Tragically Hip, the rock band which immortalized Barilko in the song "Fifty Mission Cap," presented both Anne Klisanich and the captain of that Leaf team, Sid Smith, with hand-written lyrics to the song, mounted in a beautiful display with the actual hockey card that inspired lead singer Gord Downie to write those lyrics.

Watching the proceedings from his seats in Section 306, Row 11, Seats 5 and 6 was Tom Gaston. Anne is eager to tell one more story about Tommy: "When the Maple Leafs moved to the Air Canada Centre, Tommy Gaston was fortunate enough to have his choice of just about any purple seat he wanted. He carefully chose the section and row, but specifically chose seats 5 and 6. I was touched and more than a little honoured to find that Tommy had chosen those seats to commemorate the two numbers that have been retired by the Toronto Maple Leafs: number 6 for Ace Bailey and number 5 for my brother Billy!"

Toronto sportscaster Bruce Barker, who is also the public-address announcer at home games for the Mississauga IceDogs of major junior hockey and the Toronto Rock lacrosse team, reveals how he benefited from Tom Gaston's bottomless well of hockey knowledge. "I had the distinct pleasure of working on a Hockey Hall of Fame acquisition group back in the mid '80s. Tommy gave me the best tour of the Hockey Hall of Fame I have ever had.

"It took us nearly four hours to go through everything, because for every item we looked at, Tom had a story about the game it was from or how the Hall had obtained the artifact. I can honestly say that Tommy Gaston was one of the best history teachers I ever had. He also taught me to respect the game and those who played it. Tommy Gaston has incredible passion for the game of hockey, and I am honoured to call him a friend."

Philip Pritchard joined the Hockey Hall of Fame in 1988 while it was still on the CNE grounds. Today he is the director of the Resource Centre and of acquisitions for the Hall. "From the first day I started at the Hockey Hall of Fame, Tommy treated me as a friend, a family member and a co-worker," attests Phil.

Within the Resource Centre at the Hockey Hall of Fame, Philip Pritchard oversees and nurtures an operation that gets an enormous amount of work done, but leaves room for people to have a lot of fun in the process. "Day in and day out, Tommy pushed his blue and white Maple Leafs on me," Pritchard says. "Every spring during the playoffs I would tease him, asking him which golf course the Maple Leafs would be playing on today. Tommy, being the dedicated fan he is, would say, 'Maybe next year' or 'We're just one or two players away, just wait and see.'

"Each year I wait," Pritchard smiles.

"Through dinners, banquets, induction ceremonies, parades and awards galas, I have learned more about the history of Toronto Maple Leafs from Tommy than any book could tell me – and I thought I was supposed to be the historian," laughs Pritchard. "I have heard all about King, Conacher, Turk, Teeder and many more. With each one of them, Tommy has an untold story that one could listen to for hours. I used to tell him, 'Put the stories into words, it would be a great book.' For a while in the late '80s and early '90s, I had Tom writing in the Hockey Hall of Fame's quarterly newsletter, Teammates. Tommy wrote a feature called 'A Voice from the Stands.'"

Philip Pritchard knows Tommy Gaston professionally as well as anyone. He has even memorized Tommy's inimitable daily routine. "Tommy comes into the Hockey Hall of Fame resource centre and never fails to make his regular stops along the way. First, to the closet to hang his jacket; then to the coffee room for his morning pick-me-up. Then he stops at Jan Barrina's office for his morning smile. Jan is the manager of guest services. Eventually, he makes his way down to my office to try and convince me that this might be the year for the Leafs, or ask who I would trade if I was in charge of the Maple Leafs. I never have the answer, but I would often wonder how he knows all these possible trades and/or facts about the Maple Leafs before they are even public knowledge. He must have an inside track or something!

"Tommy keeps me posted on everything that he is going to donate to the Hockey Hall of Fame," Phil continues. "There are ticket stubs, programs, personal notes and equipment, just to name a few. That doesn't include all of the items he has already donated to various Halls of Fame around the country over the years.

"Tommy would say, 'You know boy, I don't know what I would do if it wasn't for you guys here at the Hall.' But I think it is more appropriate to say we wouldn't know what to do if Tommy wasn't coming around here. It has been thirteen years since I started working with Tommy, and for the Hockey Hall of Fame's sake, let's make it another thirteen. If I had a choice, Tommy could keep all of his souvenirs at home – I would much rather have Tommy. I guess that is not a good thing for a curator to say, but then again, not all curators get to enjoy the company of Tommy Gaston. Personally, I think Tommy is the real curator at the Hockey Hall of Fame. But that's okay, as there is no one else that I would rather learn from!

"As for the Maple Leafs and their golf – well, I don't really say that much anymore, as my team is usually golfing way before his team nowadays," he smirks.

Craig Campbell, the manager of the Resource Centre and Archives at the Hockey Hall of Fame, offers another kind of appreciation for Tom Gaston. "By definition, my role at the Hall is primarily concerned with photographs. Well, Tommy has handled more photographs than anybody at the Hockey Hall of Fame. There are more than 600,000 original negatives and transparencies archived in the Resource Centre, and I wouldn't be surprised if Tommy has handled 200,000 at one time or another. He has such a love for the game, and such generosity to the people around him.

"I have to laugh when I think about Tommy and Ruth working together at the Hall. Do you know that cartoon with the two lovebirds sitting on a telephone wire? That was them – just like that. Usually, they would sit in separate areas – after all, as Ruth would remind Tommy, they were there for business, not pleasure. Whenever Tom launched into one of his extended storytelling episodes, Ruth would make a comment or give Tommy a look that told him to get back in line. They were a wonderful couple. I miss Ruth – she used to take care of sorting my business cards, which was a nightmare job. Even today, every time I get a business card, I think of Ruth."

Marilyn Robbins takes care of customer and office services at the Hall, and she has worked closely with both Tom and Ruth through the years. "Ruth was an angel," smiles Marilyn. "She was just delightful to have around. Every once in a while, if Tommy was off talking about hockey and not paying enough attention to his work, she'd give him that look that mothers give their kids when they need them to behave. Tom would get right back to his desk and buckle down. They were the sweetest couple. But Ruth didn't spend every second with Tommy. She and the girls at the Hall enjoyed their time together, too. But as much as we enjoy having Tommy at the Hall, we really miss Ruth. She was very special."

"There is one story I think of the most when I think of Tommy," muses Craig Campbell. "When he was a working man, it didn't matter how the day went, he always looked forward to getting home. He'd walk up the steps to his house, open the door, and the kids would be there, all excited that Dad was home. If the day had been hellish, it didn't matter anymore. Those little faces erased all the difficulties of the day. I'll always remember Tommy telling me that, because that's something that's important to me, too."

After nearly twenty-three years of volunteering at the Hockey Hall of Fame, Tom Gaston can still be found in the Resource Centre three or four days each week, dressed immaculately in shirt, tie and jacket. He mingles amiably with the staff, most of whom were born thirty years after Tommy bought his first Toronto Maple Leaf season tickets. Quick with a joke, and not afraid to flirt harmlessly with the ladies on staff, Tom Gaston soon pulls his chair up to the desk in his cubicle and begins the task at hand. Some days, he'll stop long enough for a hamburger at lunch, but quite often he will work without a break. On most days his assigned role is to clip hockey-related stories from newspapers, but he lives for the opportunity to identify some long-forgotten player from in the annals of hockey, or to recount a tale meticulously pulled from the recesses of his incredible memory. Hockey players often stop by the Hockey Hall of Fame – sometimes on business but usually for pleasure. Most take the time to search out Tom and spend several minutes chatting about hockey. One day it will be Marcel Dionne; the next, Billy Harris. Red Kelly might make an appointment to visit the Hall, and then inevitably fall into conversation with Tom. Gordie and Colleen Howe stop by, and Colleen insists on getting a photo taken with Tommy. It's just another day in the life of the Toronto Maple Leafs' number one fan.

Ruth

"When Ruth died," Tom Gaston says, "the lamp of my life went out."

Ruth was born on May 10, 1921, in Crediton, Ontario, just north of London. Her father, R.A. Brook, was a minister who moved his family around frequently – the Brooks lived in smaller towns throughout southwestern Ontario, such as Milverton, Hensall and Goderich. "Her family were all well educated," Tom says. "Ruth was a nurse. It's funny, but she always wanted to be an airline stewardess – I guess they call them flight attendants now. And back then, to get a job as a stewardess on Air Canada, you had to be a registered nurse."

Before he met Ruth, Tommy says, "I had never dated very much. I'd gone out with a couple of girls, but there was never anything serious." After the injury that cost Tom the sight in his eye, there was a long period of bed rest. "I used to hear the church bells ringing from my hospital bed – they were wonderful to hear. They were the bells of Metropolitan United Church, right downtown in Toronto. Quite often, the minister from Metropolitan United would come by the hospital doing his rounds. He would often stick his head in to see me. I decided that once I got out of the hospital, I was going to attend that wonderful church. When I got out of the hospital, I went into Metropolitan United and sat in the very last row. But I was made to feel comfortable, and started to attend regularly.

"I started going to Young People's at Metropolitan United – a group of young adults would get together for Bible study and social activities. I really enjoyed it. I was living quite a long way north of the church, so the people I met there were all new to me, but they made me feel very welcome. I was a little self-conscious about my eye, but nobody at Young People's made any kind of fuss about it, so over time I came to forget that I wasn't just the same as everybody else."

The Reverend Dr. G. Malcolm Sinclair is the minister at Metropolitan United Church where Tom dutifully attends Sunday services, and he has played a significant role in the lives of both Tom and Ruth Gaston. Reverend Sinclair describes how Tom and Ruth met. "Ruth was a 'preacher's kid,' and Tom was ordered to Sunday school by a dutiful father. Tom first heard of the Metropolitan Church by literally hearing it – the bells of the church carillon soothed his soul. He made a promise to seek out the place. Upon his arrival, Tom was put to work. Someone invited him to usher. If Tom had a dark suit, white shirt, black shoes and a respectable tie, the job was his. Soon Tom was a regular on the church door.

"He first noticed Ruth when she came to a Young People's executive meeting in his family home. Afterward, he was invited by friends from church to go for coffee after a service. He would need to bring a date. Tom spotted Ruth across the room and he told his friend that if she would be his date, he would go with them. She did, and that was that."

Reverend Sinclair continues the story. "The two became inseparable. Ruth was living in the nurses' residence across from the church. Each evening, Tommy would hurry home from work, change his clothes and head back downtown to meet his girl. Ruth had to be back safely under lock and key by 10:00 p.m., so time was of the essence."

Tom concurs. "Sometimes, we'd head over to the Sunnyside Amusement Park. It's long gone now – they got rid of it when they built the Gardiner Expressway. If you drive along Lakeshore Boulevard, just west of the Exhibition grounds, you can still see a few remnants of Sunnyside – there's the Sunnyside Bathing Pavilion for one, and the Palais Royale was a spot where a lot of the big bands would come to play.

"We used to like to play miniature golf. Actually, we would do that quite often. Sometimes, we would go to the pictures. And we used to like to dance. We'd go up to Casa Loma, where a lot of the great bands would play. One way or another, Ruth and I would enjoy our evening, holding hands and having fun. But I would always make sure there was a little time left for some old-fashioned smooching!

"I never knew what Ruth saw in me," admits Tommy. "Her family was well educated and I'd only gone as far as public school. She met me after I lost my eye, too. I remember saying to her – and I was only half kidding – 'You must have picked me because all the good guys are overseas with the war.' And she said, 'No, Tommy. I did the choosing and I chose you.' I was forever grateful that such a remarkable woman was put in my life. To this day, every night I look heavenward and say, 'Thank you for sending me my wonderful wife!'"

Tom beams when he speaks of Ruth. "We had so much in common. There were three boys and a girl in the Brook family, and there were three boys and a girl in the Gaston family, too. Ruth and I shared the same values and the same ideas on how to raise our family. But just as important, Ruth and I both loved hockey. Ruth was a hockey fan from the word go. She had some hockey connections, too. She graduated from nursing school with Flash Hollett's sister, Genevieve, and she knew one of King Clancy's daughters after nursing at St. Mike's. But we started going to hockey games together fairly early on. I had already had my season tickets for a few years when I met Ruth in 1943. Ruth really enjoyed going to the games. In fact, when I used to talk about selling my seats for the odd game, she'd snap, 'Go ahead and sell your ticket, but don't you dare sell mine!' We would both laugh.

"Ruth was the first real girlfriend I ever had," Tom divulges. "I was a little bit older when I met her – I must've been 26 or so. We dated for quite a while. When we talked about getting married, Ruth wasn't sure that she was ready. We decided to break up, but after a couple of days apart, we both realized that we couldn't live without each other – especially for the rest of our lives. I remember Ruth saying they were the worst two days of her life, which made me feel pretty good.

"Ruth and I got married September 7, 1946. It's true – I insisted we get married on the seventh because that was my favourite number – it was King Clancy's number. It was a beautiful day, and Ruth was an absolutely beautiful bride. We got married at our home church, Metropolitan United, and had two ministers oversee the wedding. One was Dr. Peter Bryce, the senior minister of our church, but the other was Reverend R.A. Brook – Ruth's father. That was very special!"

Reverend Sinclair continues the story of Tom and Ruth. "They never missed a Sunday at worship. Church musical events and picnics gave them endless happy hours together. When Ruth and Tom married and began to raise a family, they decided to join a church closer to home. As their children met their school friends in the church basement, Tom took his familiar place at the church door. Years later, when the children were grown and gone, Tom and Ruth made their way back home to Metropolitan."

"We waited a few years to start our family, but when we did, we had two adorable little girls – Gayle and Jayne. It was a perfect little family," beams Tom. "It's funny how things develop. Jayne is very much like her mother, and Gayle takes after the Gaston side of the family." Gayle recalls winters as a young girl: "Dad would take us to Trace Manes Park in Leaside, where there was a real outdoor ice rink to skate on. Dad was pretty nifty on his blades, and he would do his best to teach us to skate."

"I know that I was born loving hockey," Jayne says. "I'm sure that if Gayle and I didn't love hockey, we would have been put up for adoption!"

Tommy picks up the conversation. "When the girls got a little older, I'd take one of them to one game, then the other girl would go with me to another game later on." Jayne has fond memories of attending Leaf games. "The times that Dad took me to a game were so special. We would get dressed in our Sunday best and leave early so that we would be there in plenty of time for the warmup. Before we left the College Street subway station, Dad would always buy me a block of Ganong fudge – sometimes maple and sometimes chocolate. Then the excitement would build as we climbed the stairs toward that hallowed shrine – the home of the Maple Leafs. The voices of the scalpers would rise above the babble of those streaming together toward the doors.

"Once inside, you'd blink a few times to adjust to the blinding lights. Smartly attired ushers would rip our treasured tickets in half. Usually, we would be there early enough for Dad to head into the coffee shop, which was just inside the front doors. It was there that I was introduced to King Clancy and, on one occasion, Harold Ballard. We would eventually make our way up to the front row of the greys. As we wound our way through Maple Leaf Gardens, so many people would say hello to Dad, and I would always be introduced. I was quite proud to be there. At some point during the game, Dad and I would 'take our bellies for a sleigh ride' with an ice cream sandwich. Dad would take me to four or five games a year. I loved being there in that huge shrine to our beloved Maple Leafs. They were my heroes when I was growing up, especially Dave Keon and Frank Mahovlich."

Gayle also remembers visiting the Gardens as a little girl. "I remember many Saturdays going with Dad to the 'Taj Mahal' of Canada (as far as I was concerned) – Maple Leaf Gardens. I would end up standing in the corridor just outside the dressing room, looking up in awe as the players passed by on the way to the warmup. Dad would talk to the celebrities as though they were good friends, which I thought was neat. On my sixteenth birthday, Dad took me to Doug Laurie's sporting goods shop and I was allowed to pick out a really special gift – a Toronto Maple Leaf jersey with the number 27 on the back. Darryl Sittler, one of my favourites, was captain at the time. Frank Mahovlich, who also wore 27, had been a previous favourite. My daughter Aynsley now wears this prize."

But the enjoyment of hockey wasn't restricted to attending games, says Jayne. "For as long as I remember, hockey has played a role in my life. If we didn't go to the game, then we watched it on TV. It was with great anticipation that we would sit through The Beverly Hillbillies and then The Jackie Gleason Show to see if the Leafs were ahead. If the game wasn't on television, then we listened to it on the radio.

"My friends also loved the game," admits Jayne. "Now, looking back, I'm not sure if we got together because we loved the game to start with, or if they grew to love it because of our Gaston enthusiasm. As we got older, Saturday nights would be Hockey Night at the Gastons'. We always had a good television set – in fact, that was one of the items Mom and Dad made sure they had before they assumed the financial responsibility of children. We had a colour television before many other people did. It was an absolute necessity for those nights when Dad did not go to Maple Leaf Gardens. Whenever the Leafs scored, we would all jump up and cheer, and Chippy, our dog, would bark. Those were wonderful, fun evenings which we all look back on with fond memories.

"Two of my friends were branded as turncoats – in a good-natured way – because their favourite players were Derek Sanderson and Bobby Orr of Boston. However, these same two friends went to a Leaf game and stayed afterwards to chase Davey Keon down Church Street so they could get him to sign a picture. Then they blew the picture up to poster size and it became one of my most treasured Christmas gifts ever," laughs Jayne.

Gayle has her memories of watching Hockey Night in Canada, too. "On the Saturdays when we didn't go to the Gardens, I have wonderful memories of the fireplace being lit and popcorn popped as we watched the game on television. After I met the man who would become my husband, we would watch the game in the basement with our friends. Dad would watch upstairs, and every time a goal was scored, Dad would run downstairs to evaluate the play. He also could always predict, with uncanny accuracy, the three stars. We always thought Dad should have been a hockey commentator, as his insight into the game was amazingly astute. And he would offer solutions to the various Leaf malaises – which, unfortunately, were prevalent at the time."

"Ruth and I found our own little routine, especially after the girls were grown up, married and moved away," Tom says. "We'd eat at Swiss Chalet, then walk over to the Gardens. Ruth would go straight up to her seat and read her book or knit. I had my ritual – I'd stop by the penalty box and say hi to Joe Lamantia, the penalty time-keeper. Joe had been at the Gardens as long as I had. Then I'd say hi to my buddies, the goal judges – David Keon Jr. and Bill Wellman. Dave Junior is a classy guy just like his Dad. He works for the National Hockey League in their public relations department during the day. And Bill Wellman works with me over at the Hockey Hall of Fame. I'd always stop to give my regards to Jim Proudfoot – the hockey writer for the Toronto Star. I'd also say hello to Al Wiseman, the head of security for the NHL. Then, about ten or fifteen minutes before the game was set to start, I'd make my way up to my seat, saying hi to my usherette friends on the way. One of the nicest ones was Amy Cable. She was beautiful, and she later married Dougie Gilmour.

"Ruth and I knew everybody all around our seats. Most of them had been subscribers for more than twenty years. That's one of the things I miss at the ACC – I only know the people on either side of me. In the 1950s, all the people from the area around us at the Gardens would go out for coffee after the game. A bunch of us would go to Toronto Marlboro playoff games together, too. In fact, we got to know the fans around us so well that when Ruth died, the man who sat behind us – Dave Scarrow – sang "God Will Take Care of You" at the funeral. He has a magnificent voice, and when I heard him, it brought tears to my eyes. Just thinking about it is doing the same to me now.

"Most of the ushers knew us by name. We had known them for years. As we'd head up to our seats, each usher in turn would welcome Ruth and me with a handshake and a hello. It was wonderful. In fact," Tom says, growing solemn, "at the first home game after Ruth died, the head usher and a couple of the others we knew a little better came up to my seat with a beautiful bouquet of flowers, all done in the Leafs' blue and white. The card was signed 'From all the ushers from Maple Leaf Gardens and the Air Canada Centre.' That really touched me."

"Long before there was that loud rock 'n' roll music they play today, there was just an organist who provided all the music. We even got to know him – well, not really, but we'd yell out, 'Hey, Ralphy – play us Harold Ballard's favourite!' and he'd play 'The Beer Barrel Polka.' Everybody around us would just crack up!'"

"Ruth and I raised the girls the best way we knew how. I think it helped that my wife was a nurse, but I'm very proud of how they turned out. Gayle is married to Bob Osborne, and the two live in Picton, Ontario. She owns a florist's shop up that way, and her husband runs the funeral home there. Bobby Hull's father was buried out of my son-in-law's funeral home. And Jayne married Tony Asselstine. They live up near Barrie, Ontario, and Jayne works at the library in Stroud."

Tom's son-in-law Tony experienced some of Tommy's good hockey fortune firsthand. "After Jayne and I started going out, I went to the Gardens with Tom, and we stopped for a coffee and a soft drink at the coffee shop behind the ticket wicket. As we were waiting, I heard a gruff voice say, 'Tommy!' I looked around, thinking whoever it was had said, 'Tony,' but Tom just signalled that we should get our drinks and move around the corner to the end table. As we approached, it became clear to me that we were about to have drinks and a conversation with Ace Bailey, King Clancy, Harry Watson and Teeder Kennedy. As a Leaf fan, I was thrilled. We were truly among Leaf royalty!"

Jayne talks about the third generation of hockey fans in the Gaston clan. "It was a given that any of my dad's grandchildren would have to love the sport and play it. When my daughter Jennifer was born in October 1981, she was soon wearing a very special hockey sweater, with the Toronto Maple Leaf emblem on the front and the number 1/2 embroidered on the back. Years later, she would again be sporting a special hockey sweater, but this time, it was a Leafs sweater with number 93 on the back. She was on bob skates by the time she was four, and continued to figure skate for many years until she went away to university. She also works part-time at the Hockey Hall of Fame.

"On the day my son Jonathan was born in March 1985, he was given a hockey stick and a puck by his aunt and uncle. He was skating before he was two, and continues to do so today." In fact, Jonathan Asselstine was the fifth pick of the Kingston Frontenacs, drafted in the sixth round of the Ontario Hockey League priority selection draft on May 5, 2001. "Nobody could be prouder than his Grandpa. In fact, his Grandpa is the source of much of Jonathan's love of hockey. He just loves hockey – he has a life-size poster of the Stanley Cup in his room, and that's the first thing he sees when he opens his eyes every morning."

"You bet I'm proud!" Tommy enthuses. "Dan Maloney, the former Leaf, lives in the Barrie area and he told me Jonathan was good enough to get drafted. The other day I ran into George Armstrong, and the first question he asked me was whether my grandson got drafted. Isn't that something?"

Gayle's children, Wendell, Garrett and Aynsley, also enjoy hockey. In the spring of 1988, all five of Tom's grandchildren were invited to a hockey festival promoted by the Canadian Hockey Association. They dressed in Toronto Maple Leaf sweaters and got to skate on the ice at Maple Leaf Gardens.

Forty years ago, Tommy Gaston bought a home in Leaside, just a short drive from where he was born. "It's a beautiful, peaceful neighbourhood, and we've had so many wonderful neighbours through the years," Tommy says. One of those neighbours is Susan Pearce. "When I moved into my little bungalow in 1979, I discovered that I was next door to a celebrity: Tom Gaston, the 'King of Crofton,'" she says. "Crofton is our street in Leaside. Tom's queen, his loving partner in everything he did, was his late wife, Ruth. Together, they were a couple who made you feel good just seeing them. It wasn't just Tom's status as the biggest Leafs fan of all time that raised his profile then. It was his status as the hub around which the whole street revolved.

"If you wanted to know anything at all about the neighbourhood and who was in it, Tom was the man to ask," Susan adds. "Even now, in his eighties, he keeps up with the new families and the changing face of the street. Everybody knows and cares for Tommy. He makes a neighbourhood feel like a neighbourhood, where you're comfortable calling 'hello' across the road or borrowing a cup of sugar. He doesn't butt in or offer unwanted advice. He simply has a strong sense of community and friendship. Tom likes to believe the best about people.

"You'd see Tom and Ruth setting off hand in hand to church, or to the grocery store, or the doctor's, or the Hockey Hall of Fame – nearly always walking to the bus stop. Ruth drove, but not often. Walking gave them the chance to see what was going on and to chat with those they encountered. Both always had a ready smile and a warm greeting, and Tom, of course, continues the tradition.

"I particularly remember the bright glint in Ruth's eye whenever she looked at Tom or talked about him. They liked to gently tease each other. It was all done with affection. Through our twenty-two years side by side, Ruth and Tom have always been the perfect neighbours. If it snowed, Tom shovelled more than he had to, help-ing me out with my endless corner-lot sidewalk. He shovels a bit less now that he's 'semi-retired' – these days, his neighbours are pleased to have the chance to help him.

"He's never really been outside of Ontario," Susan points out. "He says he'd like to travel 'when he retires.' Now, because of health issues, he will never get to fly on a plane. But I don't think he feels that he's missed out. He and Ruth treated their family and their neighbourhood as their universe. The brushes with celebrity, their association with hockey and the fine people they've encountered as a result, have provided more excitement and gratitude than any travel could have done.

"Since he's been alone, Tommy can't say enough for the kindness of others – whether neighbour, hockey friend or church supporter," concludes Susan Pearce. "He is only harvesting what he and Ruth have sown."

Nick Kypreos, the former Toronto Maple Leaf who now works as a hockey analyst for the Sportsnet television channel, has also become a good friend of Tom Gaston's. "I had the pleasure of meeting Tom and his lovely wife Ruth in the summer of '92," he recalls. "My relationship with the Gaston family happened by chance. My sister Stelle and her family were neighbours of Tom and Ruth. The Gastons were the favourite couple in the neighborhood, and it didn't take long for Stelle to understand why. When Stelle introduced me to Tom, it took me only a few seconds to see that hockey was a rich tradition in Tom and Ruth's lives. On a scorching hot summer night in July, Tom spoke of the game as if the Leafs were moments away from a seventh-game puck drop. I find it only fitting that Tom lives in a great old part of Toronto like Leaside. The community has a tradition that dates back as far as the mid 1800s. It has also been home to its share of Leafs, from Carl Brewer to the Mahovlich brothers. Tom and my family continue to live in Leaside, and every now and then we will still share our mutual passion for the greatest game on earth – even in July!"

"Yes, that's true," admits Tom. "But let me tell you what kind of a guy Nick Kypreos is. One day, I'm sitting on the porch and he sees me and comes over. He says, 'Tom, how many grandchildren do you have?' I tell him, 'Five.' Well, damned if the next time I see him he doesn't have an autographed picture for each of the grandkids. He also gave me a Frisbee and signed it, 'Friends for life – Nick Kypreos.' That's the kind of quality guy he is. When Ruth died, he was there at the funeral, too."

Tom remembers an extra-special event in his life. "Ruth and I celebrated our golden wedding anniversary in 1996. Imagine – fifty years. To be honest, I don't remember ever having a fight, although if Ruth were here, she'd probably tell you something different. Our daughters told Ruth and me that they were going to have a little party for us at a local hall. Unknown to us, Jayne and Gayle got hold of our friends at the Hockey Hall of Fame, and they planned the event for the Founder's Room at the Hall. My son-in-law came alone to pick Ruth and me up, and said somebody at the Hockey Hall of Fame wanted to see us to congratulate us. Ruth and I never caught on! When we stepped into the Founder's Room, there was great applause and our grandkids ran out. We were so surprised! Oh, we had no idea!

"That room couldn't have been more perfect," says Gaston. "First of all, the Hockey Hall of Fame is where Ruth and I had been volunteering, and so it was perfectly appropriate. But secondly, the Founder's Room is on the second level. Just outside the room is a balcony where you can look down and see all the trophies, including the Stanley Cup, in the Great Hall. Just perfect!

"Inside the Founder's Room, Jayne and Gayle had photos from our entire lives set up all around. And they invited our dearest friends and family, including some we hadn't seen for years! There was a terrible storm that night, but even so, a hundred people showed up to our party. All the living members of our wedding party were there.

"The minister made a little speech that made us all laugh. He said he had searched the church's archives, and could find no record of our wedding, and that he wasn't too sure that we were actually married! Well, you should have heard the roars. Oh, boy, was that funny! What a wonderful, wonderful time we had that evening."

"Do you want an example of how close Ruth and Tom were?" asks Reverend Sinclair. "They had a Sunday morning routine. After rising to meet the day, they headed to the subway. Once downtown, Tom and Ruth went to their favourite fast-food chain and ordered their 'regular' – one egg-and-cheese croissant, shared, and two coffees. After that, they were set for the whole day."

"We had a little routine at bedtime too," smiles Tom. "Every night, Ruth and I would read a passage from the Bible. One night I'd read; the next night, Ruth would read. When we were done, we'd say our prayers of thanks. I always thanked God for putting Ruth into my life."

Tom's eyes grow moist. Ruth's passing will always be etched into Tom's memory. "On August 18, 1999, Ruth was downstairs ironing my shirts. I heard a noise, and it was Ruth – she was crawling up the stairs on her hands and knees. I ran over to her. I couldn't figure out what she was doing, but she whispered, '911, 911.' That's when I knew Ruth was in big trouble. I called 911, and the police and ambulance were there almost immediately. Ruth was conscious, and walked with assistance to the ambulance and climbed onto the stretcher herself. But she said one more thing to me: 'Cerebral hemorrhage.' Ruth was a nurse. She knew what had happened to her. An hour later, at Wellesley Hospital, Ruth went to sleep and never woke up again."

It takes Tommy a moment to recover sufficiently to continue the story. The pain is as great today as it was then as he retells the story of Ruth's last days. "A chaplain took me into a quiet room and we had a coffee. The doctor told me that Ruth was bleeding profusely in the brain, and that she was blind from the aneurysm. We decided to leave my dear Ruth on life support until my girls could get there. At twenty to one in the afternoon on August 20 – I'll never forget that time as long as I live – it was time to say goodbye. I took her hand and said, 'Honey, you know what you mean to me,' and then I kissed her one final time. She squeezed my hand. She had understood what I had said to her. And then... I lost the most special person to ever come into my life. She was gone.

"My son-in-law from Picton took care of the arrangements. As an undertaker, he knew what to do, although I'm sure that when it's your family, it can never be easy. The funeral took place in Metropolitan United Church. I had met Ruth there, we were married there, and she left me there. So many people came to the funeral, including a lot of my friends from the hockey world. Bill Watters from the Toronto Maple Leafs came to offer his condolences. So did Nancy Gilks, Angela McManus and Kristy Fletcher from the Leafs' communications department. A lot of friends from the Hockey Hall of Fame came, too. In fact, Jeff Denomme, the Hockey Hall of Fame's president, and Craig Campbell, manager of the Resource Centre and Archives, were two of Ruth's pallbearers, along with my two sons-in-law and our two oldest grandsons. Christine Simpson and Nick Kypreos, two of my dear friends from the media, also came to pay their respects. There were so many lovely floral tributes to Ruth. The Hall of Fame executive sent a lovely bouquet, and so did the staff on the floor of the Hall. The Toronto Maple Leafs sent a special bouquet, and so did Sportsnet. Another came from Walter Gretzky.

"Ron Ellis, my special friend at the Hockey Hall of Fame, was wonderful, and he gave the eulogy. I have to include his wonderful words."

Good morning, family and friends. Before I continue, I would like to thank Tommy, Jayne, Gayle and the rest of the Gaston family for this honour.

My own personal faith gives me confidence that the soul and spirit of our beloved Ruth, the light to Tommy's path, is presently with our heavenly Father. As a matter of fact, it wouldn't surprise me if He hasn't already taken advantage of her wonderful gifts. I'm sure she is helping Him get things in order around the office and doing a little counselling as well. I do hope for His sake that our Lord is a Leaf fan. I have this image of Ruth correcting the Lord on how the Barilko goal was scored.

Ruth came to Toronto to study nursing at St. Mike's, and met her man right here at this church at a youth meeting around 1941. They were married in this sanctuary a couple of years later by Ruth's father, who was a minister. Tommy, it must have been quite a meeting between you and Reverend Brook as you tried to convince him that you were the right man for his only daughter. You must have been at your smooth-talking best, you rascal. Tommy, time has proved that you were the right man – the only man.

The song "Stand By Your Man" comes to mind when I think of Ruth. Why? She surely helped Tommy regain his confidence after a serious eye injury. While caring for the children and carrying out the demands of her nursing career, she supported Tommy as he worked through the various seats of his lodge, and with that support, he reached the highest level of honour. I know Tommy is aware of the contribution Ruth has made to their life together. Since I have known him, he can hardly utter a sentence without referring to his Ruth. After their devotion to each other, their family, their church and their careers, Ruth and Tommy never lost the passion they shared for the Toronto Maple Leafs.

As Tommy reached his sixties, he became concerned about his health, as he had experienced some heart trouble. He decided to donate his hockey memorabilia to the Hockey Hall of Fame for others to enjoy. That's where he met Lefty Reid. Not surprisingly, they became friends. Tommy's health improved, and Lefty invited him to join the Hall as a volunteer and help out whenever he wanted to come in. The Hall now had a dedicated volunteer and Tommy had a new, much needed love after his retirement. He quickly became a fixture at the Hall.

I joined the Hall in 1992. It was about this time that Ruth started to come to the Hall at the CNE with Tommy on a more regular basis, and before long, we had the pleasure of having both Ruth and Tommy as volunteers – and what a team they made! I started to observe a couple that obviously were devoted to each other, and who were living their lives to the fullest. What role models, for someone like myself, who desired a meaningful life. At the Hockey Hall of Fame, we have a small staff of dedicated people. The majority of our staff is young, recently out of school and experiencing the real working world for the first time. I have observed Ruth at her best. Quietly encouraging and giving sound advice to many whom were naturally attracted to this wonderful woman. Her contagious smile never failed to lift all of our spirits when she arrived at the Hall. She even had advice for an old hockey puck, Ron Ellis, when he got caught up in time deadlines, by saying, 'Ron, slow down. Everything will get done.' And it did.

Ruth and Tommy worked hard in the Resource Centre as they helped with fan mail, the Teammates magazine and filing information on our Honoured Members. Sometimes, Tommy would start telling stories, leaving Ruth with the bulk of the work. Ruth would day, 'Tommy. More work and less stories!'

Two weeks ago, we had Teeder Kennedy at the Hall for a fan forum. After chatting with Tommy for awhile, he said, 'Tommy, I want to see Ruth again. Please bring her down to see me.' I believe this not only says a lot about Ted Kennedy, but also about a very special lady.

This past Tuesday, a day before her collapse, Ruth still had humour to pass on to us. Tommy was having lunch with an Honoured Member on one of the private rooms between fan forums. Ruth was in the Resource Centre with the other gals when she stated, 'That darn Tommy. There he is downstairs having a gourmet lunch, and I'm up here with my peanut-butter-and-lettuce sandwich.' Yes, you heard right – peanut butter and lettuce, her favourite.

Ruth, you have had an impact on my life as a person and with Tommy as a couple. I only wish I had shared this with you. Why is it we wait until the people we love and respect are gone before we verbalize what they meant to us? Possibly, in memory of Ruth, we all could try to share our gratitude and thanks with others in our homes, churches and workplaces. I think Ruth would be pleased.

Ruth, your family is here. Your friends are here. I know I can speak for everyone when I say, 'Don't worry, we will look after Tommy.' What's that, Ruth? Be sure he takes his medication? Yep, that's our Ruth – the one we love!

The Reverend Dr. G. Malcolm Sinclair from Metropolitan United Church presided over the funeral. "When Ruth died, friends from Metropolitan United Church were there for her and Tom," he remembers. "A warm and heartfelt celebration of Ruth's life was held in the sanctuary. Friends from the congregation, the Gardens, the Maple Leafs and the Hockey Hall of Fame gathered with Tom and his family to try to ease the pain. We in the church are proud of our long-standing member. The honours which have come his way display that we are a small group among many that have found Tom and Ruth Gaston to be a number one team over a lifetime of winning seasons. As Tom says, 'We had a wonderful life together. It was just too short!'"

Christine Simpson, a hockey reporter at Sportsnet, has been a dear friend to both Tom and Ruth. "I first met Tom and Ruth Gaston when I started my job as marketing manager at the Hockey Hall of Fame in September of 1992. I learned pretty quickly how important these two 'super' volunteers were to the staff at the Hall, and in no time, I began what was to be a very special relationship with them as well."

Christine smiles, her memories vivid and warm. "After having spent five years with the Hall of Fame and another three working for the

Toronto Maple Leafs as their arena host – I did promotions at every Leaf home game during those three seasons – I saw an awful lot of Tom and Ruth. Everyone at Maple Leaf Gardens seemed to know the Gastons, from the ushers to the players to the Leafs staff to Carlton the Bear to the other fans in their section up in the greys. Tom and Ruth Gaston were as much a part of the atmosphere at Maple Leaf Gardens as the organ music of Jimmy Holmstrom or the voice of Paul Morris.

"When I had left the Hall of Fame and the Leafs to start working with Sportsnet in 1998, I had the honour of doing a feature on Tom and Ruth as part of a series we were producing on the Leafs' last season at Maple Leaf Gardens. We had a camera follow Tom and Ruth around on a game night – and if you think hockey players have a typical game-day routine, well, Tom and Ruth had one of their own, too. We followed them from the minute they got off the subway at College Street, through the turnstiles at Maple Leaf Gardens, up to their seats in the front-row greys. And you'd think they were some kind of Toronto royalty. Everyone around seemed to know them. Smiles and waves came from all corners of the building.

"I'll never forget interviewing the two of them as they sat in their seats. Tommy's eyes would light up as he retold the many stories and memories he has of his years watching the Leafs. And as was often the case, Ruth would be sitting quietly, in the background, with that big smile of hers, letting Tommy bask in the glow of the spotlight, only to get in a little zinger herself when she thought it was warranted, always followed by a chuckle.

"I guess nothing could have prepared me for the phone call I got one night saying that Ruth had passed away. It was as if a member of my own family had died. The funeral was beautiful. And I'm sure Ruth was smiling as Ron Ellis, her favourite, eulogized her. He summed up in words the thoughts of so many of us. Ruth was as great a Leaf fan as she was a person. I know Tommy misses her. All of us who knew her do, too. And much has changed since I first met Tommy Gaston – he performs his game-day routine alone, and the subway stop is Union now instead of College, and the section is the purples, not the greys. But his love of the Maple Leafs and his passion as a fan will never change."

Tommy, like his many wonderful friends, found it nearly impossible to say goodbye to Ruth. "The funeral service took place on a Tuesday, but the interment didn't happen until the following Saturday. It was just the immediate family – me, my two girls and their families. Each of us said a few words. Some read from the Bible, others spoke from the heart. It was beautiful, but so hard to leave. Ruth is buried with my Dad, Mom and brother in Mount Pleasant Cemetery – right near the gate at Bayview. There's not a week that goes by when I don't go to visit Ruth – winter or summer, sun or rain. That's our special time."

CHAPTER TWENTYTWO

A Voice from the Stands

"After Ruth died, I had to find new partners to share my seats at the Air Canada Centre," muses Tom. "It wasn't easy for me, as I had always been locked into game-day rituals that Ruth understood – and shared. I will always wear the Maple Leafs sweater with number 6 on the back that I wore when I went to games with Ruth. Ruth's number 5 sweater is left in the closet, never to be worn again. But I've found some wonderful people to share my love of the game – and specifically the Toronto Maple Leafs.

One of those with whom Tommy often goes to games is Andrew Podnieks, an exceptional author who has written numerous books on hockey, including The Essential Blue and White Book 2002: A Toronto Maple Leafs Factbook. "Saturdays and Wednesdays," Podnieks writes. "Every winter, every week. They're rituals – rites of hockey mass, and Tommy and I are regular parishioners, linked by the God of puck, adoring the blue and white maple leaf, drinking – well, one day soon, from the Cup of Lord Stanley.

"Tommy knows I hang my hat most days at the Hockey Hall of Fame, and every morning when he drops by to do some work, he'll come over to my desk to say hello. Another ritual. He always wears a jacket and tie – stark contrast to my more casual archives attire. Sometimes he'll be stirring a cup of coffee or munching on a cookie; other times he'll be reaching into his jacket pocket for an envelope or a letter. 'The Gardens sent me this,' he'll say, showing me something concerning subscribers with Ken Dryden's signature on it. He still, inadvertently but meaningfully, calls the ACC the Gardens – as I do sometimes, and as I'm sure we all do every nostalgic now and then. It'll be a notice for playoff tickets, an announcement for one thing or another, it doesn't matter, Mr. Dryden signed it.

"Or, he'll reach into his multi-elasticked envelope to give me my ticket for our next game or show me a player photo, family photo, or the Leafs schedule. If we have nothing planned, he'll make a leading introduction to his real business in saying hello – 'Leafs are playing Saturday' or 'Boston's in town this week' – and I acknowledge what a great game it'll be. 'You going?' he'll ask, pretty certain that I'm not. 'Well, shall we?' Of course. And it's set. Another game, another night of pleasure – and sometimes pain!

"Tommy and I never hook up before the game. He likes to get to the alumni booth early for his autographed photo, get to his seat early, get ready for the game. 'The Leafs gave me this,' he'll say, tugging his number 6 Leafs sweater, the same number as his seat. I'm in number five, the other retired number. Just like a breakout play or killing a penalty or a dreaded TV timeout, our conversation follows the same consistent path, an enjoyable rote of hockey talk about trades, who's playing well, who's not. If Tommy hears foul language coming from an exuberant fan nearby, he'll turn sharply and tell the offender to 'watch it' in a most rebuking tone. At intermission, he goes for a walk to keep the fluids in his joints moving, but to or fro he'll have any number of people say, 'Hey, you're the guy from that MasterCard commercial!' He holds court with the other subscribers, many of whom come over and say hi and gab about the period's play. Tommy is most in his element at the game – ACC, MLG, it doesn't matter. It's the Leafs. King Clancy's team.

"During the breaks in play, we compare notes: ice cream sellers shouldn't come up the stairs during the game; the ushers don't control fans walking about; fans no longer wait until the whistle to move in and out of their seats. The scoreboard is great, the sound too loud, this shot was amazing, that save was spectacular. Gotta get some pressure on these guys – look at the shots on goal. Who's the referee tonight? They all look the same now.

"By the third period, Tommy's mood for the night is set. If the team is playing well, he's up; if the game's a bit of a stinker, he's in a down mood. But never do we leave early – that would be sacrilege. At the final bell, we get out onto the street and walk over to the 'Green P' where I park, and we drive home. On winter nights – my favourite – the wind bites and the cold catches our every breath. The car seems a long way away, and a welcome relief when we get to it. The drive home is a recap – of the game and of Tommy's life. At a stoplight, Tommy will see an old car drive by. 'I bought my first car in...' A particular moment from the game will send him back to the good old days – not the days of the Gardens or the Cups or Clancy, but the days when Ruth was alive and his constant companion. 'After the game, Ruth and I would...' and we'd segue to a world that still keeps Tommy going, despite her passing two years ago or more. In Leaside, I drop him off at his front door, we shake hands and compliment each other for a great night, and we look forward to seeing each other at the Hall the next day. But best of all, we both know, as always, there'll be another game soon."

Besides supervising Gaston and the team at the Resource Centre at the Hockey Hall of Fame, Phil Pritchard has grown to appreciate Tom in a different milieu. "Over the years, Tommy and I have been regulars at Maple Leaf Gardens and the Air Canada Centre to watch the Maple Leafs play. Sitting there in his seats way up in the greys (and more recently the purples) is like sitting beside the King of England. Every usher, fan and popcorn vendor comes by and says hi to Tommy, and in true Gaston style, Tommy makes them feel like a million bucks. I've often wondered how many more people would come by when I wasn't there, when Tommy was there with his wife, Ruth. The two of them were inseparable, not only at Leaf games and at the Hockey Hall of Fame, but in life – like two peas in a pod."

Conclusion

"I see him on TV, I see him in the newspapers, I hear him on the radio, and I think, 'Is that really my Dad?'" says Tommy's daughter, Gayle Osborne. "He was an honest, hard-working man, out of the house at dawn, home at 5:30 like clockwork. I would meet him at the bus stop almost every night to either walk with him, or to be pulled in the wagon by him, the block and a half to our home."

That Tom Gaston has been embraced by the media as the unofficial spokesperson for the Toronto Maple Leafs seems to defy logic. He never played for the team, never worked for the team. He is just an average fan who lives and dies by his favourite hockey club. But in that last sentence, you'll find the very reason Tommy is embraced by the press, radio and television. He is the average fan, no different than you or I or any number of others. Except he has something that most people don't have – longevity.

"Oh, there are people whose families have had season tickets longer than me, but we can't find any individual who has had them longer than me," Tommy states with a leprechaun's grin. "And I know there are fans who are older than me, too, but they either don't have season tickets or don't attend religiously like I am able to do." He knocks on wood.

"I've been truly blessed, and I know it," continues Gaston. "Why should a little guy like me be fortunate enough to get the attention I get? I don't know. All I know is that I have always tried to be fair and honest, and to live my life with passion, no matter what I am doing.

"Get a load of this: there was a contest held last summer – the Leafs were looking for pictures to print on the season tickets. I sent a picture of myself standing on the float and waving to the crowd during the parade when the Leafs moved from Maple Leaf Gardens to the Air Canada Centre. I got a letter telling me I had been chosen as one of the people whose picture was going to be used. Well, they didn't just use it, it was the photograph on the ticket for the Leaf's opening game of the 2000-01 season against the Montreal Canadiens!

"I was sent a pair of tickets in the gold section for that game. One daughter sat with me in the golds, while the other used my season tickets up in the purples. A week before the game, I was called in to the ACC to read the words that were printed on the ticket – they made a recording which was played over the public-address system on opening night, while they showed my picture from the ticket on the big scoreboard screen."

Here are the words that Leaf fans heard Tommy read that night: "There is no question what moment has meant the most to me; when I was asked to represent all Leafs fans in the Maple Leaf Gardens parade. The sign on my float read, 'Superfan Tom Gaston.'"

"At the game that night, the presentation was almost over before I realized it," Tom says. "Now that was an honour that money can't buy! Then they sent me a beautiful plaque with my VIP tickets mounted and framed. I was floored when that arrived!"

In the December 25, 2000, issue of Sports Illustrated, Gaston was profiled as one of North America's "superfans." "I think Sports Illustrated called Mike Ferriman over at the Maple Leafs office. Mike is the manager of game presentation for the Leafs. They asked him if there was one sports fan in Toronto who stood out from all the rest, and he suggested me," says Tom, a little embarrassed by the attention. "Well, two guys came up here from New York and spent three or four hours with me, walking through the Hockey Hall of Fame and listening to my stories. I was so proud when somebody called and told me I was in the magazine. My article was called 'The Iceman Cometh' – I thought that was a pretty good title – and there it was, with me in my Leafs sweater cheering. A very nice article."

Tom's fame has grown since he was included in a national television ad campaign. "MasterCard taped me talking about some Leaf memories and used it for a commercial that has run for quite a while now. It was me talking about Bill Barilko's goal. There I am, cheering away for the Leafs. Just about every time I go to a Leaf game, somebody stops me and says, 'You're that guy from the TV commercial!' I used to be a little shy about it, but now I'm proud. But whenever I see the commercial I get a little misty, because it shows Ruth sitting beside me there in our grey seats at Maple Leaf Gardens."

Tom got another thrill when the Hockey Hall of Fame unveiled the Tom Gaston Book, which Honoured Members sign when they're inducted. "I was absolutely floored!" Tom says. "There it sits in the Great Hall, not far from the Stanley Cup, with the signatures of the best players ever to play the game I love. Why me? I can't explain it, but long after I'm gone, hockey fans from all over the world will still see the special Tom Gaston book and wonder who this guy Gaston was.

"I remember the day the presentation took place, Bob Stellick from the Toronto Maple Leafs also presented me with a Leafs wristwatch, a Leafs jacket and an overnight bag. Then there was a lunch for me at the Hockey Hall of Fame. They snuck my family in, without Ruth and I even knowing."

"I can't get over the lovely things people have done for me – and all because I cheered for a hockey team. Okay, not just any hockey team," Tom laughs. "There was a night when the Leafs commemorated the three arenas they played in. I had seen games in all three: Mutual Street – well, really the name at the time was the Arena Gardens – Maple Leaf Gardens and the Air Canada Centre. The Maple Leafs gave me a copy of their beautiful coffee-table book called Memories and Dreams, and it was signed by Leaf president Ken Dryden. I also got a pair of tickets for the game that night, so I was able to have both my girls there with me again that night.

"I know I've mentioned it before, but I still can't believe I was given a lifetime membership to the Hockey Hall of Fame. It's a beautiful plaque, too, which Scotty Morrison gave to me. It's one of the best honours I've ever received."

"When the All-Star Game was played in Toronto in 2000, I was given a ticket to the game and a sweater with my name on the back and the number 00. The guys from Team Canada '72 gave me a beautiful jacket just the other day, too. I have been so fortunate. So many wonderful people have done so many wonderful things for me. I'll ask again – why? I guess all I had to do was live long enough," says Tommy as he laughs at his own self-deprecating remark.

"And it's not just things I've been given," Tommy continues. "It's opportunities. I've been to every Hockey Hall of Fame induction ceremony except two over the last twenty years, watching the new Honoured Members officially enter the Hall. What a thrill it's been to get all dressed up and attend these prestigious ceremonies. The two I missed? One was held in Vancouver and the other was in Detroit. The only other year that the ceremony wasn't held in Toronto, it was in Ottawa, and the Hockey Hall of Fame sent Ruth and me and another couple of volunteers from the Hall for that induction. Oh, boy, did we have fun!"

Tommy pauses for breath, then starts up again. "I don't want you to think that all I ever had in my life was my family, my work and the Leafs," he says. "I'm a member of Metropolitan United Church. I belong to the IOF Court 333 Independent Order of Foresters. I have a life membership in the Loyal Orange Lodge 269. I belong to RBP 1202. In school, I played in the harmonica band, and later, I played in the Toronto Flute Band. And of course, there's the Hockey Hall of Fame. Several years ago, the Minister of Recreation presented me with a certificate for being a fifteen-year volunteer at the Hall. Ruth got one as well for volunteering for five years. There was a reception at the Metropolitan Toronto Convention Centre.

"There are still things I want to do when I get older," says Tommy, immediately breaking into a belly laugh. "I want to fly and I want to play golf. I'm afraid I'll never get a chance to fly because of my heart problems. I had cardiac angina several years ago, so I'm not allowed to fly. The doctor said, 'I won't tell you not to, but if it was me, I wouldn't,' so I won't. But I've never really seen very much. Other than trips to a few American cities around the Great Lakes – like Detroit and Cleveland and Niagara Falls – I've never been out of Ontario. I had planned a trip to Ireland a few years ago, but that was around the time of my heart problems, so I couldn't go."

Tommy reflects on his long life and his dreams. "You know, when I was small, I had two dreams. One was to play for the Toronto Maple Leafs. Well, I just wasn't big enough or good enough to do that. And I would have loved to have been a preacher. I have a lot of faith in me, and I certainly have the gift of gab, but a lack of education and money put a damper on that dream at an early age. But I help out at the church wherever I can. A few times, I've been called upon to speak, and I was able to get up in front of all those people and speak with confidence and passion. Ruth's dad was a preacher, and I always thought that if I could do it all over again, that's what I might have done. Hey, maybe I could have combined both dreams and played for the Flying Fathers like Les Costello!"

"Somebody asked me to list my favourite players of all time," says Tommy, as the topic finds him suddenly deep in thought. "I tried so hard to pick just one team, but I couldn't. Then I thought, why not one team of Leafs and one team of other players? But it's too hard when you've seen as many great players as I have through the years, so let me just indulge myself and name some of my favourites of all time.

"I'll start with the Leafs. In net, it would be pretty hard to deny either Turk Broda or Johnny Bower. On defence, I always liked Bobby Baun, Tim Horton, Hap Day and, of course, King Clancy. Up front – wow, this is hard. I guess I'd have to go with Charlie Conacher, Syl Apps, Ted Kennedy, Sweeney Schriner, Bob Davidson, Max Bentley and Harry Watson from the old Leafs, and Davey Keon, Frank Mahovlich, George Armstrong and Dougie Gilmour from the more recent Leafs. Wow! That'd make a heck of a team, wouldn't it?"

Tommy continues, with players who didn't play for Toronto. "Charlie Gardiner has to be in net, but I'd put Jacques Plante in, too. I know he played for the Leafs, but I'll always think of him as a Montreal Canadien. On defence? Eddie Shore, Lionel Conacher, Ching Johnson, Bill Gadsby, Doug Harvey and Harry Howell. Let me add Bobby Orr in there, too! My forwards would be Wayne Gretzky, Howie Morenz, Guy Lafleur, Bobby Hull, Gordie Howe, Jean Beliveau, Andy Bathtub – I always call Bathgate that – and Mario Lemieux. Not bad, eh? Could you imagine watching a game between those two teams?"

"I've been a lucky, lucky man" concludes Tom Gaston. "I've had a wonderful wife and I have two beautiful daughters. I have a lovely house and can put food on my table. I have a place to go as often or as infrequently as I want with the Hockey Hall of Fame. I wasn't kidding when I said the Hall added years to my life. It gave me a purpose and a new set of friends who share my passion for hockey. And I have a hockey team I will stand behind for the rest of my days. I hope I get a chance to see another Stanley Cup – I've seen eleven – but even if I don't, I'll still remain the Toronto Maple Leafs' 'fan for all seasons!'"